Praise for *TalkRx*

"The answer to the common complaint 'My doctor never has time to talk to me.' I loved reading these down-to-earth conversations with a brilliant medical doctor who has taken the time to give straightforward answers to so many common communication and health-related concerns. Priceless information from a medical doctor who is the real deal."

— **Dr. Wayne W. Dyer**, *New York Times* best-selling author of *I Can See Clearly Now* and *The Power of Intention*

"If you have ever had your mouth say yes and your heart say no, if you have ever not had a conversation because of fear, or if you have had a conversation that turned bad, then you need TalkRx. This groundbreaking, insightful view into human relationships and Doctor Neha's prescription for communication will reduce your stress, enhance your health, and free you up to experience love, energy, and success in your life."

— **Mark Hyman, M.D.**, director of the Cleveland Clinic Center for Functional Medicine and author of the #1 *New York Times* bestseller *The Blood Sugar Solution*

"When's the last time your doctor spoke with you about the way your communication impacts your health? If your answer is never, read this book. Let Doctor Neha teach you how good communication can light up the darkest corners of your relationships."

— **Dr. David Eagleman**, neuroscientist, *New York Times* bestselling author of *Incognito*

"TalkRx is just what the doctor ordered! A different kind of prescription from a different kind of physician. You will be astounded and inspired by compelling personal experiences and patient encounters from Doctor Neha's career. Your relationships will be improved when you understand how challenging communication directly connects to physical well-being. In this book are the secrets to transforming stressful interactions. TalkRx is a masterful guide to improving your life, relationships, and health."

— **Patricia Fripp**, CSP, CPAE, past president, National Speakers Association

TALK
RX

TALK RX

Five Steps to Honest Conversations
That Create
Connection, Health, and Happiness

NEHA SANGWAN, M.D.

HAY HOUSE, INC.
Carlsbad, California • New York City
London • Sydney • Johannesburg
Vancouver • Hong Kong • New Delhi

Published and distributed in the United States by: Hay House, Inc.: www.hay house.com® • *Published and distributed in Australia by:* Hay House Australia Pty. Ltd.: www.hayhouse.com.au • *Published and distributed in the United Kingdom by:* Hay House UK, Ltd.: www.hayhouse.co.uk • *Published and distributed in the Republic of South Africa by:* Hay House SA (Pty), Ltd.: www.hayhouse.co.za • *Distributed in Canada by:* Raincoast Books: www.raincoast.com • *Published in India by:* Hay House Publishers India: www.hayhouse.co.in

Cover design: Lexie Rhodes and Monica Gurevich • *Interior design:* Nick C. Welch • *Interior photos/illustrations:* Katy Putnam (Kap Art, Inc.)

Library of Congress Cataloging-in-Publication Data

Sangwan, Neha, 1970-
 Talk rx : five steps to honest conversations that create connection, health, and happiness / Neha Sangwan, M.D.
  pages cm
 ISBN 978-1-4019-4246-5 (hardcover : alk. paper) 1. Health--Psychological aspects. 2. Interpersonal communication--Health aspects. 3. Physician and patient. 4. Self-care, Health. 5. Mind and body. I. Title.
 R726.5.S264 2015
 613.2--dc23
                    2014025462

Hardcover ISBN: 978-1-4019-4246-5

10 9 8 7 6 5 4 3 2 1
1st edition, May 2015

Printed in the United States of America

SUSTAINABLE FORESTRY INITIATIVE
Certified Chain of Custody
Promoting Sustainable Forestry
www.sfiprogram.org
SFI-01268
SFI label applies to the text stock

*To my bestie, Kathy Trost—this book simply wouldn't
have happened without you.
To my parents, sisters, and niecelette, for a lifetime
of love and support.
And to my patients, who are living proof that
honest communication heals.*

CONTENTS

I WONDER . . .

How can we be missing what's right in front of us?

A world of information is at our fingertips. We can communicate instantly with anyone anywhere anytime. Yet why is it that most of humanity feels more disconnected and lonely than ever?

Even with advanced research, the latest pharmaceuticals, and state-of-the-art technology, our rates of insomnia, anxiety, obesity, depression, and addiction are on the rise. Health care costs are spiraling out of control. And with a population of only 315 million, Americans are consuming nearly three billion prescriptions each year.[1]

As a medical practitioner, I was trained to name diseases and then prescribe a one-size-fits-all medication to treat them. The problem is that medication has become our first line of defense to treat any symptom—without even exploring other options. As a society, we have come to believe that using short-term fixes over and over somehow makes them long-term solutions. However, if you've watched a pharmaceutical commercial lately—and thought the list of possible side effects flashing across the screen sounded worse than the symptoms you were trying to alleviate—you know something is off.

Maybe we're searching for connection, health, and happiness in all the wrong places.

As I began to work in a hospital, the patients I encountered were in crisis. They suffered from ailments such as heart attacks, strokes, pneumonia, or cancer. My days were punctuated by unforgettable moments of compassion, terror, tenderness, relief, and joy—each emotion magnified by the fact that this work was often a matter of life or death. As you can imagine, my job caring for these critically ill people was as exhausting as it was fulfilling.

For the most part, I was your average physician. I worked hard. I cared deeply about my patients. I got along with my colleagues. The nurses and staff regularly refueled me with sugar and caffeine from the break rooms to get me through my overnight shifts. I sometimes grumbled when I was overtired. Scrubs were my fashion statement. And I wanted to be appreciated more by the hospital leadership. But most of all, I wanted to make a difference.

In the early years, how I made a difference came from what I had learned in textbooks. I had spent the majority of my life absorbing information with the sole goal of regurgitating the correct answers on exams. At 31, as I graduated from my medical residency, I remember thinking, *Wow, I really know a lot.*

I was acutely aware that there were many subjects I didn't know about, like politics and pop culture. But I knew how to interpret blood test results and a urinalysis. Who cared if I didn't know Madonna was on world tour? I knew what I knew, and I knew what I didn't know. Or at least I thought I did.

One of the first clues that my extensive, expensive education wasn't going to save the world was what happened when I sent my patients home armed with a list of low-fat foods, directives to exercise daily, and a schedule of new medications. For the most part, following these instructions would heal their acute physical symptoms. But like a revolving door, six months or a year later I would see them again for yet another episode of out-of-control blood sugar or another heart attack.

So I did something that was unusual for a physician. I started asking them questions about what else was going on in their lives besides the illnesses that brought them to the hospital. I hoped that, together, we would gain new insight on any additional factors that played a role in making them sick. This is when I discovered that there was a lot I didn't know. My patients were about to teach me far more than my schooling ever had.

As they answered my questions, the same issues resurfaced: Unresolved conflict. Unmet expectations. Misunderstandings. Broken promises. Unspoken truth. Heartbreak. Fractured relationships. Separation and loss. Confusion. Depression. Unhappiness.

And what I started noticing was that the situations my patients were in caused them an inordinate amount of stress. Somewhere along the way, their communication—with lovers, with friends, with co-workers, with family, with themselves—had broken down, and they were unable to bridge the gap. The result was disconnection, loneliness, and isolation. My patients' inability to communicate was literally making them sick. So I began to wonder: how might improved communication reverse their symptoms, reduce stress, and create more health and happiness?

As I searched for the answers, I encountered a small problem: I didn't really know how to communicate myself.

We notice our style of communication about as much as fish notice the water in which they swim. The only time communication becomes an issue is when our relationships start to break down or become painful. Even then, we're fairly sure that if communication is the culprit, it must be someone else's poor communication that's to blame. So if you can think of several other people who need to read a book on communication other than yourself, I am here to assure you that this book is in the right hands—right now.

You might be thinking, *Communication? That's easy. I know how to communicate.* Don't be fooled. Communication is essentially simple, but it's not always easy. Many of us learn from an early age to be guarded about what and how we communicate. Few of us learn how to pay attention to our own inner voice and speak from the heart. Instead, we tune out the very information that can help us communicate more authentically. Specifically, our body's physiological responses to stress (e.g., stomach turning, face flushing, heart racing, palms sweating) often get in the way, rather than serving as clues to how we're feeling. Experiencing this physical discomfort can be a deterrent to having those much-needed honest conversations. We sabotage our efforts to communicate effectively by exploding with anger, getting defensive, or silencing ourselves altogether.

How many times have you complained to your co-worker, spouse, or best friend about your boss or your stressful day at work? We speak *about* each other rather than *to* each other. We use backstabbing conversations in order to avoid uncomfortable sensations in our body and gain allies to prove we're right. Not speaking directly to one another ultimately results in the mistrust and toxic work environments that are making us physically and emotionally sick. We may even justify this pattern of indirect communication by saying, "I can't say anything because it'll ruin my evaluation" or "If I speak up, I'll get fired or targeted unfairly."

You may get temporary relief from your discomfort through complaining, gathering allies, and avoiding the real issue, but in the long term, resentment will build inside you and your situation will remain unresolved. These can be seeds that grow into disconnection and loneliness.

At home it's a different kind of maneuvering that happens. It could be about keeping the peace or not rocking the boat. With long-term relationships, like those we have with a parent, sibling, spouse, or child, we tend to anticipate communication based on past experiences and fall into old conversation patterns. We say things like "I've had the same conversation with him a million times before, and I know how it's going to end. I'll feel frustrated and unheard, and one of us will end up angry or hurt, so no way—I'm not going there!"

If you think you're too busy to learn about communication, ask yourself a few easy questions. How much time do you waste worrying about unresolved personal or professional issues? How much energy have you invested trying to avoid conflict, only to have it resurface over and over again? How much stress, frustration, disappointment, or loneliness occurs in your life because of misunderstandings and miscommunication? Your inability to resolve conflict and build strong connections to others can weigh heavily on your heart and keep you up at night.

Think about how many conversations you have every day—from one-word exchanges to hour-long talks. When communication breaks down in any interaction—even if it's momentary—your heart rate speeds up. Next, your blood pressure, cholesterol, and blood sugar levels rise. People who feel misunderstood report a higher incidence of depression, which is uncomfortable enough, but to take it one step further, depression leads to a weakened immune system. This is our primary defense against disease. Under prolonged stress we become susceptible to ailments such as headaches, digestive issues, diabetes, and heart disease, to name a few.[2]

It's time to put the spotlight back on how we talk to ourselves, talk to others, and relate to the world around us. Communication is our primary tool for creating relationships, one of our most profound ways to connect. Healthy communication provides pathways for growth, love, support, friendship, and healing. We know this intuitively, yet somehow it's easy to forget.

DIALING 911 FROM THE HOSPITAL

In October 2001, I had just relocated to San Francisco, 3,000 miles from my family. I began working at a large HMO and dreamed of someday being voted in as a physician partner. I was hired as a hospitalist, an internal medicine doctor who cares for patients through their acute medical crises. I was part of a team who admitted patients from the emergency department and cared for them until they were discharged.

Every five days, one of my team duties would be to redistribute the patients who had come in overnight to the daytime physicians. And every five days, Tyler, a 350-pound colleague of mine, would arrive as soon as I had finished making those assignments. Tyler had a list of unwritten, unspoken rules regarding which patients he was willing to accept:

1. No liver failure patients, especially anyone requiring interventional procedures.

2. No patients in the intensive care unit—unless everyone else already had one.

3. No one with a thick chart, long medical history, or multiple admissions.

4. Patients with uncomplicated chest pain, pneumonia, or strokes were acceptable.

And on and on. I soon realized the bottom line was this: no complicated patients could go to Tyler. If he thought I had violated these rules, his face would turn red, he would take a deep breath and puff himself up, and then he would begin swearing and pointing his finger in my face, saying things like "God dammit, don't you dare give me Mrs. X! That's *#@%^ inappropriate! Give that patient to someone else; otherwise, I'll be here until midnight. And remember, payback's a bitch."

Confronted with Tyler's rage, I would back away and say, "Okay, okay." And I would put Mrs. X's file on another colleague's pile and find a straightforward chest pain case for Tyler.

By early afternoon, Tyler would be done seeing his patients. He had mastered the art of delegating to the nurses and doing what we called "telephone medicine" from his desk on the seventh floor. Then, he would just hang out—playing with electronic gadgets, talking about the latest sports car, or bragging about how many women wanted him.

We all spent our time dancing around Tyler. I tried to befriend him, hoping that if he cared about me, the dynamic would change. No such luck.

It didn't take long to realize I had a big problem on my hands.

The tipping point came when Tyler confronted me about Jacqueline, a fellow physician who had just spent her lunch break pumping breast milk for her four-month-old twins. "This place stinks! When is leadership going to stop hiring all these women of childbearing age?" he exclaimed.

I marched down to my physician chief's office and declared that something needed to be done. "I'm being bullied and intimidated, and I need your help," I said. I went on to describe all that had happened, concluding with Tyler's politically incorrect comments about women.

"You see, Neha," my chief replied, "Tyler's already a partner in this organization. He sees the highest number of patients and has the quickest turnaround times for discharging them. That's valuable. If you hope to be a partner someday, you're going to need his support . . . and mine. I suggest you put your head down and get back to work instead of complaining. You're the only one who feels this way."

I couldn't believe my ears. Was he serious? Did he really think I was the only one who had issues with Tyler?

I polled my colleagues, inquiring if they had experienced anything similar. Examples of inappropriate and egregious behavior emerged, each one more preposterous than the last.

I made an appointment with the head of Human Resources. Surely she would be able to help if my chief wouldn't. I mean, the department's name was Human Resources. They were there to handle these types of issues, right?

Much to my amazement, the woman I talked to said it wasn't the first time she had heard this. But no one really knew how to handle this type of behavior—especially from a physician partner. She went on to say, "You see, once you become a partner, you're untouchable. You're tenured for life. Since you're not a partner yet, you might want to learn some skills to better handle his temper."

I was dumbfounded by how Tyler's bad behavior had somehow become my problem.

That night my friend David told me about a communication workshop that he thought could teach me how to navigate my emotions and communicate more openly. So two weeks later, I was on a flight to Eugene, Oregon. As the plane took off, I remember thinking, *I AM a good communicator. I even talk to families when their loved ones are dying. This better be good, David.*

As I entered the lecture hall, I saw 30 strangers who looked nothing like me. I began to think I had made a big mistake. Then the lead facilitator, Kris King, took the floor. She was classy, elegant, and well put together, so I decided to move past my doubts and give her my full attention.

An hour into the workshop, she paused, looked around the room, and said, "So, I'm curious. Why are you here? What do you hope to gain?" And her eyes landed on me.

I stood up and walked to the front of the room. "I don't know how to deal with a co-worker who's causing everyone problems." I went on to tell the class what an angry, obnoxious bully Tyler was. "But he's not here, so there really isn't anything I can do about him," I said as I began walking back to my seat.

"Hold on, Neha. Don't sit down yet." I stopped and turned around. "Are there any other times in your life when someone has gotten angry and you felt bullied?"

I stood silent for what seemed like an eternity. I didn't want to admit what immediately came to mind.

Finally, I replied, "Well, my dad has a temper."

"So what happens when your dad gets angry?"

I slowly began moving back toward the front of the room. "Well, he starts talking faster, his tone gets louder, and then he starts swearing."

"Okay. Then what happens?"

"I'm usually on the phone with him, since he lives three thousand miles away. I interrupt him and say, 'Dad, I gotta go. I don't think I can talk about this anymore. Let's talk later.' And then I hang up. We don't talk for a couple of days, and then one of us initiates calling the other. We talk normally and pretend nothing ever happened. This has been going on more than twenty-five years."

"Tell me about the first time you remember experiencing your dad's temper. How old were you? Where were you? All the details."

"Well, I think I was six or seven years old. I remember standing in the corner of the kitchen watching my mom cook and reach for her glass of wine. Then my parents started arguing about money, and I got really tense. My dad got angry, picked up an empty plate in front of him . . . and smashed it on the table. I still vividly remember it shattering—almost like it was in slow motion. I crouched in the corner behind a plant. Then my mom told me to go upstairs to my room."

"What lesson did you learn from that?"

"I learned that if you make people mad, things break. This time it was the plate. Next time it would be me."

"I want you to notice something, Neha. In your story, you were little and your dad was big. That's not true anymore. You're a grown-up. But the little girl in you is getting triggered each time someone's anger reminds you of that situation."

She paused. I was bewildered, but I knew I was buckled in for the ride with 30 participants eagerly watching. I cared way too much about what everyone else thought of me to stop now.

Kris continued, "Can you tell me what age group has temper tantrums and it's considered normal?"

"The terrible twos? Toddlers are pretty notorious for that," I replied.

"Exactly! So, why do toddlers have temper tantrums?"

"Because they are out of options and having difficulty communicating what they need."

"Yes. And that's exactly what your dad is experiencing when he starts yelling. He doesn't think he has any other way to get your attention. So the next time you hear your dad's voice escalating, getting faster and louder, and you hear him start to swear, those are your warning signs. When you notice them, take a nice, deep breath and calm yourself down first, so you can shift out of your normal state of emotionally shutting down. Then imagine him in diapers."

"But that is so disrespectful!" I argued. "I can't do that. In my culture, we're taught to respect our elders."

"I didn't ask you to imagine him naked, Neha. I just asked you to imagine him in diapers, so you can change the dynamic of your being 'small' and his being 'big.' If you can see yourself as the grown-up now and see that he's the one struggling because he can't communicate with you, you'll have much more compassion for him instead of being scared and shutting down.

"It's the same in dealing with someone like Tyler. Remember, it only takes one person to change a conversation, and that person is you. But you have to manage yourself first."

Kris went on to coach us on the importance of pausing, listening deeply to what others are saying, and then thoughtfully responding.

Three days later I was in the Eugene airport waiting to return home. I thought about what an amazing experience the workshop had been. But I still wondered, *Will this really change anything?* I had 30 minutes before we boarded, so I checked my voice mail. I had missed several calls from my father regarding our family's small jewelry business. Before I could call him back, he called again.

"Hi, Dad," I answered. "I haven't had a chance to listen to your voice m—" But he cut me off.

"God dammit, you didn't mail me that package, did you? I needed it for a client. You don't care a thing about me, do you?"

As he continued to yell, I was consciously aware of his escalating tone, the quickening pace of his speech, and his swearing. I recognized the triggers. It was as if he were talking in slow motion. Instead of hanging up on him, I simply took a few deep breaths. And then the most amazing thing happened: He stopped talking. He was done. There was only silence. And I wasn't shattered.

With a calm voice, I began, "Dad, I heard the tone of your voice change; you were talking louder and swearing. I hear how frustrating it is when you think I'm not responsive to your calls. Did you happen to forget that this was the weekend I was at the communication workshop in Oregon and wouldn't be checking my cell phone? I mentioned it to you and Mom last week when we were on the phone. I'm at the airport right now. I'll be home in two hours. If you let me know what you need, I'll send it first thing tomorrow morning."

For the first time in nearly three decades, my father responded in a way I will never forget. He said, "Neha *beti* [using an affectionate Hindi term that means "darling daughter"], I'm sorry. Your dad must be getting old. You did tell us last week. I totally forgot. Could you send out three strands of black pearls in the morning? We don't have any left."

As I hung up, I looked at the phone in disbelief. Kris had been right. By responding differently, I had changed the outcome of our conversation. I suddenly got a glimpse of how much less stress would be in my life if I mastered the art of communication.

TURNAROUND

When I returned to the hospital Monday morning and started using my new communication skills, my work environment began to shift. When confronted with frustration, anger, or conflict of any kind, instead of physically leaving or emotionally shutting down, I began using what I'd learned from the workshop to manage myself first. As soon as I was triggered, I would breathe and calm myself down. Then, instead of getting scared, I would imagine the person who was angry as someone who needed my compassion.

But I still had to face my dilemma with Tyler.

I waited until we were on a break together and then asked him if we could talk privately. He hesitantly agreed. I finally told him what I thought of his behavior and how it had negatively impacted me. For the first time, I found the words to express myself both compassionately and honestly. Armed with the awareness of how I had been triggered by his temper, I was able to manage myself better and stay engaged. It felt good.

This is when my relationship with him transformed: I had broken the pattern of talking *about* Tyler and found the courage to speak *to* him.

To my surprise, Tyler received my feedback with grace and understanding. He even apologized and told me that he wasn't trying to avoid hard work. He loved his patients and loved being a doctor. But he'd had a traumatic experience that served as a turning point in his career.

He had been treating a 56-year-old woman with lung disease. As he prepared her for discharge, Tyler suggested that she stop smoking. She reacted with immediate hostility. "Why should I listen to you? You're a doctor and you're obese. Quit giving me advice and take some of your own medicine!"

From that moment on, Tyler had assumed that patients wouldn't respect him as a physician because of his appearance, so he avoided any situations that would require him to directly interact with them. This was why he was so determined to get the more straightforward cases, and this was why he preferred telephone medicine.

The truth was disarming. My heart melted. I had made up so many stories about Tyler being lazy, mean, rude, and insensitive. Now I realized that his outrageous behavior was an attempt to protect himself from getting hurt again. I couldn't even imagine how painful the encounter with that patient must have been for him. He was so smart and talented, yet he felt as if he needed to hide his physical appearance in order to seem more credible. My compassion for him grew—and I no longer feared his temper.

I was hooked on this new way of communicating. When I interacted with patients, with co-workers, with friends, and even with my family, I listened, empathized, and then made decisions I thought were fair. As a result, I discovered an inner freedom: even if other people didn't change their behavior, if I changed how I responded to a situation, I could change the outcome.

Before this realization, I had been so focused on blaming Tyler's bullying that I hadn't even considered that my defensive reaction was the other half of the problem. What I learned was that in any interaction, if I was willing to focus on my own behavior, I could receive the gift of honest, direct communication. In other words, I held the key to solving my greatest dilemma. And so did my patients.

Because my patients were often hospitalized in critical condition, long-lost friends and loved ones would frequently show up to visit them. Suddenly a college roommate who was finally willing to forgive and forget would appear. Nephews who had been too busy to visit suddenly had time. Or an ex-husband or a disowned daughter materialized. All of these people sat outside the intensive care unit like a collection of missing socks, giving my patients the opportunity to mend important relationships long gone astray.

I began teaching my patients the communication techniques I was now using. And as my patients mustered the courage to open up in ways they never had about their emotions and desires, something magical started to happen. Their symptoms began to reverse.

A 58-year-old woman with chronic insomnia got her first good night's sleep in eight years. A 47-year-old corporate executive with chronic back pain made it through the night without anxiety medication or painkillers. Blood sugar levels began to normalize. Asthmatic patients were released ahead of schedule. And nurses were getting paged half as often.

That's when I realized that a patient's ability and willingness to communicate had the power to vastly improve their health.

The Awareness Prescription

The last place I wanted to be on Christmas Day was on call at the hospital. Nobody else wanted to be there, either. To make a long day longer, I was repeatedly being paged by Debbie, the nurse, regarding a new patient. Andrew Akins was a 56-year-old man with a long history of uncontrolled diabetes. He had been admitted for an emergency amputation of his gangrenous left foot. The nurse had been calling me because his blood sugars were off the charts and he needed additional insulin.

I walked in to quite a scene. The patient was yelling, "When the hell is a doctor going to get me out of here? Or is everyone on vacation?" as Debbie cleaned up green Jell-O splattered across the floor. I looked down and noticed two candy bar wrappers in the wastebasket.

I took a deep breath and began, "Hi, Mr. Akins. I'm Dr. Sangwan." Then I looked at the bloody IV line he'd pulled out of his arm and tossed on the floor. Saline was dripping everywhere. *What a mess*, I thought.

I continued. "I can see that you're frustrated. It looks like we're both having a tough day. I'm sure we could think of better places to be on Christmas Day than here, so let's do this: Why don't we each try to think of just one reason we're thankful to be here today? I don't know what it is, but there's got to be something good about this."

He didn't look convinced, but he nodded reluctantly. I went to see my next patient, all the time trying to come up with something I was grateful for.

A few hours later Debbie paged me again, and I went back to Andrew's room. He still looked pretty unhappy, but at least he'd stopped throwing food.

"Andrew, Debbie told me you've given our exercise some thought. Why don't I go first and tell you what I came up with? I used to be a mechanical engineer, and I switched to medicine because it felt lonely to be in a cubicle with equations and numbers all the time. I wanted to directly help people. And now that's what I get to do. I'm grateful to be here on Christmas day and for the opportunity to connect and be in service to other people when they can't be with their families. What did you come up with? What are you grateful for?"

"Well, I guess I'm grateful that you're a doctor who actually cares enough to listen. I suppose I owe you and Debbie an apology."

My heart softened as I moved toward him and sat down on the edge of his bed.

As Andrew and I talked, we were able to connect the dots and get a better understanding of what was going on beneath his anger and elevated blood sugars. He realized he was all alone this holiday because his unyielding anger and impulsive behavior had finally driven his loved ones away. I introduced him to some of the communication techniques and resources that had helped me and wished him good night.

Much to my amazement, the next morning Debbie reported that Andrew hadn't required any additional insulin and that his blood sugars were only slightly elevated.

Six months later I received a thank-you card from Andrew telling me that after leaving the hospital and using the ideas I had suggested, he had lost 30 pounds and had begun reestablishing relationships with his family.

That was the moment I realized that how I talked to Andrew was the way I should be talking to all of my patients—not just the ones in crisis or throwing green Jell-O tantrums. I needed to ask them questions that would reveal what else was going on in their lives—the issues they might not be aware existed *underneath* their symptoms. Their answers would serve as a catalyst to inspire and engage them in their own self-care. They'd be better able to manage themselves and their stress levels, which in turn would accelerate their healing.

Over time I developed what I refer to as the Awareness Prescription. Once my patients were medically stable, I would write five questions on my prescription pad to prompt them to discover any links between their physical health and the other aspects of their lives.

Question 1: Why this?

Why was the patient suffering from this particular ailment? Why a stroke? Why pneumonia? Why a heart attack?

There's the physical explanation for why a particular part of the body breaks down. That's the pathology. But I'm talking about more than the bacteria that cause a disease or a hormonal feedback loop that stops working. When the body breaks down on a physical level, it's important that we look beyond the textbook definition of a disease, the numbers from a blood test, or the results of an X-ray. Often, exploring beyond the malfunction of a specific organ or system reveals an underlying mental, emotional, or social correlation.

If a patient had back pain, maybe he felt as though he had the weight of the world on his shoulders or didn't feel supported. Maybe he wasn't standing up for himself.

For Andrew, it took a surgical amputation before he was in enough pain to make the connection between his severed foot and the severed relationships in his life.

Question 2: Why now?

Why was this happening to the patient at this particular point in time?

Maybe the stress in his life was steadily increasing until his body simply wouldn't allow him to ignore it anymore. Or possibly his pattern of behavior toward others had created a negative impact on his relationships, and this was how his body forced him to admit feelings of remorse. Perhaps some wound or pain from the past had been suppressed for so long that his body was finally pushing him to confront it.

Andrew's alienation of his family had reached the point that hospitalization on Christmas Day was the only way he could fully experience his loneliness and acknowledge the hurt he had caused himself and others.

Question 3: What might you have missed?

My patients often thought that disease hit them all of a sudden—that a heart attack, for instance, was literally that: an attack. But in fact, their bodies had been changing over time and were likely giving off signals along the way. They just didn't know how to interpret them.

In retrospect, a patient might say that for the past year, climbing stairs had caused him to break out in a sweat and feel slightly winded, but he'd chalked it up to aging. Or perhaps, months before becoming bedridden with pneumonia, he had begun using his inhalers more frequently, had a nagging cough and intermittent muscle aches, and wasn't sleeping well, but he had pushed through it.

Andrew had been using sugar to numb his feelings of anger and loneliness. That's why he even brought his favorite candy bars with him into the hospital. Andrew had repeatedly experienced mood swings associated with his blood sugar highs and lows, along with a progressive numbness in his left extremity, long before he was scheduled for emergency foot surgery.

Question 4: What else needs to be healed?

The physical ailments the body exhibits usually also reflect the pain and suffering, the miscommunication, the disconnected relationships, and the imbalances in someone's external life. These unresolved issues create the stress that in turn breaks down the body's ability to prevent illness and heal.

Did the insomnia that a patient said he'd always had actually begin when he started a high-pressure job a decade ago? Was there any parallel between the excess weight he was unable to lose and the protection he felt he needed from a partner's angry outbursts? Could chronic constipation have anything to do with his need to control the events in his life?

The feelings of anger and isolation that plagued Andrew needed to be treated as much as his diabetes did. It was only when he turned his attention to healing the fractured relationships in his life that he no longer needed his daily sugar binges. Now his stress had decreased and his physical health could improve and be sustained long term.

Question 5: If you spoke from the heart, what would you say?

When patients heard this final question, they often sighed in relief. It was as if I'd given them permission to speak the truth out loud after keeping it hidden for so long—even from themselves.

Most of us speak from our heads. We will gladly share what we think or observe. We're happy to reveal our opinions about the actions of others, and we offer advice whether it's asked for or not. But how often are we willing to travel those 18 short inches from our heads to our hearts and talk about what we truly feel and desire?

It took more than half his life for Andrew to converse with his family in an honest way—to give them a heartfelt apology and admit how much he loved and missed them.

When I asked these five questions, I wasn't asking my patients to cross items off a to-do list. Rather, I was posing these questions as a launchpad, inviting them to speak about whatever resonated with them. All that mattered was that they began connecting their physical well-being with their external circumstances, their patterns of behavior, their relationships, and their emotional truth.

After more than 15 years of seeing patients and exploring the roots of physical illness, I'm convinced that communication is inextricably tied to our overall health. I'm not just talking about our emotional and social well-being; I'm talking about our physical health—the quality of our day-to-day lives, our energy, our stress and anxiety levels, the quality of our sleep, and even our ability to heal.

The simple but startling effects of clear, direct communication would ultimately change the trajectory of my career. Since 2005 I have worked with medical teams, companies, and in my private practice to reveal the powerful link between our ability to communicate and our health. In addition to being a doctor of medicine, I now see myself as a doctor of communication, empowering people with the tools and skills not only to heal their physical bodies, but also to transform their lives.

THE I-FIVE CONVERSATION

The same practical communication tools that I discovered for myself and my patients will also help you. Once you know how to communicate clearly, you'll improve your relationship with yourself and with the world around you while simultaneously improving your health—long before you end up in an emergency room.

It starts with your everyday conversations—whether you're handling a challenging exchange at work or simply sharing something with a loved one. You no longer have to wait for someone else to change in order to express yourself clearly.

If you take responsibility for your own communication, you can turn around some of the most challenging interactions in your life, which will decrease your stress level and have you sleeping soundly again. The conversation begins internally and helps you get crystal clear about what you want before engaging in conversation with another.

I call these tools and this communication framework the i-Five Conversation.[3] The "i" stands for *interpret* and *integrate*. The "Five" represents the five key components of clear communication.

1. Interpreting Your Body

2. Interpreting Your Thoughts

3. Interpreting Your Emotions

4. Interpreting Your Desires

5. Integrating These into Action

How you interpret and integrate these five key areas of the i-Five Conversation will determine your success in relating to yourself and others. The i-Five Conversation will help you become a clear, concise, and direct communicator.

THE i-FIVE CONVERSATION

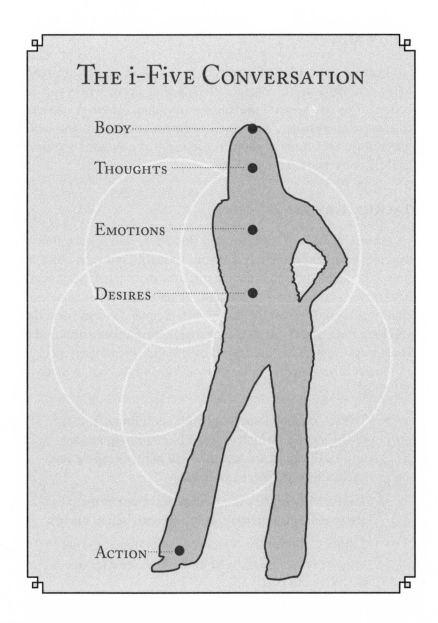

BODY

THOUGHTS

EMOTIONS

DESIRES

ACTION

i-Five Moment

Learning the i-Five Conversation will lead to new insights. i-Five moments are unexpected twists that occur when you see connections that were previously invisible. These experiences change everything, and you'll begin to connect to the world differently. This book is about those magical moments—and the healing conversations that follow.

TalkRx Toolkit

As you work your way through this book, you'll learn how to interpret your body's signals and your thoughts, emotions, and desires. You'll learn how to integrate this information into your everyday conversations, and you will also be prepared to navigate more challenging conflicts. At the end of each chapter, I recommend that you keep track of any insights or realizations that have occurred to you. I have created some resources to enhance your experience.

To get instant access, go to DoctorNehaTalkRx.com, where you will find:

- TalkRx Journal: Download your complimentary copy of the journal, which offers personalized questions and additional exercises that will help you apply the i-Five Conversation to your life.

- TalkRx Videos: Watch how practical these principles are in real-life situations as I work with actual clients.

- TalkRx Community: Share your experience, garner support from like-minded individuals, and receive exclusive offers.

INTERPRETING
YOUR BODY

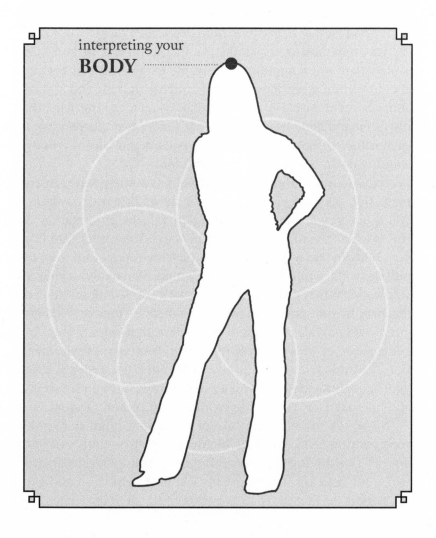

interpreting your
BODY

Your body's talking. Are you listening?

I don't know about you, but for a majority of my life, I treated my body as a vehicle to transport my head. To school. To work. To meetings. To various places where I could analyze data, give advice, and solve problems. I had given my brain so much power that it had become a little dictator. My mind thought it could overrule anything—including my body, stress, fatigue, the need for sleep, or even an extra ten pounds. Even though I didn't take care of or listen to my body, when some physical part of me broke down, my mind took over and blamed my body for being weak. *Why am I so tired? That's ridiculous. So what if I didn't eat breakfast? It's not that big a deal. Just push through and keep going.*

It's embarrassing to admit, but in the process of becoming a physician, my schooling and my life experience had been all about overriding my body to endure intense training and 36-hour shifts. Somewhere along the way, I had bought into the belief that my mind and body were entities that functioned independent of each other. It took several years of patient care and my body's shutting down before I changed my mind.

Externally and internally, your body is a finely tuned instrument that allows you to experience the multisensory world. If you listen to your body, you will gain valuable information. So this is where the i-Five Conversation starts. You gather data from your body in two ways: your senses pick up information from the outside world, while your physiology sends signals about your inside world. When you're tuned in, what's happening outside you (changes in your environment or in someone's tone or body language) will provide clues about your interactions with others. And being aware of what's happening within you (your physical reactions to those changes) will give you important feedback about your thoughts, emotions, and desires. Tuning in to both external and internal data is critical to creating clear communication.

So, if you make the mistake of using your mind to override your body, as I did, you'll be highly productive—until you burn out. It's like driving at breakneck speed toward your destination while not noticing that your Check Engine light is on and your gas tank is on Empty. To arrive successfully at your destination, you need to pay attention to the internal condition of your vehicle while paying attention to the external driving conditions. You need to maintain what I call "double vision."

Double vision in the i-Five Conversation means paying attention to two levels of awareness—in this case, how your body is talking to you and how you're engaging with somebody else. Without this feedback, you will be at a distinct disadvantage in any conversation. Ignoring your body is the equivalent of slapping duct tape on your car's Check Engine light. How effective is that? In the short term, you may buy yourself some time, but the problem doesn't go away. And if you ignore it long enough, it's likely to result in a catastrophic physical breakdown.

Listening to your body gives you an advantage in conversation because it provides early clues about your responses and reactions. Being conscious of your internal state of being is essential for navigating communication effectively with others. Knowing when you need to ask more questions or want more time are just a few important insights that result from being tuned in to your physiology. *Interpreting your body* is the first step to understanding yourself and getting clear about how to respond in any situation.

CHAPTER 1

Missing What's Right in Front of You

Brandon was a 52-year-old triathlete and successful businessman. Early one Saturday morning as he was biking up Mount Diablo, he collapsed. He was rushed in an ambulance to the emergency room.

Brandon's blood pressure was elevated at 220/120, half of his body was limp, and he was slurring his words. After getting the results of a CT scan of his head, I admitted him and wrote orders for the clinical treatment of an acute stroke.

Three days later Brandon was swallowing and speaking normally. His body was physically strong, and his recovery was quick. I went to Brandon's room to let him know that if all went well overnight, he would be heading home in the morning. On the way there, I wondered whether stress was playing a role in his illness.

"How are you, Brandon? Knowing you and how fast you're recovering, I bet you'll be climbing Mount Diablo this weekend!" I said jokingly as I entered the room.

Brandon smiled back at me. "I'm good, Doc. How's my blood pressure?"

"Much better," I responded. "Were you aware you had high blood pressure before this hospital stay?"

"Not really. I feel a throbbing in my head and neck sometimes, but otherwise nothing. It's been that way for years. I don't remember the last time I had a checkup. Once I had a migraine for three weeks while we were on a tight deadline, and I just pushed through it. I'm used to high stress and I thrive on the adrenaline rush."

"It sounds like it wasn't even on your radar. That's why they call high blood pressure the silent killer. Many people don't even realize how harmful it is until they have a heart attack or a stroke. It's important that you follow your blood pressure closely. As we get you ready for discharge, would you be willing to consider a few questions I like to ask my patients?"

He nodded, so I asked him my five questions as I began jotting them on my prescription pad:

"Why a stroke?

"Why now?

"What might you have missed?

"What else needs to be healed?

"If you spoke from your heart, what would you say?"

Before I could hand him the Awareness Prescription, he began, "If I could speak from the heart, I would say, I've worked my whole life to make my father proud."

He shook his head and looked down at his blistered hands as he began listing his accomplishments. "I'm an Ivy League grad. I'm married with two beautiful children. I'm a triathlete and always pushing my body to do more. I have to confess that I usually get annoyed when my body slows me down. I just sold my company for millions of dollars. And somehow none of it's enough. I keep pushing for the next achievement, pushing to climb the next mountain, hoping peace is on the other side. But when I get there I don't find peace; I just find another mountain to climb."

"Wow, you've accomplished an amazing amount, and I hear how important that is to you. What makes you think your father isn't proud of you?" I asked.

"Well, my father was a professor, and I remember the tension in the house whenever report cards came out. One time in particular, I had gotten straight A's and one B+. I proudly handed over my report card to my dad.

He raised his eyebrows and pointed at the paper, shook his head, and asked, 'B+?! What happened? Mediocrity will get you nowhere, son.'"

As Brandon recalled the story, I could see the pain on his face—almost as if he were once again that dejected little boy. "You must have been so hurt and disappointed," I said. "Did you ever ask your dad if he was proud of you?"

"I never even thought to ask him. My dad was a man of few words." He took a deep breath, then continued. "Doc, the craziest part is that my dad died five years ago, and I'm still struggling to prove myself. It's just that I don't know exactly who I'm trying to make proud.

"This stroke forced me to a halt. I had no choice but to slow down and listen to my body. I didn't even realize how exhausted I was. Being admitted to the hospital is an odd way to get three days of much-needed downtime. Can someone actually be grateful for a stroke? Now that I've regained function, I kind of am."

"Sure, that makes sense. So what else needs to be healed?"

"I usually sleep four hours a night—and to make that happen, I have to knock myself out with Ambien. Maybe now that I understand what's driving all of this, I won't be in such a panic to do more. If I could get seven or eight hours naturally, that would make a huge difference. I suppose some forgiveness for my dad would be a good place to start."

I placed my hand on his shoulder. "That's great insight. And I really like the plan you've come up with. I think it will address both your physical and your emotional healing. One last thought: how about showering some of that forgiveness you're planning to give to your father on yourself? I think you deserve some grace and kindness for how hard you've worked."

After talking with Brandon at length about forgiveness and next steps, I shared some books and additional resources to help him lower his stress levels and begin to listen to his body.

The next time I heard from Brandon, he said, "You're not going to believe this, Dr. Neha. I feel great and I'm more relaxed. I'm on half the dose of my sleep meds, and there have actually been nights that I didn't need any at all!"

Observing Your World

Hopefully, it won't take a stroke for you to learn the importance of interpreting your body's external and internal communication signals.

Let's start this process in the way that is easiest for most people to grasp—by looking at the external world. Your body is an incredibly complex instrument, continually taking in and processing data through your five primary senses (sight, hearing, taste, touch, and smell) so you can effectively navigate the world.

Gathering data through your senses provides you with raw, objective information. You may see someone walk into a room. While talking to him, you may notice that he crosses his legs. You may hear certain words. You may hear someone whispering. You may smell smoke. You may touch something wet on the chair. You may taste a sour lemon. These are examples of objective data your body is picking up from the outside world.

Objective data is similar to what a video camera would pick up in a room. It might pick up that there is red paint on the walls and a tan couch and chair with a brown table between them. It might also pick up hardwood floors with two muddy footprints and eight crumpled papers in the trash can.

What would a video camera "see" if it saw you reading this book right now? It would record your hands holding a book or an electronic reading device. It would record the location where you are sitting or lying down and the movement of your eyes back and forth. A video camera might "hear" audio in the form of your mumbling or sighing or my voice speaking from an audiobook. It might just pick up silence. Unfortunately (for the video camera) it can't touch, taste, or smell, but you get the idea. A video camera doesn't interpret the facts to mean anything specific. It just records them.

Every day we are human video cameras taking in data. Fortunately, our human technology is more advanced than that. We go on to integrate that data and make meaning of the information we've observed. To communicate effectively, it's essential to understand the difference between objective data and our interpretations. If you know how to navigate this external data, then you can recognize that what you think are facts are actually your observations mixed with your thoughts, beliefs, ideas, and perceptions. There's a big difference! Being able to distinguish different forms of incoming data allows you to make decisions and navigate conflict with ease.

Let's use Brandon's example. He picked up the external data from his dad—he saw the raised eyebrows and the shake of his head. He heard his father's tone as he exclaimed, "B+?! What happened? Mediocrity will get you nowhere, son." Those were the external signals Brandon was receiving. He obtained this external data the same way we all do when we're communicating with others—through three main aspects of communication.

THE PRIMARY ELEMENTS OF COMMUNICATION

There are three main components of external interactions: words, tone, and body language. Research varies in terms of which components account for what percentage of the message. In the 1960s, psychologist Albert Mehrabian reported that 55 percent of communication came from a person's body language, 38 percent came from tone, and only 7 percent of the message was conveyed through the actual words. While there has been much debate about Mehrabian's studies and much evolution in our modalities of communication over the past few decades (think e-mail, text, chat, etc.), current research still indicates that nonverbal communication makes up the majority of face-to-face exchanges.[4]

It's clear that communication is a multisensory experience. While impressive as a fun fact at parties, knowing the percentages of the different components of communication isn't going to make you a more effective communicator. While research provides important context and helps to convert skeptics into believers, I advocate doing your own research. Yep! Right here. Right now.

Imagine if I were right in front of you, say at a conference delivering the content of this book in person. How would you be gathering data from me? Primarily you would be using your sight and hearing. You would be picking up on my *body language* + *tone* + *words*. Your "research" would give you valuable information about my message, and your body would start responding to what you picked up.

Most people are aware of the concepts of body language, tone, and words, but they don't often understand the importance of how these components of communication can assist in any conversation. Subtle (or not so subtle) shifts in body language, tone, and words are often an early indication that something has changed in an interaction. It may be as simple as someone crossing his arms, breaking eye contact, or getting quiet. When you feel confused, it's often because of a mismatch of these three important components. This misalignment holds the key to unlocking the mystery of *What the hell just happened?*

SAME MESSAGE, DIFFERENT DELIVERY

I've got an easy scenario to show you how aligning body language, tone, and words can create communication synergy—and determine how effective your message will be.

Suppose it's two days after you've made a health resolution to lose a few pounds. You've just enjoyed your carrot sticks and steamed fish for dinner, and for dessert you've splurged and had two slices of apple. Suddenly the doorbell rings. There at your threshold is an adorable, seven-year-old Girl Scout with curly red hair, pigtails, and freckles. She's shivering. Pointing at her backpack, she bashfully inquires, "Hi, ma'am. I'm Mandy. Can you please buy my last two boxes of cookies?"

She drops her head slightly and lowers her voice. "They are only four dollars each, and I'm trying to raise money to go on a camping trip. It's for a very good cause!" And then her big blue eyes stare up at you with gentle curiosity and eternal hope.

You think, *It's only eight dollars. And after all, I don't have to eat them all myself!*

What's going on in this communication scenario? What are the three different ways the Girl Scout is communicating with you?

First there is her *body language*: her blue eyes staring up at you, her tilted head and bouncing pigtails, her gesture toward her backpack with its last two boxes of cookies. What is her body language conveying? Why, of course, without knowing she's sending a very clear message: "Forget your health resolutions—how can you possibly resist all of my cuteness?"

Can you hear her? Her *tone* is her second deadly weapon. With certain words, she lowers her voice and speaks shyly. In other words, she musters her courage to convey the bleeding hope of her innocent heart. Her message? "This is really important. Haven't *you* ever wanted something this badly?"

Her third and final strike comes from the actual *words* she uses. She's a pro. She starts off personal by introducing herself. She brings her etiquette to show respect. She stuns you with her detailed request and directness. She makes a sales pitch that would have you not only funding a charitable cause, but also making an investment in her own life skills and education—all while enjoying something that tastes good. It's nearly impossible to resist.

If you were the one who answered the door, what part of her communication would have influenced you most—her body language, tone, or words?

Words Only Are Lonely

What if you had only received a text or an e-mail from the Girl Scout? You would have missed a lot of information. While it might have been more convenient to receive the message on your own schedule, how effective would the communication have been (from her point of view)? And would it have been easier for you to reply NO? Bottom line: The communication would have likely been less persuasive and a lot easier for you to turn down. But the good news is you'd probably still be on your diet.

Words are important. Your choice of words makes a difference. The problem is that when you send communication in the form of words only, the interpretation of those words is left entirely up to the reader. It's almost as if the reader gets to insert the tone and body language they *think* you're using to convey the message. In this very moment, although I'm writing with a very specific tone and intention, you get to decide what tone you think I'm speaking in and what you think I mean.

There are lots of good reasons to communicate in the various mediums that use words only, such as text, tweet, e-mail, and chat, for example. These mediums are great for conveying information, asking a quick question, making a request, or confirming instructions. Often they are the most efficient, effective, and convenient ways to dialogue about factual matters. The written word engages one of your senses—sight.

Some people use the written word for clarity in agreements or to provide an e-mail trail for legal purposes. Others use the written word because they think it's more polite and less invasive. Some people like writing because it allows them time to think and get it "just right." Unquestionably, it's one of the most convenient ways to give and receive communication.

Don't be fooled, though—communication strategies aren't always noble. Using words only can make it easy to avoid conflict, a common desire. Some people know if they get on the phone with Aunt Nellie, they'll undoubtedly get roped into another awkward social gathering. Or worse yet, others may use e-mail, text, or chat to avoid difficult in-person conversations, like breaking off a romantic relationship.

For others, writing behind the screen of their laptops or their smartphones helps them muster the bravado to express opinions they wouldn't dare say in person. Unfortunately, some use the safety of anonymous electronic communication as a way to lash out and channel their anger, fear, or hatred. Whether it's tears, frustration, or awkward silence, some people will do anything to avoid facing their own or others' emotions. This allows them to have more perceived control.

Take a moment to reflect on whether you ever use words-only communication to hide or avoid conflict.

As I've said before, while there is much that can be expressed through the written word, it leaves the most room for flexibility and interpretation *by the reader*. Although e-mailing, texting, tweeting, or posting may be the most convenient way to communicate, you need to know *when* these methods are most effective. This will make a big difference in how you communicate with others. Some situations call for words only, but make sure you're aware of why you're using a particular medium and what to do if it doesn't create the intended effect.

Words-only communication works best when the content is purely factual or a question requires a simple yes or no. For example:

- The party is at 347 Harley Street at 6 P.M. tonight.

- Can you pick up milk on the way home?

- Do you want to go for a run?

Have you ever written an e-mail when you were upset or angry because you thought it would convey your message more clearly? It may have allowed you to think through the situation and given you a controlled environment in which you could express yourself. That's true. While writing an e-mail can help you get clear, the downside is that it can leave a lot of room for misinterpretation on the receiving end.

How words are spoken adds more meaning and context to the message, but it requires your body to get involved—specifically your vocal cords.

Words + Tone: Things Are Getting Friendly

Imagine that the Girl Scout had called you rather than showing up at your door. What would have been missing in her communication? Well, those blue eyes, freckles, and pigtails and the oversize backpack full of determination couldn't have tugged on your heartstrings. It probably would have been a lot easier to say no if she weren't standing right in front of you.

So consider how communication changes over the phone—with words + tone. You are now using your sense of hearing, and you're picking up two forms of communication. Tone adds an animated, auditory dimension to words, allowing you to convey your message with emotion and personality. The good news is that spoken communication creates a dynamic personal connection between two or more people in real time (unless you leave a voice mail, of course).

Pay attention to tone in a conversation and you can gather more information—and also identify when words and tone don't match up. This is one of the biggest external clues your senses pick up on, and you can use it to decipher mixed messages. We'll talk more about unraveling complex communication in Chapter 5.

The tone of your voice comes across through:

- Pace and volume

- Points of inflection (an inflection at the end of a statement can indicate a question)

- Rise and fall of intonation (pitch and emphasis of certain words)

These physical cues express the intention and emotion behind the words being said. Tone gives underlying clues about what is really happening.

Let's take a relatively neutral word like *oh* and see what happens when you use tone to give it meaning. (It'll make you smile.)

1. Say *oh* out loud like you are surprised.

2. Say *oh* out loud like you are angry.

3. Say *oh* out loud like you are skeptical.

4. Say *oh* out loud like you are disappointed.

5. Say *oh* out loud like you are pleased.

Okay, you get the idea: Tone matters!*

This is where objective data and subjective interpretation start to mix. We typically associate a particular meaning with a certain tone. Or we use tone to animate our communication. Tone changes the interpretation of what's being said. For those of you who

---

* If you've never thought about this, right now you may be experiencing one of those i-Five Moments I referred to at the beginning of the book.

are thinking, *I know how to get tone across in an e-mail, and I can tell when someone is yelling at me in a text*—that's your interpretation, but it may not be true.

Granted, in our written communication we've come up with ways to convey tone—those wonderful emoticons and emojis that tell the other person you're happy or sad when you text. Adding color and images to our words-only communication enhances the message by conveying an attitude or emotion, just like tone does.

Let's talk about how this might get confusing. In an e-mail or text, what do ALL CAPITAL LETTERS mean? Yelling? Anger? Excitement? Emphasis? All capital letters can be interpreted in various ways. What we know is that the interpretation is ultimately left to the reader of the message, and not the sender.

I learned this firsthand in July of 2008. The phone rang, and on the other end was my colleague Dr. Jim Gordon.[5] Jim had just received an invitation from Saudi Arabia that read, "The Prince Sultan Cardiac Center is honored to invite you to speak at the second International Conference on Advanced Cardiac Sciences: 'King of Organs'"—a conference focused on the heart. They wanted Jim to speak about the link between depression and heart disease.

Jim said, "Neha, I have a conflict, and I need you to represent my work in Saudi. Are you available?"

When I told my parents about the opportunity, the panic began. They pleaded, "Neha beti, please don't go to the Middle East. We grew up amidst Hindu-Muslim conflict. It's dangerous."

My colleagues said, "Don't go. You'll be treated like a second-class citizen because you're a woman."

As you can imagine, my excitement was rapidly turning into anxiety. I called Jim back and asked, "Are you sure I'm going to be safe?"

"Absolutely. But why don't you reach out ahead of time to one of the men traveling from the U.S. and get to know him? Then you'll feel more comfortable."

Logically, it made sense. *Why not?* I thought.

One of those gentlemen was Dr. Paul Rosch, the founder of the American Institute of Stress. I decided to e-mail him: "Dr. Rosch, my name is Neha Sangwan, and I'll be joining you in Saudi on behalf of Jim Gordon. I wanted to say hello and connect before we meet. Have you ever been to Saudi? Or is this your first time? I'm curious what to expect."

His response arrived in all caps:

"I'M SORRY JIM WON'T BE JOINING US. I WAS VERY MUCH LOOKING FORWARD TO MEETING HIM. WE HAVE CORRESPONDED BY E-MAIL ABOUT HIS BOOK, UNSTUCK. IT IS MY FIRST TRIP TO SAUDI. IT'S EVERY-ONE'S FIRST TRIP."

This is when I began to make up stories in my head:

- Paul wishes Jim were going instead of me.
- Paul must be writing in all caps so I "get it."
- Paul doesn't think a woman should be joining three men on a trip to the Middle East.
- Paul is being really condescending.

My anxiety continued to grow. I noticed that I wasn't sleeping well and my throat was constantly constricted. It dawned on me that I didn't have very much information in the e-mail from Dr. Rosch. So I decided to use the Curiosity Tool that I teach to so many of my clients. All I needed to do was to state what I had observed and then get curious.

I picked up the phone. "Hi, Dr. Rosch. It's Neha." After a bit of small talk I said, "I noticed your e-mail was in all capital letters. What does that mean?"

"Oh, sweetie, when you get to be eighty, you'll see what hap-pens to your body. Not only do I type with one finger, but some-times I write in capital letters because I can't see worth a darn!"

Talk about a stress reliever! On top of that, when I met Paul in person at the airport in Saudi Arabia and body language came into play, it completed the picture. He reminded me of a nurturing grandfather. It was clear that Paul didn't have a condescending bone in his body.

Words + Tone + Body Language: A Communication Party

The third aspect of external communication is body language. Body language—everything from a firm handshake to slouched shoulders or folded arms—speaks volumes. It can encompass facial expressions that are conscious or unconscious. On my Saudi trip, everything changed when I saw Paul Rosch's gentle smile. When I observed my patient Brandon shaking his head, looking down, and taking a deep breath before he spoke, his body language conveyed the gravity of what he was about to share. And I know that if that Girl Scout had been at my doorstep, batting her eyelashes and bouncing her pigtails, she would have had me at "Hello."

Even on its own, without tone and words, body language silently sends its own message. Let's look at a few common scenarios:

- If you were to tell a teenager to clean her room, and she rolled her eyes and stomped up the stairs, her body language would give you a big clue as to what she thought about your request.

- Have you ever been in traffic and cut in front of someone—even unintentionally? In the rearview mirror, if you see the driver behind you mouthing words and waving his fist, you get information about his response to your action.

- Think back to a recent social gathering you've attended with your partner or a friend. Without a word being spoken, could you tell when he or she was ready to leave? You know the look.

Of course, body language is not universal. For instance, depending on cultural upbringing, using or not using eye contact can have different meanings. In the U.S., direct eye contact often signifies clarity, confidence, and trust. Yet some Asian countries consider looking away to be a sign of respect toward authority. Understanding cultural nuances gives us context in which to think about how body language may be influencing our cross-cultural relationships.

The presence or absence of body language, tone, and words plays a big role in clarifying communication. And the more awareness you have about how you gather and sort external data, the easier it is to problem-solve when communication challenges arise. Understanding body language, tone, and words helps you identify when mixed messages are being sent. It allows you to figure out what is missing or out of alignment for yourself or others.

The way you do this in a conversation is by first stating objective data (e.g., what you heard or saw) to create neutral ground. This clarifies for the other person what you've observed. Then it's time to get curious and gather more information. In equation form, the Curiosity Tool is: external data + curiosity = clarity

For example, have you ever been with someone who raises her voice as she exclaims, "I am not angry!"? You may be confused. And you might be inclined to say something along the lines of "You *are* angry! You just never admit it."

However, now that you're aware of how she is communicating, through body language, tone, and words, you could respond with this: "I saw your face turn red [body language] and heard your voice get louder [tone] as you said, 'I am not angry' [words]. What happened [curiosity]?" This gives the other person clarity that what you've experienced—the external data—doesn't seem to match up. Presenting her with what you saw and heard gives the other person a chance to reconcile what's actually happening. Often it's something you couldn't have even guessed!

Deciphering external data is the foundation on which to build your everyday conversations and even your most challenging ones. Clear communication starts with gathering external data through your five senses. But here's the catch: this isn't the only data you're receiving. A parallel internal conversation is also happening inside you, and it affects your external interactions whether you're paying attention or not. This internal dialogue involves your body's physiology. This might sound complicated, but it's not, really. You're already familiar with what I'm talking about.

◆ ◆ ◆ ◆ ◆

TALKRX TOOLKIT

Curiosity Tool

When in doubt about what just happened:

1. State what you observed (external data).
2. Ask a question (curiosity).

YOUR I-FIVE MOMENT

- To identify how you give information to and receive information from the outside world, answer five personalized questions in Chapter 1 of your *TalkRx Journal*. Go to DoctorNehaTalkRx.com to download your complimentary journal.

- Share with the TalkRx Community any insights, discoveries, or questions that came up as you read the chapter.

CHAPTER 2

KNOCK, KNOCK. GUESS WHO?

Your body is polite. It knows you're busy. So it first communicates with a whisper—you know, that annoying tightness in your shoulder or your neck. But when you brush it off, it begins to speak louder and you develop an aching upper back. If you're still too busy to pay attention, it raises its voice again, and you'll wake up with a stiff neck and lower-back pain. Push on through, and your body will have no choice but to knock you out with a two-by-four. Next thing you know, you'll be flat in bed and calling in sick to work. (And the best part is, you'll be surprised by it all.)

By the time Brandon wound up in the hospital, his body was screaming. He learned two crucial lessons—the hard way. The first was that he was using work and extreme sports to relieve stress and override those early signals in order to prove something to himself (not his dad). And the second lesson was that his body was talking to him long before he listened.

As a child, Brandon had paid attention to the data he gathered from the external world (his dad's facial expressions, tone, and words that "mediocrity will get you nowhere"), but he had missed the other half of his body's communication—his internal signals. Brandon didn't articulate what was happening inside his younger self when he showed his dad his report card, but I imagine his stomach was in knots or his heart was pounding.

In his adult life, Brandon worked crazy hours and pushed his body to its physical limits to accomplish what he thought would make his father proud. Except the fact was, by the time Brandon landed in the hospital, his father had been dead for five years, so it was clear that the only person driving Brandon was Brandon. He discovered how unaware he was of his body's internal dialogue when I asked him if he knew he had high blood pressure. He mentioned that he had periodically noticed a throbbing in his head and neck and that he'd had a migraine for three weeks but just pushed through it. It wouldn't surprise me if Brandon had had high blood pressure for many years before I met him. Once he started paying attention to his internal signals and let go of the pressure he was putting on himself, Brandon was not only happier but also able to sleep better.

Can you see the importance of listening to the internal conversation your body is having with you? The problem is that most people don't know what it's telling them. If you pay attention to only one type of conversation—either external or internal—you're missing a lot of information. Understanding the ways your body simultaneously communicates with others (external) and with you (internal) will provide you with a new and refreshing sense of clarity in conversation. This is the foundation that frames your everyday i-Five Conversations and will also serve you when situations get tough. Now let's decipher this internal conversation.

Your Body's Unique Language

Many people aren't even aware of how their body is sending them messages. Instead, they treat physical sensations as a nuisance or simply don't know what to do with them. Everyone's body has a unique way of speaking, including yours.

It's important to become familiar with your body's messages and what they mean. If you pay attention, even subtle signals such as muscle tightness, flushing, or tingling in your hands or feet can give you valuable information. These physical signals are the way your unconscious mind talks to you through your body. Slight bodily changes are the earliest signs telling you that you need to pay attention to what's happening within you and around you. I refer to these as intelligent signals because they are a part of your body's physical intelligence.

WARNING: Sometimes physical signals have their root in physical causes. For example, chest pressure and sweating can indicate a heart attack. But other times, the same physical sensations can result from experiencing an emotional reaction to a situation. So first, rule out any potential medical concern. Once you have a clean bill of physical health from your doctor, pay attention to what else your body might be saying.

Take a look at the body map illustration on the next page to get a few ideas of how your body might be speaking to you. It's time to map out your body's signals. Place a check mark next to any sensations that you commonly experience.

Headaches
Heaviness
Fatigue
Going Blank   Jaw Clenching
Shallow Breathing
Throat Constriction   Neck Stiffness
Shoulder Tightness
Heart Racing
Chest Tightness
Flushing
Sweating
Stomach Turning
Stomach Knots
Butterflies
Stomach Dropping

Tremors

Muscle Tightness

Numbness
Tingling

Body Map

Pay attention to your physiological signals*

*Warning: While these sensations can signal getting out of your comfort zone, they can also signal a serious medical condition. Please discuss them with your health professional.

Your body is on call 24/7 to pick up the highs and lows of every conversation and interaction in your world. The signals it sends can help you efficiently and effectively make decisions.

Sometimes, even before your conscious mind has time to process what's happened, your physiology lets you know that:

- Something is important to you
- Something is out of balance
- Something is different from what you expected
- Something isn't quite right
- Something is just right (kind of like Goldilocks and the Three Bears)

Here are five everyday scenarios and some physical sensations that could accompany them:

1. If you're asked a question and you don't answer honestly, your throat may constrict, your muscles may tighten, and your jaw may clench.

2. When you're watching your favorite sports team score a goal, you may experience your heart racing and a rush of energy that causes you to jump out of your seat and cheer.

3. When you agree to take on another project at work (even though you already have too much on your plate), you may develop a headache or a backache.

4. If your mouth says yes while your body is saying no, you may experience a knot in your stomach or your energy might drop. That night you may even have difficulty sleeping.

5. When you kiss your child or a loved one goodnight, you may experience warmth in your body, your muscles relaxing, and your heart rate slowing.

Pay attention to your body talk. If you're thinking, *I don't have time for that*, I want you to know it doesn't take extra time. It just takes awareness.

———————————◆—◆—◆◆———————————

Let's try an exercise. Begin by noticing where your hands and feet are placed and if they are warm or cool. How does your head feel—heavy or light? Can you feel your heart beating? Do you feel any sensations in your chest? Is your breathing shallow or deep? What about your abdomen? Your legs? Do you feel any tightness or pain? Are there any other signals your body is sending you?

Now that you're waking up to your body's physical intelligence, you have important information that will guide you. You need to know this data so you can interpret what your body is saying. So become aware of your body's signals when you're not reading this book. The next time you're interacting with someone, do the same exercise and become familiar with the feedback your body gives you. This time note what is happening externally as well—the topic of conversation, whom you're with, where you are, and the event immediately preceding each sensation. You will use this awareness to decipher how your body's feedback will help you clarify your thoughts, emotions, and desires to take effective action.

———————————◆—◆—◆◆———————————

If you learn to recognize and make meaning of your body's physical intelligence, then you will be able to respond more effectively in any situation. For example, if you realize that butterflies in your stomach often accompany a situation that makes you nervous but generally turns out well, you'll give yourself the green light to go ahead with whatever you're doing. If you know that you get a headache when you've been pushing yourself too hard, you'll know that it's in your best interest to turn down an upcoming project. For me, I noticed that when my colleague Tyler or my dad got angry, my muscles would tense up and I would nearly stop breathing. My gut reaction was to physically leave the room or hang up the phone. Now when I feel those sensations, I slow down, take a few deep breaths, and paraphrase what I heard the other person say. This allows the other person to know I heard them while giving me a few seconds before I respond.

Let's do another exercise to make this theory practical. On a scale of 1 to 10, where 1 represents an unpleasant experience that you hope to forget and 10 represents a joyous experience, bring to mind an event in your life that you would categorize as a 1, such as losing something dear to you, like a loved one, a pet, or a job. Maybe someone said something that really upset you. How did your body communicate with you that this experience was unpleasant? What physical sensations did you feel? Scan the Body Map (page 24) for clues, and jot them down in your journal.

Next, imagine an event that you would categorize as a 10, such as a celebration, a new addition to the family, or the completion of a hard-earned goal. What physical signals did your body send to you then? Just by thinking about it, your body may experience similar sensations. Try to get as specific as possible. Jot those down as well.

Paying attention to these signals in your everyday life—even the more subtle ones—will bring you a greater awareness of your body's unique language.

AT THE EDGE OF COMFORT AND BEYOND

Since you're reading this book, you've probably either (a) been given an ultimatum by your doctor or a loved one or (b) taken it upon yourself to reduce your stress, improve your health, strengthen your relationships, and save yourself time. Either way, this process takes courage—and you can't be comfortable *and* courageous at the same time. So settle in, because it's time to get comfy with discomfort.

Some aspects of your life are working well. Keep those! And then there are the aspects of your life that aren't going so smoothly, that you avoid or deny altogether. How do you know which is which? Your body always knows.

I was introduced to the idea of body zones at the communication workshop I attended in Eugene. I picture the zones as three concentric circles that we move in and out of depending on what we're experiencing. These zones are dynamic and flexible. The innermost circle is the comfort zone, the middle one is the learning zone, and the outermost is the panic zone. Our body's physiology lets us know when we are transitioning between zones. I learned that my body speaks to me in different ways and at different volumes depending on the situation. And so does yours.

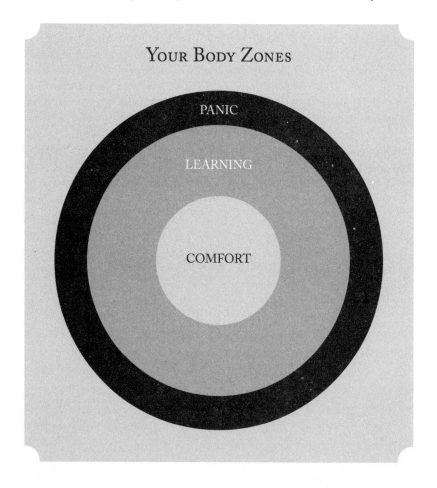

YOUR BODY ZONES

PANIC

LEARNING

COMFORT

How will knowing what zone you're in help you communicate more effectively? Once you recognize the sensations associated with each zone, you'll be able to quickly navigate situations. For instance, if someone you think is attractive winks at you and your heart starts racing, it might mean that you're moving out of your comfort zone. You have a choice in that moment about how to communicate—stay in your comfort zone by looking away, or move boldly into your learning zone by holding eye contact and winking back. In the same scenario, suppose you are introduced to this person, and in mid-conversation you realize that he is your ex-spouse's attorney in your divorce case from a decade ago. You feel nauseated and start stuttering, and you recognize you've hit your panic zone. If you're aware of your body signals and the zone you've entered, you can pause the conversation and excuse yourself so you can process what's just happened and figure out next steps. But let's back up and take this one step at a time.

The Comfort Zone

We'll begin with your comfort zone and what happens when you venture out of it. Think of your comfort zone as a place that's cozy. You probably find that certain people, situations, and tasks are easier to handle than others. Any familiar interactions, skills, patterns, habits, and strategies have likely become a part of your comfort zone.

For example, if you enjoy being in nature, going on a hike may be in your comfort zone. If you grew up in a large family, it may feel natural to be surrounded by noise and chaos. If you've lived in the same city or worked at the same job for a number of years, navigating your commute may require little or no effort on your part. For one person, to prepare a meal and throw a dinner party for 20 may seem like a natural activity. I, on the other hand, would be paralyzed by the idea and would have to coerce my mom or a friend to help.

The comfort zone is known. So it requires very little energy and effort. It's the path of least resistance, such as watching your favorite show with a friend or catching up over coffee. Spending time in the comfort zone is rejuvenating. It can be easy and safe, but staying too long causes big problems.

Bad habits, behaviors that aren't getting you what you want, resistance to change, and plain stubbornness can also be part of your comfort zone. In other words, don't mistake the word *comfort* to mean *good for you*. For me, in the face of anger, my comfort zone behavior was to physically shut down and remove myself from the situation (with Tyler) or hang up the phone (on my dad). While it temporarily soothed me, it didn't solve my problems.

Those who stay only in the comfort zone often describe feeling stuck or bored. The problem with staying there too long is that there's little to no growth. Think of a time when you stayed in a relationship or a job too long. C'mon, I know you have. How did you know? Whatever the physical signal, you may have found yourself checking out, feeling trapped, or making excuses.

The Learning Zone

When you move away from what is known and familiar, you will have some sort of reflexive response. Your body will wake up and start sending signals. They're like updates from the Weather Channel to help you plan for upcoming changes in your environment.

For example, if you're a person who prefers to be curled up on the couch with a good book on a Friday night, you may feel tongue-tied or nauseated as you enter a dinner party.

This is when many people feel the urge to shift into reverse and head straight back into their comfort zone. This is completely natural. If you can stay put for just a little longer—and get a little comfy with discomfort—a wonderful new world awaits you in the learning zone.

What I know for sure is that I don't need to let the uncomfortable sensations in my body stop or control me. Otherwise, I'll miss valuable information and the opportunity to create the life I want. I just need to get clear about what's happening in the moment. It can mean I'm afraid or upset, or maybe I just need more time to figure something out. My body is simply telling me that I'm moving into unfamiliar territory and I need to pay attention.

Taking risks and venturing into the learning zone is a courageous and bold act. It allows you to learn and improve your relationships and your life. Simply reading this book might be in your comfort or learning zone. And you may find that taking action on what you've read sends you into your learning or panic zone.

The learning zone is where you grow. You might be trying something new. For me, I spent my life studying until I was 31 years old, so higher education was part of my comfort zone. When I had to apply that knowledge to solving real-life problems with patients, that's where I entered the learning zone.

I am often in the learning zone when I speak in front of an audience. My heart races and I tremble. Sometimes I even ask the audience to take a deep breath and I say, "This one's for me." I notice that when I acknowledge my fears, they often subside. It's when I pretend they aren't there that they grow bigger.

The potential drawback of the learning zone is that you will likely feel some physical discomfort or awkwardness. You might avoid this zone because of fear or intimidation. Most often, the uncomfortable feelings you experience in the learning zone are temporary. They show up to let you know that you're moving away from the familiar. The key is learning how to work with those sensations in order to use them as feedback to grow and become a better communicator.

Just like transitioning from a tricycle to a bicycle, at first it's wobbly and you may fall. But before long, the wind is blowing in your hair and you're bragging to anyone with ears, "Look: no hands!" The empowering part of entering the learning zone is that once you spend time here, these new experiences will expand the edges of your comfort zone.

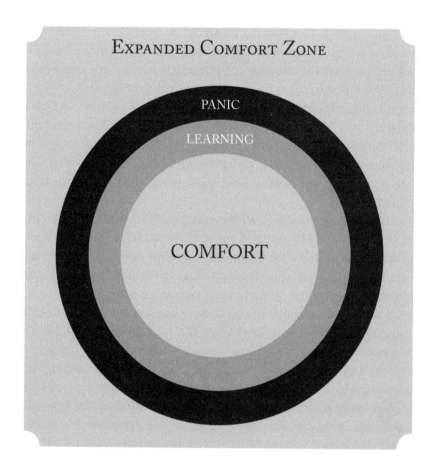

When you enter your learning zone and grow, the benefit is that your comfort zone expands. When you get to the edge of the learning zone, you may feel nervous, anxious, or fearful. It's not the end of the world, but it might feel that way. The third and final zone is the panic zone. Some people refer to it as the danger zone.

The Panic Zone

Being in the panic zone is more than having a little fear or apprehension. It means: *Danger! This is not safe!* It's crucial to listen to your body at these times because then you'll know what to do next. The signals may be the same as those encountered in the learning zone, only exaggerated, or they may be completely different. Only you know when you've entered this zone because everyone responds differently—even to the same situation. So don't expect other people to know when you've hit your panic zone. It's your responsibility to recognize it and voice what you need. For example, you can choose to remove yourself from a situation or ask for time and space.

At this point, your body sends alarm signals telling you when you've gone too far or exceeded your limits. You may feel numb or shocked. Your mind may go blank. And your heart may feel as if it's pounding out of your chest. When you are in this zone, you have exceeded your capacity to think creatively, explore, and learn. Jumping out of an airplane would send a more cautious person into the panic zone. For a thrill seeker, the very same opportunity might be in his comfort zone because it makes him feel alive. It all depends on who you are.

Think back to Brandon. Although he pushed his body so hard for so long, if he were to go to the other extreme of attending a ten-day silent meditation retreat, he would probably enter his panic zone. That much stillness could surely drive a man that active nuts! So the key was for him to find the sweet spot of his learning zone. The way he did that was by committing to get clear on why he drove himself so hard and to get more sleep at night. This might still have been uncomfortable for him, but he soon got used to slowing down a bit and found the right balance.

Everyone visits the panic zone now and then for short periods of time. The panic zone helps you identify when you've exceeded your limits. It helps to define the boundary between learning and panic.

My own body sends very clear signals letting me know when I'm moving out of my learning zone and into my panic zone. My mind goes blank, and I feel as if I'm in a soundproof room. It's as if I have headphones on and can just hear the hum of external noise, but I can't decipher what it is.

COMFORT TO PANIC IN LESS THAN 60 SECONDS

During the first year of my residency, I was launched into the panic zone when I awoke to my first code blue, an emergency situation that indicates a severe decline in a patient's health. At 11 P.M., after a long evening of making rounds and admitting patients, I collapsed onto the rock-hard bed of the call room. Not 45 minutes later, an overhead speaker loudly broke through the silence: "Code Blue! Third Floor East! Code Blue!" I jumped out of bed and sprinted down the hall.

I made my way through the crowd of medical personnel and saw an elderly woman lying naked on the bed amid syringes, shock paddles, and an oxygen mask. As soon as I entered the room, my mind went blank. I had read the protocol for a code blue many times, but this was my first time *on* the code team.

I froze. I could hear the commotion going on around me. I looked at the patient and couldn't remember what I was supposed to do. I could see mouths moving, calling for oxygen, for a chest X-ray, for a heart rhythm, and then for shock paddles, but the sound was muffled. After each item was called out, my mind tried to locate where that item fell in the algorithm of a code blue. But I couldn't think, and my body wasn't moving.

Going from my comfort zone (sound asleep in the call room) to my panic zone (facing life or death with a patient) called forth a slew of physical signals as my body tried to protect me. I had recited the code algorithm to myself so many times and chosen the correct answers on so many tests. No matter how many years I had spent preparing for this moment, nothing was like the real deal. I felt a huge weight of responsibility to save this woman's life—to figure out what had gone wrong. I simply wasn't able to respond. And time was running out. I stood there wide-eyed and open-mouthed.

Thank goodness the ICU nurse and the third-year resident had the situation handled. The patient's heart rhythm was successfully restored.

Afterward, when I apologized for my lack of assistance, my third-year resident said, "You're in the first month of your residency. Go easy on yourself. This was your first code; your job was to observe. Next time, just listen to whoever is running the code and get them what they're asking for. That's all you have to do. Don't put so much pressure on yourself. You have a team that will help you."

I let out an enormous sigh of relief.

To my amazement, by the end of my first year, I was running codes. My uncomfortable bodily sensations surrounding a code blue never completely went away, but I had moved from the panic zone into the learning zone. This wasn't a matter of being desensitized or numb to the gravity of the work. I no longer panicked because, by then, I had had this experience repeatedly and gained more confidence. And even more important, I realized that I needed to quit feeling responsible—that the root of my panic was thinking that if this person died it was somehow my fault and I had failed.

My biggest realization was that even with all my preparation, the science of medicine couldn't save everyone. My job was to be present and execute the code with great care, attention, and expertise. If a patient's time to leave the earth had come, then my role—equally important—was to be a comforting presence to him and his family during this critical transition, and to answer questions as best I could. There were times I simply didn't have all the answers. And that was okay, too.

GETTING IN THE ZONE

Are you ready to join the internal conversation with your body? With or without you, your body has been talking. Your physiology has valuable information that helps you navigate everyday situations in order to communicate clearly and confidently. Your body is where it all begins—long before you enter a hospital. So many patients realize—but only after they experience a medical crisis—that they've ignored countless signals from their bodies. In your daily life, you may have already formed a habit of shutting down your body's signals as a strategy to make it through the day, the week, or your next deadline. Beware: there's always a trade-off.

◆ ◆ ◆ ◆ ◆

TALKRX TOOLKIT

How Your Body Talks

Your body's physical intelligence = your body's senses gathering data (external) + your body's physical sensations (internal data)

Body Map (page 24)—a tool to decipher the unique way that your body talks to you

Get instant access to your free personalized Body Map at DoctorNehaTalkRx.com

Your Body Zones

Comfort Zone = familiar, known

- Staying here too long can lead to feeling stuck or bored.

Learning Zone = full of adventure and growth

- This zone may be associated with some physical discomfort.

Panic Zone = dangerous, beyond safe limits

- Your body may override your ability to take action.

Your 1-Five Moment

- To make this practical and figure out how your body talks to you, answer five personalized questions in Chapter 2 of your *TalkRx Journal*. You've got a complimentary copy waiting to be downloaded at DoctorNehaTalkRx.com.

- Share with the TalkRx Community one way you plan to get out of your comfort zone.

CHAPTER 3

NUMBING OUT

If your body can provide all this important information that helps you better navigate the world, why aren't you listening to it? It's as simple as this: you don't like discomfort. Nobody does. And sometimes the signals your body is sending are uncomfortable. Ignoring them or trying to make them go away can be a natural response because it seems much easier than addressing the root cause of the problem—in the short term, anyway.

Various ways exist to shut down the body. Some people use a double latte and a chocolate chip cookie. Others use a beer or a few glasses of wine. Some rely on over-the-counter or prescription medications. Others get lost in the virtual world of video games or the Internet. Some people buy themselves temporary happiness through retail therapy. The list goes on and on, but no matter the coping strategy, they all have one thing in common: they work to numb you so you don't have to face the real issue at hand, such as:

- You're in a relationship long past its expiration date.

- You're in a job that doesn't fulfill your soul.

- You need to have a conversation that you've been avoiding.

- You have taken on too much and feel overwhelmed.

- Your finances are in a downward spiral.

When you ignore your body's physiology, no matter how uncomfortable, you miss important information about what's going on and the ability to pick up signals early. Hitting the snooze button on these sensations can also create ongoing stress, resulting in physical illness. As if that weren't enough, when you're confused on the inside, there's no hiding it on the outside. Your body language, tone, and words will not be aligned, and others will pick up on your confusion. Your communication will be unclear.

I learned this firsthand.

THE BODY RULES

Throughout my medical school training and residency, I lived at a distance from my body. Not a quick-trip-to-the-corner-store distance, but a New York–to-Tokyo distance. I endured 36-hour shifts. I missed out on food and sleep. When we were short-staffed, I told myself that since I was single (and didn't have kids or a family to take care of), I was the one who should stay and cover the overnight shifts.

I perfected a formula to numb out any physical signals coming from my body. It was a time-tested equation that would help me survive the night shifts. It went something like this:

32-ounce ice-cold Mountain Dew + 1 king-size Snickers Bar =
Surviving a 36-hour hospital shift without sleep

My body was sending me low-energy signals letting me know that it needed rest, proper nourishment, and balance, but I wasn't listening. My internal physiology was going crazy with exhaustion, and I was tuning it out with sugar and caffeine.

I had a more challenging time, however, with a different signal that went off in my body. At first I noticed that during times of high stress, such as finals week, my throat would tighten up. I had trouble breathing, I got hoarse, and when I ate, my food would get stuck when I tried to swallow. Sometimes it felt like I was choking.

As medical school progressed, so did the intensity of my throat constriction. I'd even have to periodically leave class for fresh air so I could breathe more easily. After a while, my throat was in a continuous state of constriction.

I spent my days learning about various types of cancer and the endless options for treating them. I saw patients who were devastated by their illnesses, and I became convinced that something was physically wrong with me as well.

In casual conversation with my colleagues, I would declare, "I keep feeling like I can't get enough air, like I've got something lodged in my throat. Do you think it's a mass?" Needless to say, that was a conversation killer.

I consulted two gastroenterologists. Each one sedated me and used a camera to look down my throat. And each one came to the same conclusion: there was nothing physically wrong with me.

"Are you sure?" I pleaded, following the second procedure.

"What else is going on in your life? What kind of work do you do?" the doctor asked.

"I'm a fourth-year medical student," I said proudly.

He chuckled and said, "I guess I should have asked you that first. You're just overworked, stressed out, and abusing your body. This is temporary. You'll be out of med school soon. You're young and you'll get through this. This is your body's way of talking back. It doesn't seem like you're listening. You need to learn some good stress management techniques. Get a massage or practice yoga. That'll help."

Huh? My body's sending me physical signals? That's odd, I thought. *How could I almost be graduating from medical school and not have learned about this? More important, what am I supposed to do with these signals?*

I was bewildered as I read my doctor's assessment and plan:

Symptoms of throat constriction secondary to high stress (fourth-year med student)

1. Endoscopy negative (no findings). Biopsy pending.

2. Advised to learn relaxation & stress management techniques.

I was elated that I didn't have cancer, but the truth was, I still didn't know what to do with the discomfort in my throat. So whenever I got stressed, his words rang in my head: "This is temporary. You'll be out of med school soon."

I wish I could say that I learned my lesson and began taking better care of myself. But some habits die hard—especially when they are the driving force behind an overachiever.

I completed medical school and residency and was working to become a physician partner when my body finally punched me out. Instead of acknowledging the warning signals my body was sending, I silently fumed, becoming increasingly impatient, stressed, and irritated. I powered through shift after shift, fueled by caffeine, sugar, and a fear of failure. But eventually the grueling pace, erratic sleep schedule, and blatant disregard for my own physical, mental, and emotional well-being led to burnout.

I remember the day very clearly. It was June 17, 2004. I was on the last day of a five-day rotation and was moving at a snail's pace. I didn't even realize exactly how slow I was going until I noticed that it was 11:15 A.M. and I had seen only 2 of my 18 patients.

I walked to the nurses' station and asked, "Nina, did the patient in Room 636 get forty milliequivalents of potassium?"

She looked at me, bewildered. "Dr. Sangwan," she said, "that's the fourth time you've asked me that question. Are you okay?" It was only in that moment that I recognized that I might not be.

I walked into the sterile, white bathroom, took out my phone, and called a psychiatric colleague. "Roger, it's Neha. When is the earliest I can see you?"

"Great to hear your voice. How about at the end of the day—say five o'clock?"

I shook my head as I looked at my pale, weary face in the mirror and said, "How about right now?"

"Come over right away. I'll squeeze you in."

Roger took one look at me and exclaimed, "Neha, tell me what's going on. You look like a zombie."

I proceeded to explain what was happening. After we talked for an hour, he told me that I was experiencing burnout and recommended that I take a few months of medical leave to focus on self-care. As I left his office, he gave me a prescription for Prozac.

I filled the prescription, but as I was driving home, I remember thinking, *I'm not sure why this is happening, but I know it's not a Prozac deficiency.* I got home and collapsed on my bed. I'd figure it out in the morning.

Burnout is fascinating. It's a gradual process, but its victims are usually so tuned out that they're oblivious to the signals their bodies have been sending. Then, when they finally crash, it feels like someone has hit the light switch and suddenly left them alone in the dark.

I had no idea how hard it was going to be, staying at home with nothing to do except face the critical thoughts in my head about how I had somehow failed everyone—my colleagues, my patients, my parents, but mostly myself. I couldn't believe it: my hands and legs functioned but I couldn't go to work.

THE TRUTH WAS MY ANTIDEPRESSANT

On medical leave I began to work with my psychiatrist to understand patterns in my life that had contributed to my situation. Each week, Roger clarified how my desire to be a team player caused me to make choices that were unhealthy for me. He explored how I had come to believe it was a badge of honor to push through my symptoms instead of caring for my body.

After a month I showed signs of improvement. My energy was returning, and I had started sleeping through the night. Much to my amazement, my throat constriction began to subside. I was getting more comfortable being still rather than running on adrenaline.

At my fifth session Roger began, "Neha, that Prozac is really working. You look much better."

Confused, I said, "Roger, I filled the prescription, but I wanted to see how our sessions went before I began taking the medication. I haven't taken any Prozac. I was more scared of the side effects than of how I was feeling. I'm doing much better now, so I don't need meds, right?"

In a surprised tone he said, "If you're not on medication, I technically can't be the one who sees you. As a psychiatrist, I can't bill for someone who is not on medication. I'm happy to give you a letter for time off, but you'll have to find another provider."

I was stunned. Wasn't it a good thing that I didn't need the medication? Somehow in this moment, it wasn't.

Fortunately, Roger gave me excellent recommendations and I found another provider who helped further my progress. After three months, I returned to work with a new and improved approach—one that included listening to my own needs as well.

What I learned during my time off was that my body didn't begin its dialogue with me at the onset of debilitating throat constriction or burnout. It had actually been talking to me all along. I had just become accustomed to overriding my own physical intelligence. First, the signals were subtle. I remember being much younger and having that sensation in my throat when my older sister would say or do something that I thought was unfair. One of her pet peeves was when we both wore a skirt to school on the same day, because "everyone would know we copied each other." No one had ever made any such comment, but I silenced myself whenever she insisted that I change my outfit, in order to avoid conflict. My frustration manifested as tightness at the base of my tongue. Since I didn't know how to interpret that signal (other than as an annoyance), I ignored it.

As a teenager, I felt the same sensation whenever my parents insisted on chauffeuring me to social engagements because my peers were, to quote my mother, "too inexperienced to drive."

I remember experiencing throat constriction during study groups and examinations in college. I managed it with repetitive throat clearing and drinking carbonated beverages.

Because I was searching for ways to numb these sensations, rather than getting curious about what they were trying to tell me, my body began screaming. My intermittent throat constriction progressed to a constant sensation that led me to seek medical treatment. I continued to push through until it was no longer sustainable and I burned out. Then I listened.

Numbing Strategies

Now that you understand that your body talks to you, let's see if you try to tune it out. Do any of these common strategies sound familiar?

- You worked all month to meet the deadline, and your presentation was criticized by your boss in front of the entire team. You feel sick to your stomach. Then the Sugar-Caffeine Buzz Strategy kicks in and you think, *I'm going to grab a chocolate chip brownie and a Red Bull so I can get back to work.*

- You've been in a relationship way too long. You don't have the energy to deal with a breakup today. Your back and shoulders are killing you. The Dull-Your-Senses Strategy kicks in and you think, *A few drinks and some ibuprofen will take the edge off and get me through the night.*

- Your life gives you a headache—literally. If you call your brother for emotional support, he'll probably ask if he can borrow money again. So the Internet-Escape Strategy kicks in, and as you log on to social media you think, *My virtual world is much easier to control. At least there I can steer clear of family drama. I get to showcase the glamorous highlights of my life, and no one has to know what's really going on.*

Whether you use sugar and caffeine, numb out with drugs or alcohol, or escape to the Internet, these strategies all have something in common. They work—for a few minutes—to change how you feel. If you're really good at numbing out, these strategies might work for months or even years. Call them what you will; the truth is they're all Band-Aids. They're temporary strategies that allow you to tune out, but they don't resolve the underlying problem.

———————————————◆◆◆———————————————

When you experience internal discomfort, what do you turn to?

- Taking a nap
- Reading a novel
- Alcohol or recreational drugs
- Surfing social media
- Sugar, sugar & more sugar
- Your personal favorite: _____

If you gave your numbing strategies names, what would they be?

———————————————◆◆◆———————————————

Even activities that seem healthy can be numbing strategies. For instance, you may be used to running every day before work to alleviate stress. Or you may work longer hours instead of dealing with the conversation you've been avoiding at home. When you notice yourself using more and more of a strategy over time, that's one clue that your strategy is a form of tuning out rather than tuning in.

You might be wondering, when does a strategy become an addiction? Addiction is an extreme version of numbing out. As a physician, I know firsthand that it is more common in our society than we think. Author Tommy Rosen provides one of the clearest definitions of addiction in his book *Recovery 2.0*: "Any behavior you continue to do despite the fact that it brings negative consequences in your life." If this applies to you, it's important to seek help immediately from a qualified professional and get support.

Once you become aware of which strategies you use to tune out, you can pay attention to the real issue at hand. Sometimes it's easier to notice these numbing-out behaviors than it is to notice the signals coming from your body.

One important idea to keep in mind: Your numbing strategies have served you for a period of time. They may have protected you when you didn't have the words or the resources to deal with a situation. These strategies were useful, and it's important to be grateful for them. They bought you time until you could come up with another plan.

Be gentle with yourself; your intentions were good. It's just that tuning out can limit what's possible and stand in the way of your getting what you want. Tuning into your body instead will help you manage yourself, your relationships, your work, and your life better than ever before.

◆◆◆◆◆

TalkRx Toolkit

Name That Numbing Strategy

When you feel discomfort, become aware of your numbing strategies:

- Sugar-Caffeine Buzz Strategy
- Dull-Your-Senses Strategy
- Internet-Escape Strategy
- Other: _____

Your 1-Five Moment

- To understand how your numbing strategies are impacting your life, answer five personalized questions in Chapter 3 of your *TalkRx Journal*. Go to DoctorNehaTalkRx.com to download your complimentary journal.
- Share creative names for your numbing strategies with the TalkRx Community.

CHAPTER 4

TUNING IN

Congratulations! You've bravely named your numbing strategies and now understand how they have served you. But times have changed. And left unchecked, these coping mechanisms can damage your health or, at the very least, leave you feeling stuck. They also block you from experiencing what you're truly feeling, so you aren't able to communicate or address conflict in an effective way. This can result in situations that don't benefit your health or your happiness.

If you don't know how to manage uncomfortable physical sensations, you'll default back to your time-tested numbing strategies. The good news is that you can learn to tune in, rather than tune out. With practice you can easily interpret what your body signals mean.

You don't have to be in conflict or burned out to practice tuning in. You can do it anytime. Tuning in is essential to be effective in everyday conversations. As you tune in to your body, it will guide you to what your next step needs to be. But before you can tune in, you have to slow down.

Slowing down gives you time to notice your internal signals while simultaneously paying attention to external data. Slowing down provides an opportunity to pause and get clear, in order to save time and be more productive in the long run. So, in essence, you're slowing down to speed up!

YOUR PAUSE BUTTON

Luckily, pause buttons aren't just for watching videos or listening to music. Each of us has one; we just need to learn how to use it. When we're outside our comfort zone, sometimes it's easier to say yes in the moment and then deal with what comes next: our own discomfort. For example, suppose someone we care about makes a request we would rather decline. In an attempt to avoid discomfort and save time, if we immediately agree, we may end up wasting more time and energy on the back end trying to figure out how to get out of the commitment.

When you physically pause, your brain has a moment to re-engage its critical thinking capabilities and gain additional perspective. This allows you to come up with creative options as you navigate daily interactions. When someone makes a request, if you pause, you'll realize there are many options. You can ask for time. You can ask for resources. You can ask for additional information. You can say, "Thank you for thinking of me, but I can't make it."

Learning to effectively use your pause button can help you respond confidently while taking both yourself *and* others into account. This is possible to do not only with a simple request but also when considering a complex situation. The pause button is so important because it creates the opportunity for double vision. Simultaneously tuning in to your external and internal worlds and ensuring they line up will lead to clear and effective responses.

And I say *responses* because there is a big difference between reacting and responding. A reaction is an immediate, knee-jerk, reflexive answer that comes from fear, self-protection, the desire to please someone else, or an attempt to avoid conflict. One of the biggest mistakes people make in communication is providing an answer to a question right away without thinking it through.

The belief that *answers must be given immediately* is a misperception. For example, you may react by saying yes to a request to go out on a Friday night because you want your friend to be happy (even though you are exhausted from the workweek). When you answer without pausing, you'll soon find yourself overextended and resentful. That's when you'll hear yourself making statements like "I hate Friday nights."

A response, on the other hand, takes into account the other person's desires as well as your own needs. So your response to a

Friday night invitation may sound more like "I would love to go out with you, but I am so exhausted. How about Saturday?" If you can pause long enough to step into the learning zone, it may be a little uncomfortable, but you'll be able to come up with creative options that work for everyone.

You can learn a few simple tools to activate your pause button in order to better manage yourself and your everyday interactions with others.[6]

Pause Method 1: Use Your Breath

In our busy lives, it's common to move quickly and take our breathing for granted. Thank goodness our body takes over when we forget!

Our brains need a steady supply of oxygen in order to function optimally. The problem is that most of us are shallow breathers. But the best oxygen exchange occurs at the base of our lungs when we breathe slowly and deeply. Deep breathing engages your body's relaxation system, effectively slows down your physiology (heart rate, blood pressure, etc.), and helps you think more clearly. And as a bonus, deep breathing soothes those uncomfortable signals coming from your body.

When we're relaxed and taking deeper breaths, the cortex (the outermost part of the brain) engages in creative thinking. But how many times a day do we do that? Deep breathing may happen in a yoga class or on a run, but it doesn't usually happen without our focused attention.

The kind of breathing I'm talking about is soft belly breathing (see next page).[7] It may sound elementary, but stick with me. When you soften your belly and relax the muscles of your abdomen, the rest of your body also relaxes.

Your lungs are huge. To see for yourself, take both hands and, beginning at your collarbone, follow the outline of your rib cage all the way down to your mid-waist. Your lungs expand throughout this space.

Now breathe in as deeply as you can. Pay attention to what it takes for you to fill your lungs completely. And slowly release your breath. Go ahead; I'll wait.

Soft Belly Breathing in Five Simple Steps

1. Place the palm of your hand on your relaxed belly.
2. Let gravity pull your shoulders down.
3. Slowly and deeply inhale, allow your abdomen to expand, and notice the hand on your abdomen moving outward.
4. As you exhale, move your belly button back toward your spine and notice your hand moving inward.
5. Repeat three times, and pay attention to any shifts in your body and your level of relaxation.

You can use soft belly breathing anytime, not just in crisis situations. The next time you're in a conversation, a meeting, or heavy traffic, consciously take a few deep breaths and notice how it helps you relax and think more clearly.

The key here is to breathe correctly. When people feel anxiety or fear, they often resort to reverse breathing—contracting every muscle as they inhale and collapsing as they exhale—which only further fuels their anxiety.

When I was working in the hospital, there wasn't a soul in the emergency department who didn't think they were going to die. I used to teach them exactly what you've just learned, and once they began this new way of breathing, they felt much better.

Go to DoctorNehaTalkRx.com for access to the video tutorial "Soft Belly Breathing" if you want to see just how this is done.

Pause Method 2: Ground Your Body

Another way you can pause is to become present in your body. Whether you are sitting or standing, you simply bring your attention to the force of gravity holding your bottom on the seat.

Start with soft belly breathing. Then, as you take another deep breath in, become aware of your rib cage expanding and contracting. Next, notice the location of your hands and your feet and whether they feel warm or cool. Continue breathing for as long as it takes to slowly move your attention to your chest, then your abdomen, next your legs and calves, until you get to your feet making contact with the ground. This is a great way to get out of your head and into the present moment. Yep, it's that simple.

Pause Method 3: Tense and Release

Another option for hitting your pause button and getting reconnected to your body is to tighten and loosen different muscle sets.

- Begin by noticing where your feet are placed.
- Then wiggle your toes.
- Tense the muscles throughout both feet as tightly as you can.
- Hold for three to five seconds.
- Release and relax.

The engineer in me likes to start at my feet and work my way methodically upward until I get to my facial muscles as a full relaxation exercise. For example, I begin with my toes, then I do the same tensing and releasing exercise in my calves, my quads, my buttocks, my abs, my chest, my arms, my shoulders, my jaw, and my facial muscles. You don't have to be so linear. Just do what feels good.

Any of these three pausing techniques can be done alone or in combination with one another. When you master internal pausing, you can use this strategy in real time. You don't have to wait until you get home. You can manage yourself right in the middle of a conversation (with soft belly breathing or grounding your body).

Once you pause internally, you can combine that internal presence with a variety of activities in your external world that synergistically help you tune in, such as getting a massage, going for a walk, or taking a hot bath. Maybe you prefer journaling, talking to a friend, or meditating.

Getting familiar with pausing will bring you into the present moment while you develop the habit of tuning in to your body's physiology. It will soon become natural to let your body's signals guide you in every conversation, and especially when it matters most.

◆ ◆ ◆ ◆ ◆

TALKRX TOOLKIT

Soft Belly Breathing

1. Place the palm of your hand on your relaxed belly.

2. Let gravity pull your shoulders down.

3. Slowly and deeply inhale, allow your abdomen to expand, and notice the hand on your abdomen moving outward.

4. As you exhale, move your belly button back toward your spine and notice your hand moving inward.

5. Repeat three times, and pay attention to any shifts in your body and your level of relaxation.

A few quick ways to hit your internal pause button:

1. Use your breath.

2. Ground your body.

3. Tense and release.

TalkRx Video: Go to DoctorNehaTalkRx.com for the video tutorial "Soft Belly Breathing."

YOUR I-FIVE MOMENT

- To discover how you best tune in and feel grounded, answer five personalized questions in Chapter 4 of your *TalkRx Journal.* (Go to DoctorNehaTalkRx.com to download your complimentary copy of the journal.)

- What are your personal tips for tuning in and grounding yourself? Share them with the TalkRx Community.

MIXED MESSAGES

Numb out. Tune in. Who cares? What's it got to do with improving conversations anyway? The answer is *a lot.*

Your body is constantly gathering data from your external and internal worlds. When those two worlds match and words, tone, and body language send the same message, the resulting communication is authentic, clear, and direct. On the other hand, when they are not aligned, a communication catastrophe looms.

If the primary elements of communication are not in harmony with one another, it's the equivalent of listening to an orchestra that's out of tune. The result is a mixed message. While mixed messages may seem minor, they are often the culprit of unraveling relationships and business deals. Usually people know something's amiss, but they aren't sure what happened and don't know how to sort it out. Bottom line: even with the best of intentions, communication signals can easily get crossed.

What causes mixed messages? One reason is internal conflict—when an individual is trying to balance his or her own needs with those of another. Such a situation may arise when you:

- Are uncertain about what you want

- Wish to avoid conflict at any cost

- Say yes when you really mean no

- Feel pressure to give an answer right away

- Feel trapped because you don't think you have a choice

You may not consciously know it, but competing intentions can cause an internal struggle that outwardly creates confusion in your relationships. Your internal body's signals affect your external communication. Let's look at some practical scenarios that illustrate mixed messages.

Need for approval. As a leader, you ask someone on your team to work an extra shift on a weekend. He responds with a sigh as he simultaneously slumps in his chair (visibly losing two inches of height) and says, "Oh-kaaaaaay." His collapsed body language and his dejected tone are in contradiction to his words.

Unmet expectations. Suppose one partner has promised a quiet evening at home with a candlelit dinner and instead gets the opportunity to go to a sporting event with friends. With great excitement, he may say, "Hey, you don't mind if I go to the game with Steve, do you? We can have our date night this weekend instead."

His partner folds her arms tightly across her chest and purses her lips. "Sure, fine," she says. "Do whatever you want." It's clear that although her words indicate it's okay, her body language is closed and saying something like "I'm feeling upset and disappointed. Our relationship is not a priority."

Feeling guilty. Think about the dad who has been to every soccer game this season for his twin ten-year-olds. He finds out his favorite comedian is coming to town for a one-night-only show and his buddy has front-row seats. What a welcome break—he hasn't had a night to himself since his divorce four months ago.

Over dinner, his boys begin to talk up their upcoming game against their biggest rival, and one of them asks, "What time will you be there, Dad?"

His heart sinks as he realizes it's the same night as the show, and he pauses and looks down at the floor before saying, "Your mom will be there instead of me."

"No way!" they exclaim with distraught faces. "Mom doesn't even know what a foul is!" As guilt kicks in, he sighs and gets up from the table. Reluctantly he says, "Okay. I'll be there at 7 P.M." While he is dedicated to being an excellent father, his body language and resigned tone signal that he has a competing desire to enjoy quality time at a unique opportunity with his good friend.

Do you feel your own body responding to internal conflicts like these? It's completely normal if you do. These play out all the time in our conversations. That conflict has to come out somehow—and the body conveys the mixed message of your internal world with what you're saying to the external world.

DOUBLE-TALK

Misalignment of body language, tone, and words is not the only way mixed messages are sent. Cultural nuances also play a role in miscommunication. Have you ever heard someone say one thing, and afterward you realized they meant something very different?

Growing up in Michigan and New York, I experienced cultural differences when I traveled below the Mason-Dixon line for winter break. Southern charm was abundant. And a common phrase I heard was "Bless his little heart . . . ," except if he actually heard what was coming next, it would probably *crush his little heart.* You know what I mean. It's when you hear someone say, "Bless his little heart, he's not the brightest bulb in the box," or "Bless his little heart, he's dumb as a doorknob," or any number of personal attacks smoothed over with words that seemingly contradict one another.

Another kind of mixed message comes from cultural gaps where the same words or gestures have varied meanings across cultures, depending on how and where you have been raised. One gesture with many meanings is placing your palms together at your heart. Go ahead. Try it. In the U.S., unless you're in a yoga class, if your hands are in that position, I'd venture to guess you're in church or begging your parent, partner, or child for a favor. Yet if you're in India, placing your hands together at your heart would mean *namaste,* a friendly way to greet one another.

Getting Back on Track

You can see how important it is to pay attention to mixed messages. It's easy to assume other people are the ones sending mixed messages or misinterpreting your signals. They might be. But it's an act of bravery to begin by figuring out whether or not *you* are. Yes, I just made the (not so subtle) suggestion that you might have something to do with an interaction going awry. To rescue any communication, you have to start with yourself. Here are three questions to ask yourself about your part in any miscommunication and get back on track in no time.

1. How did I know there was a communication breakdown?

What did my body's external senses and internal physiology tell me?

Externally, what did I notice in my environment? Did something change? Did I hear someone say or do something? Did I receive an e-mail, text, or voice mail? Did the body language, tone, and words I received match up? Was there a period of silence?

Internally, what physical sensations did I feel?

Pay attention to your physical signals and what those signals are responding to in the outside world. For example, by merely seeing the name of a particular person in your in-box—before you've even seen the message—have you had a strong internal response? If so, the strength of your body's reaction may have limited your ability to communicate.

Or maybe you were in a conversation and noticed that after listening to someone's opinion, your heart started racing. That's a good indication to pause before responding (unless, of course, you're thrilled). If you forgot to hit the pause button and instead reacted immediately, this could be precisely where the communication went awry.

2. Did the method (of communication) equal the importance (of the conversation)?

It's important that you choose a method of communication that gives you the best chance of successfully conveying the content and significance of your message. Since you already know the combination of body language, tone, and words is delivered only in person or on video, make sure you align the method you use with how important the conversation is to you.

If you recognize a breakdown, identify which method of communication you used.

- Method 1 (low): Words only (text, e-mail, chat, or tweet)
- Method 2 (med): Words + tone (phone, conference call, voice mail)
- Method 3 (high): Words + tone + body language (in-person, video)

Now identify how important the outcome of this conversation was to you. Give it a number.

- Level 1 (low): e.g., saying yes to a simple request or thanking someone for their kindness
- Level 2 (med): e.g., changing plans at the last minute or asking for a favor
- Level 3 (high): e.g., breaking off a romantic relationship or delivering bad news

Did the method equal the importance? If the number assigned to your communication method did *not* at least equal the level of importance, this is probably one reason why you didn't get the response you were hoping for.

Moving forward, how do you make a better choice? For starters, the importance of the conversation is naturally elevated once you realize you've had a miscommunication (if you care about the relationship or outcome). You therefore would want to use as many aspects of communication as possible to relay your message effectively and understand what happened for the other person.

- If you sent a text or e-mail, do you need to pick up the phone to hear the person's tone of voice?

- If you made a phone call or left a voice mail, would adding body language be an asset?

The more aware you are of the method you communicate in and why, you'll effortlessly choose the most effective and efficient mode for each situation. While a quick text can seem efficient up front, it may lead to additional work on the back end to clear up misunderstandings. At the same time, a sit-down conversation, while thorough, isn't necessary for making dinner plans—unless you're asking someone on a first date (be classy and do it in person).

3. Did I send a mixed message?

Moi? Are you talkin' to me? Yep, it's time to take a look at whether *your* words, tone, and body language matched up. Did you answer in a way that corresponded to what your internal sensations were saying? The funny part is, most people think they're really good at hiding their emotions. But has your parent or your partner ever told you that you were in a bad mood before you even realized it? The truth is, other people can pick up on your misaligned body language, tone, and words sometimes even before you do.

So now that the cat's out of the bag, here's how to get clear. Ask yourself three clarifying questions:

1. Did my words match my body language and tone?

2. Am I thinking or feeling something I haven't expressed?

3. Am I holding back because I'm concerned about the other person's reaction?

Now you know how to investigate the most important part of any conversation that breaks down: your contribution to the outcome.

You Can See Clearly Now

Once you're clear about what happened, you can use that knowledge as an opportunity to build a stronger connection with the other person.

Remember my first e-mail interaction with Dr. Paul Rosch, when I received his one-finger-typed response in all capital letters? In that exchange, I had only the letters on my screen, which I now know was very little information. I wasted so much time and energy creating scary stories about what I thought he meant. I got myself all worked up for no reason. It was embarrassing—but also freeing—to realize the truth: that the method I used, e-mail (Method 1), didn't match the high level of importance (Level 3) of this conversation.

Since Paul lived in New York City and I was in San Francisco, I wasn't able to have an in-person meeting with him. Thank goodness I chose to pick up the phone. Once I heard Paul's voice and got curious, it was clear that his use of all capital letters had to do with his eyesight and typing technique—details I couldn't have possibly gauged over e-mail. In retrospect, I can see that I didn't have enough data. I'm so glad I got curious!

Connecting the Dots

By now I hope you recognize how interpreting your body's signals, both from your external world and your internal physiology, is key to simplifying communication. Learning to pause and respond rather than react is crucial. This concept may seem simple, but don't be fooled—knowing how to accurately interpret your physical body is the foundation of becoming a masterful communicator.

Everyone's body is talking, so you can see how a simple conversation can actually be complex when internal signals are going on while external dialogue is happening. And it's easy to get mixed up, especially if not every individual is aware of what's happening inside. Now, this is the deal: Don't worry about all those other people. Just stay focused on *you*.

The i-Five Conversation will help you sort out exactly what's happening. And you've already completed the first of five parts—Interpreting Your Body. But this won't be the last time we talk about it. You'll need your internal signals, your breath, and the awareness of your body language, tone, and words as we move forward.

Your body is talking. Now that you know how, are you listening?

◆ ◆ ◆ ◆ ◆

TalkRx Toolkit

[My (internal + external) data + your (internal + external) data] x infinite ways to deliver the message = lots of opportunity for miscommunication

Back on Track Tool

When there's a communication breakdown, ask yourself these three questions:

1. How did I know there was a communication breakdown?
2. Did the method equal the importance?
3. Did I send a mixed message?

Your i-Five Moment

*   To get clear about a recent miscommunication in your life, answer five personalized questions in

Chapter 5 of your *TalkRx Journal*. Your free journal can be downloaded at DoctorNehaTalkRx.com.

- Do tell the TalkRx Community about the latest mixed message you've given or received.

INTERPRETING
YOUR THOUGHTS

BODY

interpreting your
THOUGHTS

Since you know how to interpret your body, you've got lots of good information. Now it's time to figure out what that data means. That brings us to the second step of the i-Five Conversation: Interpreting Your Thoughts. Here you'll make sense of what you've observed and identify how your thoughts are influencing your communication.

Your body and thoughts are so intertwined that sometimes it's hard to separate what you're observing from what you're thinking about what you're observing. For example, there's a difference between watching someone throw a brick through a car window (data) and the thought that he is an inconsiderate jerk (story).

Once you've experienced a situation, the raw data you've gathered travels to the frontal cortex of your brain as you begin to create thoughts, which I also refer to as stories. By *story*, I mean any kind of interpretation or meaning you deduce from your external and internal data. You might be thinking, *I don't make up stories!* Don't worry; most people aren't aware that they do this, but it's natural to fill in the gaps about what you have observed. And the possibilities are endless. For example, if the data you witnessed was a man throwing a red brick through a car window, you may have a thought (or story) about the incident such as:

- He's an inconsiderate jerk.
- I bet his wife is in labor and his keys are locked inside.
- He's trying to steal the radio.
- He's a stuntman and it's all fake!
- He's getting something important out of the backseat because the car is about to explode.

The story you make up may be true. It may not be true. All you know for sure is that you've pieced together the data in a certain way in order to make sense of it.

How can people interpret the very same data in different ways? Your thoughts, your beliefs, and your unique view of the world are formed in your childhood, from your family and cultural upbringing, your education, and your past experiences. Based on those influences, you form certain perceptions. So it can be hard to understand why other people don't think the way you do. And sometimes the mistake is assuming that they do. This is when communication can get complicated.

> The good news: Each of us has a unique perspective.
> The bad news: Each of us believes that his or her perspective is the right one.
> The cure: Get curious, not furious.

If you aren't aware of how your life experiences—the good, the bad, the ugly—bias the way you interpret information, it's easy to believe that your thoughts are the only perspective. In reality, there are probably as many perspectives as there are people.

Imagine someone raised in a home where meals always involved lively discussions and noisy debates about politics. From that person's perspective, a dinner where people are interrupting each other and raising their voices might be interpreted as *This is a close-knit group.* Now imagine a guest at the same dinner table who was raised in a family that valued quiet politeness above all else. This person could observe the exact same situation and conclude, *This is a very dysfunctional group. How rude.* In other words, two people's unique perspectives have led to completely different interpretations of the exact same situation.

The stories you make up may or may not be true. We know they're true for you—because you have evidence from your life experience to prove it. As you form thoughts, it's common to confuse fact with fiction. Yes, I said fiction. In the moment, it can be hard to distinguish the two. But not for long.

I know I've felt this way about certain topics. But I realized that even if I believed something strongly and gathered plenty of allies, I still had to interpret my thoughts. My i-Five Moment came when I realized some of the thoughts that I swore were true were, in fact, fiction. And more alarming, these stories were at the root of my miscommunication.

Beware! Reading from this point forward may radically shift your perspective.

CHAPTER 6

FACT VERSUS FICTION

It was 8 A.M. as I made my way up the stairs to the second floor. I was curious to see how Lilly, a patient who had been admitted with severe pneumonia, was doing after being gradually taken off her ventilator. The nurse had called to let me know Lilly hadn't had a fever for 12 consecutive hours and her white blood cell count was trending back to normal. I was hopeful. Lilly greeted me with a fragile smile.

"It sure is good to be using my own lungs to breathe again. How am I doing, and when do I get to eat?"

I chuckled. "You've answered your own question. Being hungry is an excellent sign. You're definitely doing better. Let me listen to your lungs."

She proudly sat up and began, "I've always taken breathing for granted. Now I appreciate the miracle of taking a simple, deep breath."

I smiled and leaned in with my stethoscope. "You sound so much better using your own equipment to breathe. Your fever is gone, and your body is responding to the antibiotics. You'll be up and out in just a few short days. I'll transfer you upstairs to the medical floor later today."

"So, what comes next? How do I make sure I don't end up here again?" she asked.

"There are many reasons why people get sick. On a physical level, you caught a bad bug this time. As part of a natural process, your body's ability to fight disease often gets weaker with age. Exercising daily and getting eight hours of sleep are both great ways to strengthen your physical body. On a mental and emotional level, stress can also weaken your immune system, your body's defense against disease.

"Would you be willing to reflect on a few questions that have helped many of my patients discover the answer to what you asked?"

She nodded in agreement as I reached for my prescription pad. I began writing as I spoke. "Why do you think you developed pneumonia? Why do you think this happened now instead of two years ago or two years from now? What signs might you have missed along the way? Besides your physical symptoms, is there anything else in your life that needs to be healed? And if you spoke from the heart, what would you say?

"How about if you reflect on these questions overnight, and we'll talk in the morning?"

Lilly looked down and away. "I've been too scared to ask myself those kinds of questions. But since it's doctor's orders, I'll journal about it and see what I discover."

The next day, before I could even say, "Good morning," she said, "Dr. Neha, I thought about those questions like you asked me to, and there's something I need to tell you. My son married outside of our faith, so I disowned him. I've had a knot in my stomach ever since. I mean, after all that his father and I had done for him, I just couldn't believe he would abandon us along with his Jewish heritage. I couldn't bear that my grandchildren wouldn't be Jewish—and that meant that I had failed as a mother."

"Wow. That must have felt awful," I said.

"It was," she replied with tears in her eyes. "I wish I were close to my six grandchildren. I only know them through pictures my son shares with me. I've missed their high school graduations and even missed two weddings.

"I thought a lot about why I got pneumonia. But after needing life support, I've realized that what I have to do is open my heart again and breathe back in the beauty of life . . . which to me is family.

"What else needs to be healed? Well, the truth is that my son has raised his children to attend synagogue on Saturdays, and his wife goes to Hindu temple on Sundays. The kids sometimes go to both. My daughter-in-law's name is Anjali. I don't really know much about her except that her parents are in India. Eventually, I reconnected with my son, and he comes to dinner once a month at our house, but I told him I prefer he come alone. I've built such strong walls of protection around me that I don't know how I'll ever break them down in order to heal.

"If I could speak from my heart, I would say: I tried to punish my son, but in the process I cut off my own oxygen."

THE FILTER THROUGH WHICH WE SEE THE WORLD

I was stunned by Lilly's clarity. It took a near-death experience and the courage to answer a few simple questions to bring her to her own accountability in this situation. She had made a bold choice many years earlier that had changed the trajectory of her and her family's life. And she had made up a story—about what it meant that her son married an Indian woman—that colored all of her interactions with her son and led her to choose a course of action that separated her from his family. It wasn't until she looked at these events from a new perspective that she realized that there were other options.

Lilly couldn't control whom her son fell in love with. What she did control, however, was how she responded to that information. It's the same for each of us. We may not be able to control what someone else says or does, but what we do control is how we respond. Each of us has a choice in how we show up—in every interaction and every communication, every day.

How do we honor our beliefs while simultaneously staying open to and curious about another's perspective? This is where most people get stuck—just like Lilly did—all alone on Self-Righteous Island. Don't worry. As long as you keep reading, that won't be you.

You observe the facts and take in data, but there are many ways to make meaning of those facts. How you choose to piece them together determines what you think and, ultimately, how you respond. How you do this determines everything else.

ALL THOUGHTS ARE NOT CREATED EQUAL

Let's take a glimpse into the power of your thoughts. Your thoughts literally impact your body's physiology. One easy way to think about this is when you dream. Have you ever had a nightmare in which, for instance, someone is chasing you or has broken into your house? When you wake up, what's actually happening? Usually, all is quiet and calm in your external environment—but not in your internal environment. Your heart may be racing. You may be sweating. Your body actually doesn't know the difference between what's real and what's imagined. That's why the quality of your thoughts matters.

Communication gets easier when you can differentiate your thoughts. There are the public thoughts you share with others and the private thoughts you keep to yourself. And then there are the thoughts running around in your subconscious mind—the ones you're not even aware of. It has been estimated that the brain receives data at 11 million bits per second from the senses; however, the conscious mind is capable of processing only 50 bits per second.[8] So there's a lot we're not aware of. It's time to shine some light on what's happening in that pretty little head of yours.

An important point to understand about how we make choices is that we all have identities and roles that influence our perspectives. As a child, I grew up thinking that there were only two sound career choices: engineering or medicine. Once I realized they weren't mutually exclusive, I pursued both. That decision came from my role as a dutiful Indian daughter who wanted to make her parents (and the Indian community) proud.

We all play different roles, often without even realizing it. Lilly saw the world through her Protective Jewish Mother filter. One point was clear: she was devastated by her son's choice to marry outside the family's faith. She told me that her son came to her years ago and said, "I love Anjali. You know we've been dating for the past nine months. I'm thinking about marrying her, and I wanted your blessing." Those words were so hard for Lilly to hear that she shut down and never gathered any more information.

As a mother, Lilly's worst nightmare seemed to be coming true. The story she made up was that since her son had fallen in love with a Hindu woman, it meant that *he was not committed to creating a family in the same way that she had.* She took that information a step further and in her own mind and heart decided that it meant *he was abandoning his parents and his Jewish culture.* Worse yet, it meant *she, herself, had somehow failed as a mother.* No wonder she took such drastic action. The only problem was, her stories weren't true.

Let me clarify. They might have been true. They might not have been true. She actually didn't know yet because she shut down and didn't ask any questions. She pieced together what she heard him say and filled in all the blanks with her own stories about what it meant about the future. The problem was, Lilly never challenged her own thinking. She assumed her fear-based thoughts were true, which ultimately created much of her own despair. Lilly got furious rather than curious.

So now, let's separate fact (objective data) from fiction (the stories Lilly made up).

Facts

1. Lilly's son married a woman named Anjali who was raised Hindu and whose parents lived in India.

2. Lilly's son and Anjali had six children.

3. The children had been raised going to synagogue on Saturdays and Hindu temple on Sundays.

4. Lilly told her son that when he came for dinner, she preferred he come alone.

5. Lilly said, "I wish I were close to my six grandchildren. I only know them through pictures my son shares with me. I've missed their high school graduations and even missed two weddings."

Fiction

1. The way Lilly had raised her family was the right way, and her son should do the same.

2. Her son didn't value his faith or his family.

3. Lilly had failed as a mother because her son fell in love with someone who wasn't Jewish.

4. Lilly's grandchildren wouldn't be raised in the Jewish tradition.

5. Lilly had no choice but to sever ties with her son's family to make her point.

After Lilly's near-death experience, she had her own i-Five Moment. Through journaling and getting curious, she discovered connections that she hadn't previously noticed. She saw that her son had actually remained committed to his relationships with his parents, his family, his Jewish heritage—and his own heart. Lilly, however, who remained stuck in her perspective, had shunned her son's wife and kids and, as a result, had limited her own joy by depriving herself of what mattered most to her: family.

Lilly created her own destiny by her thoughts. Her definition of being a good mother meant her son would listen to her and follow her beliefs, making the same decisions she had made. In reality, Lilly's son was everything she had raised him to be—and more. She was so focused on blaming him that she didn't see how her own thoughts had created the divide she feared so deeply. She never asked her son about the facts; instead, she let her fears create horror stories about what might happen, based on incomplete data. And she resisted including facts that were right in front of her, stuck as she was in her unwillingness to change her perspective. That stance came at a huge cost.

The world works in mysterious ways. As a patient, Lilly arrived at the hospital helpless and vulnerable. I just happened to be the physician on call. Timing and circumstance put her in the care of a female Indian physician of an age and appearance similar to Anjali's.

As we partnered to restore her health, she did something she had never done before. She let her guard down. Because of that, we were able to build trust and a strong, tender bond. When she opened up about the pain she was experiencing, her perspective changed. Amazingly, what had seemingly broken Lilly's heart and come between her and her son—an Indian woman—was exactly what served as a catalyst to connect her more deeply to her own heart and begin to heal it.

When I ran into Lilly the following year on her way to her primary care doctor's appointment, she was thrilled to report that she had made amends with her son and his family. She exclaimed, "I've not only strengthened my relationship with my son, but I've gained a daughter and six grandchildren!" She was also elated that she had made it through her first winter in a decade without catching a cold. Lilly had been exercising and even felt inspired to sign up for a 5K walk. She felt stronger with each passing day.

This is one example of how we make up stories that limit us. The tragedy is that, based on that misinformation, we can make life-altering decisions that lead us away from our hearts.

The stories you make up matter. They matter because they define what you think is possible, they affect how you communicate with others, and most important, they determine whether your doors to connection, health, and happiness are closed or wide open.

◆ ◆ ◆ ◆ ◆

TALKRX TOOLKIT

Data + your unique perspective = the story you make up

YOUR I-FIVE MOMENT

- To discover the stories that may be holding you back, answer the questions in Chapter 6 of your *TalkRx Journal* (DoctorNehaTalkRx.com).

- Share a crazy story you've made up with the TalkRx Community.

CHAPTER 7

MIND CHATTER

Let's face it: all of us have stories from our childhood that suck.

We've buried them deep inside our hearts because, when they took place, we didn't have the tools to voice what we were experiencing internally, so we simply endured. Or we might have cried or yelled to let it all out. Whether we shouted from the rooftops or stifled our thoughts about these experiences, often the end result was that we didn't feel seen or heard.

Until now, if you have successfully evaded those parts of your life, you're a pro at recycling thought patterns. What do I mean? Well, have you ever said to yourself:

- "Let sleeping dogs lie."
- "Isn't the past in the past?"
- "I don't have time for this."

If any of these sound vaguely familiar, yep, I'm talking to you. Here's the problem: those experiences and memories are still inside you, influencing your thoughts and limiting what you can create in the world. What if I told you that exploring these thoughts and getting curious don't have to take a long time but are essential to improving how you communicate every day, even with the most challenging personalities?

During childhood we begin to develop survival strategies to navigate our relationships and the world around us. From our experiences we make up rules with multiple clauses, such as:

- If I cry, I get attention (at the grocery store or in other public places).

- If I cry, I get spanked (at Mom's house).

- If I cry, I get ridiculed (if my sisters and brothers hear me).

- If I cry, I get my favorite ice cream (at Dad's house).

- If I cry, I get my way (especially with Grandma).

These early experiences are the foundation for our thoughts and beliefs. We developed strategies to survive; to communicate that we need help; or, even more important, to command love, affection, and attention. These thought patterns had a critical role in how we learned to get our needs met.

Except now we're grown up and not in that same environment. And just like our physical numbing strategies, our outdated thought patterns are mental strategies that keep us in our comfort zones. They may have served a purpose early on, but now they hold us back. Very often, when we use those same ways of thinking that worked when we were young to navigate our adult relationships, we experience problems. While I advocate recycling in the physical world, recycling 30-year-old thought patterns can be hazardous to your relationships, your stress levels, your health, and your happiness.

Think about a few simple scenarios: Take the only child who had so much attention showered on her that, as an adult, she still expects others to dote on her. She wonders why she has trouble forming long-term friendships and has been called selfish by more than one ex-boyfriend. Or take the child of divorce who sees himself as the cause of his parents' split and spends his life trying to please everyone around him so no one will leave him.

Every life experience writes on the slate of who you are. These defining moments shape what you believe about the world—whether you believe it's safe or dangerous, whether you believe people are friendly and play by the rules, whether you feel a sense of belonging in your family or community.

These thoughts developed from a combination of what you heard, saw, and experienced from your family, friends, teachers, religious institutions, media, and environment. What you observed was as important as what was absent. For example, if you grew up in a family with parents who didn't outwardly show affection, it would be easy to understand that you would think it's inappropriate to hold hands or hug in public. Suppose you were raised with a parent who worked a lot and was rarely home, you might find yourself seeking a partner who is always at work or lives far away.

THE "IF ONLY" STORY

Growing up, we may have had a person with a voice louder than our own—like an overbearing grandmother, a domineering parent, or a bullying sibling—who made it difficult to know what story was ours and what story was theirs. We've all been hurt and disappointed by our families or wished our upbringing would have been better if only . . .

- If only my dad didn't have a temper.

- If only my older brother didn't beat me up.

- If only my sister didn't drink so much.

- If only we had more money.

- If only my parents got along.

If only, if only, if only . . .

Once we're adults, we get to choose how long it serves us to recycle those stories. Some of us actually never let go. But we have a choice, even when it doesn't feel like it.

While it's important to learn from our families, our cultures, and our upbringing, it is equally important to challenge our own thinking so we can recognize when thought patterns are no longer useful or when we're dealing with a new situation. Sometimes this happens naturally when we enter new arenas—a job, a relationship, a neighborhood. We apply the same rules to new situations and wonder why we're not getting the results we hope for.

How you choose to interpret your thoughts will determine what you believe about yourself, others, and your environment, and what you think is possible. Specifically, I refer to the stories you make up about yourself as self-talk. And the stories you make up about other people and the world are your assumptions, judgments, or opinions. Let's explore these.

SELF-TALK

Try sitting in a quiet place, close your eyes, and try to empty your mind for 60 seconds. Observe any thoughts that spontaneously arise.

What happened? When most people sit in silence, they suddenly become aware of just how many thoughts are going through their heads that they haven't even been aware of. You may be distracted by sounds around you or begin thinking about what someone said recently. A very important part of challenging your thinking is what you say to yourself in the silent moments—about *you*. Ta-da! I'm referring to your self-talk.

Self-talk can seem like background noise, but it's powerful. These thoughts will expand or limit what you think is possible for you, and they are among the most powerful influences on your communication.

Your self-talk started long before you were aware of it. The common way self-talk forms is by trial and error. For instance, you were successful at something, and because of that, decided you were capable of anything. Maybe you won the ring-toss game at a carnival. Rewarded with a life-size stuffed panda bear, you decided, *I'm athletic and talented.* Or at your friend's wedding, maybe a raucous crowd circled you, hooting and hollering as you showcased your latest dance moves. So you thought, *I'm a ladies' man!*

Experiences such as these can often result in self-talk that expands what we think is possible. Expanding beliefs include thoughts such as *I'm kind. I'm strong. I'm smooth. I'm hopeful. I'm hardworking.*

On the other hand, perhaps you tried certain activities that didn't have the outcome you had hoped for and decided, *I'm a disappointment* or, even worse, *I'm a failure*. If you got injured while running a race, you may have thought, *I'm clumsy and weak*.

Culturally, we have become a society that focuses more on limiting beliefs than on expansive thinking, and this begins when we are still toddling around. A majority of the feedback that toddlers receive is "No," "Stop it," or "Don't do that." This heavy focus on negative feedback leads to an imbalance in our self-talk as we're forming our perspectives and what we believe about ourselves. Growing up with an emphasis on what we *shouldn't* do rather than what we *should* do can result in thinking patterns that produce tragic stories in our heads—long after those voices are gone.

Some of these stories become rules that we live by, such as *I'm too old* or *I'm not strong enough, smart enough, pretty enough*. We all have our own versions of this. Do any of these limiting beliefs sound familiar?

- *I'm not rich enough.*

- *I'm not brave enough.*

- *I'm not thin enough.*

- *I'm not witty enough.*

- *I'm not disciplined enough.*

Don't be bashful. We all have these stories of *I'm not good enough!* I've got my own, for sure.

It is no secret that our families are an important lens through which we learn about ourselves and the world. Their words, their actions, their presence (or absence) impact us. How we interpret and react (or respond) to our experiences with them determines what we believe about ourselves and the world around us, because human beings are genetically hardwired for connection and belonging.[9]

One of the most obvious ways to notice your self-talk is in relation to your physical appearance. Your may think your feet are ugly; your nose isn't straight; you need to be leaner; or your breasts, abs, or butt should be a different shape or size. Whatever your version of this self-talk is, pay attention to whether it's a limiting or expanding belief.

WHO KNEW CURLY + DARK = ADOPTED?

For me, it began with my grandmother nagging me to stay out of the sun. She would say, "Neha, get inside! You're already three shades darker than the rest of us, and nobody is going to marry you if you become *kala*," (the Hindi word for "black"). I would reluctantly come in from playing and think, *I do want to get married someday,* as I unsuccessfully tried to scrub the color out of my skin.

To make matters worse, my older sister, Ritu, teased me about my curly hair. She would point to our family portrait on the wall as supporting evidence and say, "See how the rest of us have straight hair? Don't you ever wonder why that is? Fuzzball, you're not even the same color as us. You're definitely adopted."

Fast-forward to my first-grade parent-teacher conference. We had drawn self-portraits that were proudly displayed on the walls. My mom circled the classroom twice and made her way back to me. In a slightly bewildered tone, she inquired, "Neha, why isn't there a self-portrait of you on the wall? Didn't you do the assignment?"

Frustrated that my own mother didn't recognize me, I rolled my eyes, fiercely crossed my arms, and marched over to my drawing, taped neatly to the wall. "*Here I am,* Mom!" I said, pointing to a fair-skinned face framed with straight, dark hair.

"But, Neha, what happened to your pretty curls?"

With disgust, I responded, "I just got out of the shower, Mom!"

Isn't it sad that I began to dislike and reject physical parts of myself? At six years old, I was already uncomfortable in my own skin. Subconsciously I wanted to change what I looked like so I would fit in with my family. Somehow I managed to twist curly hair and dark skin, beautiful attributes, into damaging self-talk that I was ugly and unlovable.

SMART SCHOOL

As a child, I didn't just make up stories about my physical appearance. I created another set of beliefs about my intelligence, my abilities, and my accomplishments.

Ritu and I are just a year and a half apart. But when I was growing up, those 18 months felt like an unbridgeable canyon. Ritu loved music and movies and just plain being in the middle of what was happening. My greatest desire was to play with my sister and her friends. I wanted to be loved and accepted. I wanted to belong. From my sister's perspective as a first-born child, my attempts to tag along were intrusive and annoying. She naturally wanted to be with her friends without her little sister in tow. Her favorite proclamation to me was "Babies aren't allowed to play with big kids!"

One of the happiest moments of my childhood was the day Ritu came home from first grade and announced that she wanted to play school with me. She declared, "Neha, it's important to remember that anything I say goes because I'm the teacher and you're the student."

"Okay," I said.

Only when I was sitting at full attention, with my legs crossed and my pencil properly held, would Ritu begin her lessons. When I began to daydream, she would say, "Neha? Tell me what I just said or we're going to stop. You have to pay attention."

In this way, day after day, Ritu taught me to read, write, add, and subtract. She taught me the secrets that only a first grader was privy to. It wasn't long before I found my time in kindergarten quite boring in comparison with the one-on-one attention I received at home.

Shortly thereafter, my teacher called my mother. "Mrs. Sangwan, I have an unusual concern about Neha. It seems that during tests and exercises, she finishes her work quickly."

"Is that a problem?" my mom inquired.

"Well, no, she definitely knows the material. The problem is that when I turn around or leave the room, she starts helping other students.

"Don't get me wrong; I like her sense of community and her desire to help, but when she tells them the answer, I can't tell what the other children know or don't know. She thinks she's their teacher."

My mother asked me not to share my knowledge with the other children, and I reluctantly agreed. But playing school with Ritu continued well into the second grade.

One day, a letter arrived in the mail. It read something like this:

Mr. & Mrs. Sangwan,

We are pleased to inform you that your daughter Neha has been selected to be a part of the academically gifted program beginning in the fall at Cook Elementary School. She has been identified as a child with academically superior performance, and we are excited to invest in her future growth and education.

When I heard the news, I was elated. I went searching for my sister to tell her. As I approached her bedroom door, I overheard her sobbing.

"I hate her!" she wailed.

After a few seconds, I heard my mother's voice. "Now, Ritu, *hate* is a very strong word. In this house, we use *dislike*. Besides, you love Neha. She's the only sister you've got."

"But why does Neha get to go to Smart School and not me?" Ritu cried. "That's not fair! Everyone will think she's smarter than me!"

I stood there paralyzed.

My mom responded, "Oh, Ritu *beti!* That's not true. You've taught Neha everything she knows. That's why she was chosen to go to Smart School—because of *you!*"

As I peeked through the crack in the door, I saw my mom hugging Ritu on her lap. My heart was racing and my stomach churning. So I ran to my room and cried myself to sleep.

I interpreted my mother's consoling words to Ritu to mean that I wasn't smart. Without my sister, I would never have been chosen for the accelerated program. My mom even said so. From that moment forward, I believed I couldn't do it on my own.

Somehow my home-schooling advantage suddenly felt as if I had cheated. Subconsciously I buried my secret: *I'm not supposed to be in Smart School. Clearly I needed extra help. They must have made a mistake in choosing me.*

In my mid-30s, I had an i-Five Moment when I realized how that interaction had changed my life. I had shielded myself with multiple academic degrees to protect my "secret." I had become a mechanical and biomedical engineer as well as a board-certified internal medicine physician. As if that weren't enough, I went on to be a certified mind-body medicine practitioner, then a certified coach, and I attended more than 50 communication workshops. There's more, but you get the point.

I highly doubt anyone suspected that at the heart of it all was a frightened little girl trying to convince the world that she really did deserve her seat in Smart School. Because of one incident 30 years earlier, I was still trying to prove that I was smart enough and that my accomplishments were not just because of my sister. There was one small problem: it's hard to prove something to others that you don't believe yourself.

What about you? By now you can see that there are endless stories you can make up about yourself or others. The stories you make up—like Lilly's story that "my son has abandoned me by marrying outside of our faith," or self-talk that *I'm not smart enough* or *I'm unlovable*—will shape what you think is possible. More important, these beliefs shape how you feel, what you want, and what you do next.

Taking Out the Trash

You take out the trash every week, right? If you don't, someone else surely does. What about the mental garbage accumulating in your mind? I carried around stories about myself that weren't true for a long time.

Let's talk about how to turn those limiting beliefs around. First you have to challenge your thoughts by getting curious about yourself, the facts, and whether the story you've made up is actually true. Once you've gotten curious about what you might be missing, the second step is to replace limiting beliefs about yourself with new thoughts called affirmations. Affirmations are positive statements made in the present tense that articulate a different story about who you are and expand what's possible right now. This is not about just making stuff up.[10] You have to replace the old self-talk with expanding beliefs that shift your perspective and guide you toward health and happiness.

The thoughts in my head regarding Smart School were:

- *I'm not smart enough.*
- *I can't do this.*
- *I hope no one finds out that I cheated to get in.*

Thirty years later, I developed affirmations that helped counteract that thinking. Anytime those garbage thoughts would appear, I replaced them with:

- *I am intelligent.*
- *I trust myself.*
- *I work hard.*

During a communication workshop, I was able to integrate these expanding thoughts into one affirmation: *I am an intelligent, magnificent woman, loving and trusting myself.*

This positively framed statement in the present tense is a tool that reminds me of who I am in those moments when I doubt myself.

Affirmations help you reprogram your thoughts toward love, acceptance, and an honoring of yourself. An easy way to get started with affirmations is to think about them as something you are reaching for or hope to attain someday.

Then you transform those thoughts into the present tense. For example:

- *I want to be patient* becomes *I am patient.*
- *I want to be flexible* becomes *I am flexible.*
- *I want to forgive* becomes *I am forgiving.*

And as you get more comfortable doing this, you may want to combine them: *I am a patient, flexible, and forgiving woman who listens deeply.*

Some of your self-talk is probably working well. By all means, keep those internal conversations alive. In regard to the self-talk that limits you, changing how you think will give you a fresh perspective.

Addressing self-talk is an important part of challenging your thinking. In addition, getting curious about the stories you've made up about others and your environment will create expanded possibilities for connection.

GET CURIOUS, NOT FURIOUS

We often limit ourselves by making assumptions, judgments, or opinions about others or the world. Sometimes we believe these assumptions because we make the mistake of thinking that others interpret information the same way we do. The problem with that way of thinking is that everybody has his or her own unique experiences, families, and perspectives; it's rare to find someone who thinks just like you (those often are the ones who become your best friends). This is why three people can look at the same piece of artwork, for example, and offer three different interpretations of it. The only safe assumption is that our own perspective is limited.

Once you get curious about the facts, you can ask another person about what you heard, saw, or observed. The missing information fills in the gaps and often expands your perspective.

When I got curious about my Smart School experience, I realized I was missing a lot of information, and this led me to ask my mother about the incident.

All these years later, I remembered the exact words (external data) that I had heard my mother say to Ritu: "You've taught Neha everything she knows. That's why she was chosen to go to Smart School—because of *you!*"

After repeating these words to my mother and telling her about eavesdropping on her conversation with my sister, I told my mother the story I had made up about their conversation: *She thought that I'd cheated by playing school with Ritu and that I hadn't really earned my seat in Smart School.* I asked her if that's really what she thought.

My mom was flabbergasted. She remembered the incident clearly and told me what was happening from her perspective—that it pained her to hear Ritu exclaim that she hated me. As the eldest of three children and the only daughter in her family, my mother had desperately wanted a sister herself. She explained that her intention in telling Ritu how she had helped me get into Smart School was to level the playing field so Ritu wouldn't feel threatened or jealous. She wanted Ritu to know how her hard work and dedication had actually contributed to my success. It was her attempt to build a bridge between us girls. And, no, she didn't think I had cheated.

Since this was so dramatically different from the story I had made up, I decided it would be worth getting curious about what was going on for Ritu as well. So I asked my sister about the external data I had heard and seen as a child.

"Do you remember the day I got into Smart School and you were crying in Mom's lap and screaming that you hated me?" I asked her. "Do you remember what was going on for you? Did you hate me? I thought you would be happy for me."

What my sister said then surprised me even more: "I was jealous and angry because you were getting all the attention. How come I didn't get invited to Smart School? I had done a lot of hard work teaching you after school and no one was recognizing me."

Ritu went on to tell me how the story she made up about this same incident had changed the course of her life as much as it had changed mine: "That experience taught me academics weren't my forte; they were yours. I'm not sure it was even a conscious decision when I was that young, but, in reaction to my pain, I had to develop a new strategy. After that, I decided to focus my energy on creative and social endeavors, including being an enthusiastic mother's helper to Sarika [our newborn sister] and developing my creative writing skills. I knew I could beat you there. I wrote poems and stories that were selected for the children's section of the local newspaper, and I won the fifth-grade spelling bee, remember?"

"Yeah, I remember," I said as I smiled gently.

Finally, after decades, I began to challenge my own self-talk and my judgments about others. Of course, as a second-grader, I had no idea that three sets of stories—all different—about the same interaction could have such a dramatic influence on our futures.

INFINITE SHADES OF GRAY

In order to simplify the world, people often think in black and white. But life isn't often that cut-and-dried. There are endless perspectives and ways to piece together data. Unless we challenge our thinking and examine the stories in our heads, we'll never know what's actually true and be able to adjust our perspective to include what's possible in the present moment.

All these years later, I'm so glad I chose to get curious with my mom and my sister. Now I have a more complete picture of what happened, and it has allowed me to rewrite my story moving forward—one that connects me to both of them. The danger of not getting curious is that you'll assume your perspective is the right one, like Lilly did, and maintain the divide between yourself and others. On the other hand, expanded perspectives identify common ground and have the power to create deeper connection and a sense of belonging.

◆ ◆ ◆ ◆ ◆

TALKRX TOOLKIT

Old stories + thinking *I'm right* = limited perspectives + disconnection

Curiosity + affirmations = expanded perspectives + connection + belonging

YOUR I-FIVE MOMENT

- To break through your recycled thought patterns, complete the Chapter 7 questions and exercises in your *TalkRx Journal* (DoctorNehaTalkRx.com).

- If you're feeling brave, share one of your affirmations to inspire others in the TalkRx Community.

CHAPTER 8

POINTING
THE FINGER

Isn't it great to get the last word in an argument? You showed them!

When conversations get heated, most of us respond with an instinctive defense mechanism that's easier to identify in others than it is to see in ourselves. There's nothing complex about this; in fact, often it can be one of those recycled thought patterns that is almost reflexive. And there is plenty of it to go around in our society today. What's more, if you harbor this defensiveness for extended periods of time, it causes high stress and undermines your health and happiness. What I'm talking about is a way of thinking that ruins friendships, splits marriages and families, costs companies in productivity and turnover, divides nations, and yes, even creates wars. Subconsciously, holding on to this common response to conflict gives you a "valid" reason not to change or move forward. What I'm talking about is *blame*.

You might be thinking, *Blame? Are you kidding me? How could blame be the cause of all this mayhem in the world? I mean, sometimes, don't other people deserve it? Shouldn't we hold them responsible for their bad behavior?* Yep! That's exactly what I'm talking about. You just did it. That's how easy it is to blame. And while you think you've "won," you've actually ended up with the booby prize. In the short term you've gotten what you wanted, but in the long run you've damaged your relationship and created a divide.

If you blame a past experience as the reason you can't achieve your dreams or have the life you want, you get to stay stuck. You get to be the victim. Not only do you get the booby prize (blame), but you also have an excuse that makes another person or people bad and yourself good. It's the endless game of who's right and who's wrong.

University of Houston research professor and author Brené Brown describes blame as the discharge of pain and discomfort. We already know what happens when we're uncomfortable in our bodies. There are many physical strategies we use to change how our bodies feel. Blame is a mental strategy that allows us to alleviate our discomfort along with any responsibility.

The amazing part is there are so many variations of blame. Let's explore a few of them.

- **Self-deprecating blame:** You blame yourself when something bad happens . . . even if it's not your fault.

- **Political blame:** You blame another (out loud) when you need to own your part in a situation.

- **Suffering-in-silence blame:** You blame another, but you don't say anything out loud. Meanwhile, you're fuming inside as your blame slowly transforms into resentment.

On a simple level, every interaction requires at least two people. When communication breaks down, a few things happen:

1. If we feel discomfort, we may want to discharge that sensation from our bodies.

2. If we feel wronged or hurt, we may want someone else to acknowledge their wrongdoing.

3. We might resist acknowledging our own part of an interaction.

What Game Are You Playing?

Did you play hot potato at birthday parties as a child? You know, when everyone sits in a circle and the music plays while each person passes the "hot" potato (which is ironically room temperature) to the next person as quickly as possible. When the music stops, the person left holding the "hot potato" is eliminated from the game. No one wants to be left holding the hot potato. It means "You're out!"

That's exactly what we do with blame. It's an endless game of tossing the metaphorical hot potato of responsibility onto another person instead of owning how we may have contributed to a situation. Once again, it's more comfortable not to be "out."

Projection

It's natural to be able to see faults in others more easily than we see them in ourselves. Projection is a type of blame that focuses on someone else's contribution to an outcome rather than on one's own. Many of us learn this skill at a young age. For example, if you had siblings, you quickly learned a game of survival called "pin the blame on your sibling."

It's no wonder that as adults, we recycle projection on others with thoughts like:

- *It's your fault.*
- *You shouldn't have done that.*
- *You messed it up.*
- *You made me do it.*

One reason people project blame onto others is self-protection. They want to create a sense of control or safety, and they do this by making someone else bad, wrong, or 100 percent responsible for an outcome. This manifests in several ways. Sometimes blamers are direct about their projections and say them out loud to the person they are in conflict with. A majority of the time, however, blamers voice their grievances to somebody else. Blamers can also simmer in silence, as you've already learned. But just because someone doesn't voice blame out loud doesn't mean it doesn't exist.

Why would someone waste so much energy on this type of behavior? Blame is seductive. It's enticing. There's a short-term (false) sense of power you get from blaming another. A sense of righteousness. A sense of justice. If you blame somebody else and you don't tell them about it, it can turn into loneliness and—depending on how important this relationship is to you—sometimes even resentment, isolation, and depression.

If you blame somebody in a repetitive, persistent, or aggressive manner, it can be considered intimidation, bullying, or badgering. These are more intense forms of blame and commonly occur in emotionally charged disagreements or in legal disputes. The blamer thinks that if he absolves himself of responsibility in a situation, he will somehow feel better and get more of what he wants.

But here's the problem. Blame is an illusion, kind of like a mirage of water in the desert. In reality, what happens is that the person blaming feels a false sense of power while the other person ends up feeling unfairly accused—they carry a disproportionate share of the blame. This results in disconnection and distance and, if it continues on both sides, ultimately a stalemate.

Why would anyone choose to be in a stalemate? Because in reality, they don't realize that they have a choice.

Now let's talk about another form of blame that can be harder to recognize.

Personalization

When we blame ourselves for something that, in fact, has nothing to do with us—and we don't have the courage to get curious about the facts—we are personalizing. This type of blame comes more naturally to those of us who beat ourselves up or want to be perfectionists. Personalization also occurs when someone is insecure about something and more worried about what others are going to think than what they themselves think. Personalization is rooted in a lack of self-esteem. Typical thought patterns that lead to personalization are self-talk that sounds like *I'm not smart enough. I'm not pretty enough. I'm not funny enough.* And so on.

When people aren't confident in themselves, they doubt their capabilities or feel unworthy. Then they gather "evidence" to prove their hypotheses. The only problem is that—even though it feels real—the evidence is often just a story.

This plays itself out most obviously when there is silence. Whether it's during quiet time in nature or the silence in a conversation with somebody else, the voice of personalization speaks loudly in the stillness.

For example, suppose you send a text saying, "Hey, honey, do you want to go to our favorite spot for dinner tonight?" and four hours pass without a response. In the silence, someone who personalizes would begin running thought patterns like this:

- *I can't keep the excitement in this relationship.*
- *I must have been too overbearing last night.*
- *I always do the wrong thing.*

Another common situation where personalization can take root is in the face of strong emotion, such as anger. The default mode for personalization would be: *I must have done something wrong*, or *Something is wrong with me.*

Projection and personalization are on opposite ends of the same spectrum. Here's an example to tie it all together so you can better recognize the many faces of blame.

Here are the facts: You're new at school, there are two teams being formed, and the captains are taking turns choosing players. You are selected 20th out of 20 players. Now, what story could you make up about that?

You could make it about the others (projection):

- *They aren't friendly.*
- *They're jerks.*
- *They don't like me.*

Or you could make it about yourself (personalization):

- *I'm not athletic enough.*
- *I'm not a fast enough runner.*
- *I'm too scrawny.*

These limiting beliefs attack your worth. They're damaging and demeaning self-talk. Notice whether the limiting belief is about yourself or about another and whether it creates distance. In this example you can see how these beliefs could undermine a relationship before it has even started.

People think there's only one way to put the facts together, and the story they create resembles the familiar one they've made up many times before. Think back to the section in Interpreting Your Body about the comfort zone, learning zone, and panic zone. You'll remember that we are creatures that like the known—even if the known isn't working anymore. We often choose patterns of thinking, patterns of blame or dysfunction, that are familiar rather than those that are not. At what point in your life, your day, or your week does it ever seem like a good time to change the rules of the game?

How about now?

Changing the rules of how you communicate may feel scary. But what if you reminded yourself that making mistakes is necessary in order to grow and learn? In order to create new pathways in your brain and your heart, you have to rebuild the connections. It's just like when you were learning how to transition from a tricycle to a two-wheel bike: Was falling down and skinning your knee part of rewiring your muscle memory and learning balance? Yes. And it was part of growing up, too. You would probably call skinning your knee necessary, right? So is stumbling a little as you learn to communicate, especially when you feel hurt or in conflict with another. It will all be okay.

SAME STIMULUS, DIFFERENT OUTCOME

Let's start with a common place where people get stuck. When things go awry, people often focus on the actual words that were said. They focus on the gesture, such as the furrowed brow and blaring horn from another driver as he speeds by. They focus on the tone with which they are told they can't have what they want. They focus on their racing heart or sweaty palms. This is good information. That's what the first part of this book was all about: paying attention to the external data and the messages coming from your internal signals.

What most people don't do is take ownership of the story they make up and their reaction to what occurs. Any interaction is the alchemy that takes place between two people. Each person contributes to the outcome. The tricky part is that it's so much easier to see someone else's shortcomings than it is to see our own contribution, which can easily be hidden in our blind spot.

The stimulus is just that—a stimulus. We often think of it as the problem. It is not always the problem. More often, the incident provides an opportunity to see how we respond to a given stimulus.

For example, you walk into a room and an eight-year-old girl is crying. That's the stimulus. Your response can be that you:

- Roll your eyes, cross your arms, and walk out.
- Say, "Please stop crying."
- Say, "Go to your room until you put yourself back together, and don't come back out until there's a smile on your face."
- Stay silent, ignore her, and keep walking.
- Give her a hug and ask her, "What happened?"

It is both the stimulus and the response that create an interaction and its outcome. For those of you who choose withdrawal and silence, it's important to realize that this, too, is a response.

In Chapter 4, you learned that when your body's physiology gives you powerful signals internally, it's time to pause and interpret them. Pausing between a stimulus and your response gives you precious time to make a choice rather than just react.

Now that you know the faces of blame, let's see how many ways Smart School could have played out.

Let's look at the facts:

- Ritu taught me every day after school for two years.
- I was selected for the accelerated program at Cook Elementary School.
- I saw and heard Ritu crying in our mother's lap.
- Ritu said, "I hate her. Everybody thinks she's smarter than me."
- Our mom said, "You've taught Neha everything she knows. That's why she got chosen to go to Smart School . . . because of *you*."
- I ran to my room and cried without saying anything to them.

The story I made up about myself was:

- *I'm not smart enough to do it on my own.*
- *I need extra help.*
- *Somehow I got in and I don't deserve it.*
- *I "cheated."*

In the game of blame, the move I chose was *personalization*. I made the experience all about *me*. I chose a limiting belief and held on to it as if it were true. It took me 30 years to have the courage to get curious.

Before you jump to defend me, remember, I chose personalization. Even though I was only seven, there were many other options. I could have made a different move in the game of blame and chosen projection instead. What if the story I made up had been about my sister?

It might have sounded something like:

- *Ritu's a crybaby.*
- *Ritu's just angry and jealous.*
- *Ritu wants Mom's attention.*

Or, if I had projected blame on my mother, it might have sounded like this:

- *Mom doesn't love me as much as she loves Ritu.*
- *Mom thinks I couldn't have gotten into Smart School on my own.*
- *Mom hugs whoever cries.*

As you can see, there are infinite ways to play the blame game. Ritu could have blamed the school for how they chose the students. My mom could have blamed my dad for not participating enough with the kids. And on and on . . .

One of the most interesting parts of this experience for me has been that I'm now grateful for Smart School and the story I made up about it. As strange as that may sound, it drove me to excel in academics, work hard, get my degrees, and prove that I could do it on my own.

For many people blame is a way of life. Choosing to let go of old thought patterns can be uncomfortable, and letting go of them, like letting go of anything, requires courage and self-trust to navigate what comes next. But once you stop playing the blame game, you'll have the mental space to expand your perspective and create new possibilities in your relationships.

◆ ◆ ◆ ◆ ◆

TALK R$_X$ TOOLKIT

Pointing fingers + enlisting others in why you're right = stalemate

Projection = disproportionately blaming others

Personalization = disproportionately blaming yourself

Personalization + projection = an endless blame game (think hot potato)

YOUR i-FIVE MOMENT

- To figure out where you play the blame game, answer the questions in Chapter 8 of your *TalkRx Journal* (DoctorNehaTalkRx.com).

- Share with the i-Five Community one example of how the blame game keeps you stuck.

CHAPTER 9

WHAT DO
YOU MEAN—MY
RESPONSIBILITY?

Often, before a relationship goes awry, each person makes the choice to blame instead of being accountable for their part. So if you're curious about exiting the blame game and healing your relationships, choose a new move—personal accountability.

> The good news: you'll have the secret to getting what you want and building strong relationships.

> The bad news: it's about *you* taking responsibility, not someone else.

Believe it or not, this is where *me, me, me* actually comes in handy. While society has taught us that talking about ourselves too much can be rude and self-focused, that is not the case here. In resolving conflict, the key is to figure out how you contributed to the outcome. Get curious about your part in a situation and endless i-Five Moments await you.

You might be asking what the difference is between taking responsibility and beating yourself up or blaming yourself. Blaming through personalization is a way of attacking the core of who you are (*I'm not worthy, I'm not smart*). Personal accountability is taking ownership of your behavior, your reaction, what you said or didn't say that contributed to a less-than-ideal outcome (staying silent, laughing, leaving the room, making hurtful comments).

How you show up (or don't) in any situation contributes to the outcome. Taking ownership of *your* part in an interaction can be uncomfortable in the short term. But in the long term, if you stop blaming others or your past, and choose to create a new path that gets you what you want, wouldn't that be worth it? Through recognizing your part in a situation and owning it, rather than getting the booby prize (blame), you are rewarded with less stress, more happiness, and deeper connections.

Taking responsibility may seem counterintuitive, especially when someone else seems soooooo wrong! Yes, there are times people say words or take actions that seem unconscionable. You may think someone is a drama queen or socially inept or even clueless. Yes, it's true. It may have even been you a time or two. Here's the key: it takes only one person assuming responsibility to turn the situation around. And in case you're thinking it's that other person, let me remind you: that person is *you*.

Don't be hard on yourself; you may not have known until now that you play a starring role in every interaction and outcome. That's a lot of pressure. But you can ease the pressure by asking yourself a few simple questions:

- What was my role in creating this outcome?
- What did I say (or not say)?
- What did I do (or not do)?

Accountability—taking ownership—is getting curious about your part in a situation. You'll know you're emerging from blame when you catch yourself having thoughts like *It wasn't my fault, it was Sally's* and change your thinking to *Wow. I was nervous about talking to Sally. I checked my phone twice and interrupted her while she was talking. That may have indicated that I wasn't giving her my full attention.*

This new awareness of your role in conflict gives you an added bonus in everyday conversations. Once you discover your part in how communication gets off track, it becomes easy to adjust your behavior to prevent conflict from happening in the first place.

CHALLENGE YOUR THINKING

Once you believe that you could have an itsy-bitsy, teeny-weeny part of the responsibility for the outcome of a situation, it's time to challenge your thinking by examining the stories in your head. It actually takes courage and awareness to open up to new possibilities.

When communication goes off track, you challenge your thinking by first taking a deep breath and pausing. Once you pause, you can get curious about what type of thought patterns you're using.

- Are you using blame?

- If yes, are you blaming yourself (personalization) or another (projection)?

  - If you are personalizing, ask: What if this isn't about *me*?

  - If you are projecting, ask: What is my role in this?

No matter what your thought pattern is, begin with the assumption that you don't have all the information, and get curious about the unknown.

I have witnessed the power of my patients challenging their own thinking. Remember Brandon and Lilly and the bridges they were able to build once they quit blaming and owned their part in the situation?

Brandon was able to see that while he spent many years blaming his father for *not being proud of him* (projection), his own part (his accountability) was that he'd never asked his dad if that projection was even true. In fact, five years after his dad died, Brandon was still blaming him. That's a great example of how someone can unknowingly stay stuck in a relationship stalemate. When Brandon slowed down enough to challenge his own thinking, he realized he had been projecting blame onto his father while holding on to limiting beliefs from his school years. It became painfully clear that there was a lot he'd never gotten curious about.

Lilly, on the other hand, interpreted her son's decision to marry someone outside the Jewish faith as a reflection on her parenting (personalization). She also felt justified in blaming her son for abandoning their heritage and causing a rift in the family (projection). Lilly's curiosity revealed the harsh reality that she had unknowingly orchestrated the demise of her relationship with her son's family. For years she hadn't even considered her part in creating the divide between herself and her son. Once she did, everything changed.

Me, Myself, and I

A critical aspect of owning your part in everyday conversations or conflicts is using the appropriate pronouns. One of the most common mistakes people make is using general statements instead of speaking on their own behalf. This is when you hear yourself using "we" or "you" when you're really talking about yourself. Owning your experience from a place of personal accountability, using "I" when you mean "I," turns up the intensity of your body's physical sensations. This is because you then experience more acutely how much a particular situation is impacting you. It gets much more personal. Therefore, making generalizations is often an unconscious way of speaking that allows you to maintain control and not let a conversation get too personal. As a society we use these pronouns interchangeably but pay little attention to their significance.

Look at the following examples of generalized statements and how accountability language (swapping pronouns) can turn it around. Say the statements below out loud to see if you notice a difference in the intensity of your body's physical signals when the statements become personal:

Generalization: "We don't appreciate receiving the check before we're done with our meal."
Accountability: "I don't appreciate receiving the check before I'm done with my meal."

Generalization: "You know how annoying it is when you're interrupted."
Accountability: "I feel annoyed when I'm interrupted."

Generalization: "Don't you get upset when the clerk is rude to you?"
Accountability: "I'm upset because the clerk was rude to me."

Generalization: "We can't stand when we get e-mails with last-minute requests."
Accountability: "I can't stand when I get an e-mail with a last-minute request."

Generalization: "When we feel unappreciated, it's natural to get passive-aggressive."
Accountability: "When I feel unappreciated, I react by getting passive-aggressive."

Why don't we swap pronouns then? Because it's easier to hide behind "we" and "us." People often think that if they want to make a bold statement, somehow there's power in numbers. Another reason is that taking ownership can be uncomfortable. Using the pronouns "I" or "me" can invite possible judgment or criticism. When people reveal their own sentiments by using "I" statements, they must be much more thoughtful about the words they're saying instead of hiding behind the words "we" or "us."

It's just as important to appropriately use "you" rather than "we" when you are actually making a request of someone else:

Generalization: "Let's make sure we take the trash out tonight."
Accountability: "Can you take the trash out tonight?"

This nuance might seem small. Don't be fooled. Using the accurate pronoun is an important part of clear and accountable communication.

Let's take it one step further. Have you ever felt nervous about addressing conflict because you were worried that the other person would get defensive or not be able to hear what you were saying? How your message is received depends heavily on the language you use. So if you start with "You made me" or "You did this" or "It's your fault," I hope you've started to recognize the blame in those statements and how they can get any conversation off to a rocky start. Change your words; change your world. Let's make a you-turn.

You-Turn Tool

Instead of using "you" to blame someone else:

1. Use "I" to share what you observed.

2. Speak from your own perspective.

3. Then get curious.

This takes some practice, but it will be much easier for the other person to listen and stay engaged. And the best part is, you'll create an opportunity for a dialogue. Here are a few everyday examples:

Blame: "What have you been doing all day? You didn't even wash the dishes."
Accountability: "I wanted to cook dinner and noticed the dishes from last night are still in the sink. What happened?"

Blame: "You made me upset. Your behavior was inappropriate."
Accountability: "I was upset at the dinner party last night when I saw you hug Marcie. Last week you mentioned that you two had dated back in college. Should I be concerned?"

Blame: "You left the door unlocked this morning. It's going to be your fault if someone steals everything."
Accountability: "When I got home, the door was unlocked. Do you know what happened?"

If you were on the receiving end of this type of communication, which version of the communication would you receive more easily? I bet you would prefer to be on the receiving end of the "I" accountability statements. How you phrase your communication with others impacts your effectiveness. Go ahead. Pay attention to pronouns at the next dinner party conversation and you'll notice how easy it is for people to get them all mixed up!

Bonus Tip: Be careful about using absolutes, like *always* and *never*. These words are generalizations as well and often send the person you're speaking to in a frenzy to find one example that disproves what you've just said. Using absolutes may undermine your message.

Transforming Our Stories

Just by challenging your thinking, using the right pronouns, stating what you've observed, and asking a few simple questions, it's easy to imagine a story different from the one you've been telling yourself—one that expands your beliefs and bridges relationships.

So here's the deal. Since you're making up a story, why not make it a good one? You already know the health benefits that result from positive thinking and the way your body reacts strongly to your thoughts, whether they are fact or fiction. If you're busy getting curious about what you don't know and if you stay relaxed, the creative part of your brain will stay engaged, allowing you to imagine expanded possibilities. On the other hand, if you panic and begin creating a horror film, your brain and body will move into survival mode, and one of the first aspects of your physiology to shut down will be your creative thinking. Instead, since you now know there are infinite ways you can put the data together and create a story, why not create one that allows you to relax and be open to listening to another person?

Making the move to personal accountability is your ticket out of the blame game. Recognizing the thought patterns you've been using is the first step. Then it's about challenging your own thinking and taking responsibility for your part in a situation. That's courage. And it's the way to create a win-win for everyone. It's your move. You choose.

◆ ◆ ◆ ◆ ◆

TALKRX TOOLKIT

Personal Accountability Tool

1. What was my role in creating this outcome?
2. What did I say (or not say)?
3. What did I do (or not do)?
4. Did I generalize or misuse pronouns?
5. Was I using blame?
   - If yes, were you blaming yourself or another?
   - If you were personalizing, ask: What if this wasn't about *me*?
   - If you were projecting, ask: What was my role in this?

You-Turn Tool

Instead of using "you" to blame someone else:

1. Use "I" to share what you observed.
2. Speak from your own perspective.
3. Then get curious.

YOUR 1-FIVE MOMENT

- To figure out your part in any situation, answer the questions in Chapter 9 of your *TalkRx Journal* (DoctorNehaTalkRx.com).

- Share any questions you have about blame versus accountability with the TalkRx Community.

CHAPTER 10

LISTENING— A SOUND DISCUSSION

As you read the title of this chapter, you might have thought, *Listening? Really? That's like needing to pay attention to my breathing. I am a good listener. I do it all the time.*

Okay, let's put some data to that. On a scale of 1 to 5, what level of listener are you most of the time (1 = worst listener, 5 = best listener)? Quick! Jot down the first number that comes to mind. You don't have to show anybody. And you'll get to reassess your number at the end of the chapter.

Listening is a primary way we take in data and form stories in our head. It's how we decide what we think in order to formulate a response. What I'm trying to say is that listening is kind of important. Listening is simple but not always easy. For example, how good a listener are you when you're preoccupied or bored? When you're feeling stressed? What about when you're angry with someone? What about when you're in a social situation and you find yourself with someone who doesn't have much to say—but that doesn't stop him? How well do you listen then?

Just like breathing, people often take listening for granted. You shouldn't. It's by far one of the most powerful tools in communication. My hope is that you'll recognize the distinct advantage that listening deeply will give you in any conversation, no matter how simple or complex.

More Data = More Options

There's an old adage, "Less is more." It may be true for some things in life, but when it comes to listening, *more is better.* The depth of our listening determines the quality and quantity of data we absorb. We already know how powerful our thoughts are and that they have a huge impact on our physiology. What we think ultimately determines what we say and do. Therefore, the better listeners we are, the more effective communicators we'll be. And the better listeners we are, the more likely we'll be able to build a bridge to others in everyday conversation and especially during conflict. This is why the quality of our listening is so critical. And *more is better.*

Even if you understand everything we've discussed in the book so far, it will be nearly impossible to change your thoughts and expand your perspective unless you understand the i-Five Levels of Listening.

The i-Five Levels of Listening

People tend to listen at different levels depending on their surroundings and state of mind. Once you get curious, listening with an open mind allows you to hear what you may have been missing. The i-Five Levels of Listening will help you improve your relationships and save you time.

Level 1: Closed Listening

There are three primary causes for Closed Listening:

1. **You're distracted.** It might not be a good time for you. Your attention is on something else. You're sending an e-mail, preparing for a meeting, daydreaming about a lover, checking your phone for the latest tweet—anything other than actually listening to the person talking to you.

2. **You already know.** You're thinking, *Been there, done that.* You might already be resistant to a particular topic or person. Or you may not be open to receiving input. Whatever the underlying cause, you think you already know how this is going to play out.

3. **You don't care.** You may be indifferent about the topic at hand. And no matter what is being said, what you hear is "Blah, blah, blah . . ."

With Closed Listening, you may say you're listening, but you're not. Your crossed arms and legs tell it all. You're probably rolling your eyes. You may be multitasking while the person is speaking. Direct eye contact is risky and not often used with this level of listening. You don't dare give the speaker the wrong message, that there's a green light for them to continue speaking. You're answering with one-word grunts: yep, nope, uh-huh. Bottom line: You're the king or queen of mixed messages. Your words aren't matching your tone and body language. You wish this were over.

Calling all level 1 listeners: Take a look around. If this is your primary way of listening, you may be all alone on Self-righteous Island. Closed Listening may allow you to multitask in the short term, therefore appearing seductively efficient. But in the long term, this type of *not really listening* isolates you from the people you love and creates distance in your relationships. It actually may require *more* time, especially if you need to revisit the conversation again later on.

Closed Listening is a form of pretending. This is about trying to make people think you're listening when you're not. It can be about not knowing how to get out of a conversation or not wanting to look rude. Whatever the reason, mixed messages are abundant.

Level 2: Head Listening

The big question with Head Listening is: who are you really listening to? Level 2 listening is self-focused. It's when you hear a sound bite of what the other person is saying and then immediately jump to how that relates to you.

When you are listening more to yourself than you are to the other person, it can play out in three ways.

1. **The Planner:** One reason people engage in Head Listening is that they want to *get it just right*. It might be that they're worried what other people will think of them. It might be that they want to sound smart and articulate. It might be that they want to avoid public humiliation. Whatever the reason, they are self-focused.

   Suppose at your family dinner or in a workshop setting, a question is asked, and, one at a time, each person is supposed to give an answer. If you're more focused on how your response will make you look in front of others, you'll move into mental overdrive. Rather than listening to what others are saying, you'll be busy running potential algorithms—judiciously planning your spontaneous answer. In the meantime, you'll completely miss listening to others.

2. **The Hijack:** This version of Head Listening can be tricky because it's natural to want to share how your own experience relates to what someone else is saying. You might be well intentioned, but the problem comes when you aren't first curious about what the other person is sharing. Instead, you take what is being said and make it about you. If you're only thinking about how you can redirect the conversation to yourself, it can backfire, especially if the other person doesn't feel heard first.

   Here's a simple example of the hijack: Maureen calls her friend, excited to share about her first vacation to the Hawaiian tropics. She got to spend an entire week on the Big Island and had her first helicopter ride over a volcano. If her friend is listening at level 2, he will think about how Hawaii applies to him, and this is what his response might sound like if he is hijacking: "The last time *I* was in Hawaii, *I* was on the Big Island, and you'll never believe what happened to *me* . . ."

Instead of asking about Maureen's trip, he pivots to talking about himself. Worse yet, he might one-up her.

3. **The One-Two Punch** (Hijack + One-Up): Some people take it to the next level. You know that friend—the one who has no clue that while he's trying to connect to you, he's doing exactly the opposite. You share something with him, and not only does he use it as an opportunity to make it about himself (a hijack), but he reminds you that his story is even better than yours (one-up). It's a one-two punch.

Let's go back to our previous example to see how this might play out: Maureen calls her friend, excited to share what her first vacation to the Hawaiian tropics was like. She got to spend an entire week on the Big Island and had her first helicopter ride over a volcano. If her friend is listening at level 2, he will think about how Hawaii applies to him and how his experience might trump hers. If he uses the one-two punch, this is what his response might sound like: "The last time *I* went to Hawaii, I went for *two* weeks. We had an oceanfront room at the Westin, and the owner took us on a tour of the islands in his private helicopter."

It's all about how his last trip to Hawaii was longer, bigger, and better than Maureen's.

Be careful: you might be the one who one-ups others. Don't fret. As soon as you realize your mistake, there's a simple remedy. All you have to do is acknowledge what the other person is sharing, ask questions, and make sure they feel heard first. Then you can share your experience with them, and you'll both feel connected.

A common trap for Head Listeners is to interrupt. If you're waiting for the person speaking to take a breath so you can begin talking, that doesn't count as listening. (Okay, it is listening, albeit a calculated and brief type of listening.) Can you imagine how unheard your friend would feel if you were to interrupt him to hijack his story and then one-up him?

Another reason people interject when others are speaking is that they feel uncomfortable. They may have a time constraint or feel anxious or defensive. Head Listeners often have an agenda, so they're interested in redirecting the conversation back to themselves or their needs.

Physicians are not exempt from this type of listening, either. Studies show that physicians listen to their patients for an average of 18 to 22 seconds before interrupting them.[11] I'm guilty of having interrupted a patient or two as I gathered their history and performed their physical. Yes, I may have been busy, but I imagine interrupting them left my patients feeling unheard and disconnected.

In addition, cultural upbringing influences how we listen. If you come from a boisterous culture where family gatherings have everybody talking over one another, you know the loudest voice wins. I come from a large extended Indian family, so we thought it was completely normal for everyone to speak at the same time. My friends who are Italian and Greek tell me they experience similar family interactions.

It's just as important to recognize when you are *not* listening as it is to learn the next three levels of listening. It's time to get out of your world. Whew! Level 3 is the first time you are truly listening to another person.

Level 3: Ear Listening (words)

If you like gathering data, this is the level of listening for you. Ear Listening is focusing on the words being said. This is great for details and facts. I like to think of it as black-and-white listening to gather content.

For example:

1. When someone tells you the party is on *October 22 at 7 P.M. at 727 Crescent Avenue*, it's important to listen to the words in order to show up at the right place at the right time.

2. When you're picking up groceries for a dinner party your friend is throwing, it's important to focus on the details of the ingredients she needs in order to make the right grocery list.

3. Similarly, if you are in learning mode, say in a class, a presentation, or a meeting, level 3 listening is important so you can take accurate notes about the subject.

Listening at this level is valuable. It is the foundation for levels 4 and 5. If you're a problem solver, an advice giver, or just more left-brain analytically inclined, Ear Listening probably comes naturally to you. Problem solvers tend to ask questions like "Why did you do that?" or "Did you think of this?" or "What about trying this?" Sometimes these questions can be helpful. However, if you don't seem to be getting anywhere, it's a good time to ask yourself if you need to listen at a deeper level.

Most people think that listening to someone is about hearing the words they are saying. It is. *And it's much more than that.* When you listen for words, you hear the content, but you can miss a lot of what's being said.

As a traditional physician, most of my listening was at levels 2 (Head) and 3 (Ear). It wasn't until I studied communication, stress management, and coaching that I realized the power of deeper levels of listening. The next two levels of listening are where I began to understand how much was *not* being said. I missed hearing my patients on an emotional level and even missed what was most important to them.

Now let's reveal the secret of people who have great relationships. I mean solid, consistent, understanding, and loving connections that last for decades. It's something you probably don't suspect. It doesn't take any extra time; in fact, it probably saves you time. It does, however, require your full attention. It's listening between the lines and hearing what's not being said. The secret is levels 4 and 5 listening.

Level 4: Heart Listening (words + emotions)

In Heart Listening, you listen to more than the words—you also listen for the emotions underneath the words being spoken. This type of listening is useful for everyday conversations, and it also has the power to de-escalate emotionally charged situations, navigate awkward moments, and resolve conflict. And if that isn't enough, Heart Listening helps to create deeper connections.

With Heart Listening, becoming acutely aware of someone else's tone and their body language is *how* you listen to more than what is explicitly being said. With level 4 listening, you hear *the words someone is saying* (content) while simultaneously tuning in to *how* they're saying it (the emotion). It's about acknowledging what's happening in the background and showing empathy.

A common myth is that empathy and deep listening take more time. In fact, it often takes less time because the person you are listening to feels heard and doesn't feel the need to repeat herself. It does, however, take more of your presence and focus.

The problem is that most people have a limited emotional vocabulary. They can name a few emotions such as happy, mad, sad, or glad. And commonly, when people are uncomfortable in their body, they can have more trouble identifying these emotions. In the next section of the book (Interpreting Your Emotions), you will learn how to expand your emotional vocabulary. This will make it easier to identify emotions and listen on a deeper level. You will also be able to recognize and manage challenging emotions more effectively.

Level 5: Open Listening (words + emotions + values)

Open Listening is a tool that will allow you to find common ground in conflict and mend relationships long gone astray. Level

5 listening has the power to restore human connection, even in the most difficult situations. It's easier to focus on what divides us (as we explored in the chapter on blame), but listening at level 5 will reveal what we have in common. Once you can listen at this level, it's easy to build a bridge between yourself and others.

When you're in a conversation with someone else—whether it's an everyday conversation or an emotionally charged one—listening between the lines is powerful. It combines level 3 (words) and level 4 (emotions) with level 5 (what the other person *values*).

Just as people may have trouble naming emotions, they may have trouble identifying their values. Often, they know that they value their health or their family, but they may have trouble articulating a broader range of values. You will learn more about values in the fourth section of the book (Interpreting Your Desires). When you make it a habit to use level 5 listening, your relationships will be strengthened.

WHY THINGS ESCALATE

Usually, in the face of strong emotion such as anger, sadness, or anxiety, people feel uncomfortable. This discomfort causes them to want to fix it, change it, or do anything to make it go away. Let's face it: all of a sudden, it's just plain weird. Now tears are streaming, faces are red, and—boom!—there's an elephant in the room. Just like that.

In emotionally charged conversations, if you respond with words only and don't acknowledge the emotion, you will most likely escalate the situation. If instead you listen for the emotion underneath what someone is saying and you learn to name it, you can easily connect to the other person in a heartfelt way.

Let's explore how your level of listening can influence the outcome of everyday interactions. For example, imagine you're the receptionist at a medical office and a frantic mother is 30 minutes late for her five-year-old son's appointment. She runs to the desk, out of breath, and says, "I had trouble parking. The doctor is still going to see my son, right? I know we're late, but I want to make sure he'll still be seen!"

- **Level 3: Ear Listening.** If you listened only to this mother's words, you might respond with something like "Sounds like you got delayed while parking? Our office policy is to reschedule if you're more than 20 minutes late."

  What do you think the response of an anxious mother with a sick child would be? Likely, her emotional response would escalate if she didn't think you understood her sense of urgency and panic about her son being sick. I promise this conversation would go on much longer if she didn't feel heard.

- **Level 4: Heart Listening.** However, if you addressed the underlying emotions, you might say something like this: "Mrs. Smith, I hear how *upset* you are about being late. It must be *scary* when your little one isn't feeling well."

  If you were that parent, might you have a different response to the second version of the conversation? Would you feel more understood if the receptionist acknowledged the emotions underneath your words and understood your plight? You'd probably sigh in relief.

- **Level 5: Open Listening:** "Mrs. Smith, I hear how *worried* [emotion] you are. And I can see how important your son's *health* is to you [value]. Let me see what we can do."

  Even if the doctor can't see her son immediately, the mom will more likely be open to other options if she feels heard on a deeper level. Listening for the emotions (fright and worry) and values (health) actually could build a bridge to her during this emotionally charged situation.

Here's another example: Your teenage daughter raises her voice as she again complains that her brother is the "favorite" child. You've heard her in the past and thought that the issue had been resolved.

- **Level 3: Ear Listening.** You might respond, "This is the second time you've brought this up. I heard you the first time. What are you complaining about now?"

  Your daughter will likely cross her arms and say, "Nothing, Mom. You never listen to me anyway." Then she'll storm out of the room.

  Now that you're at a stalemate, shift gears into a higher level of listening. You've been reading a book on effective communication and have begun paying attention to much more than the words your daughter is saying. It's only now that you realize she's not just being dramatic, but she feels unheard.

- **Level 4: Heart Listening.** So the third time the topic comes up (and you know it will), you notice your daughter is not making eye contact. You listen for the emotions underneath the words she's saying and respond differently this time. You say something like "This is the third time you've mentioned this, so it's clearly really important to you. You sound *frustrated*. Tell me what's going on."

  Your daughter may immediately break down crying and express that she's not *frustrated*; she's *angry* because her brother can apparently do no wrong. Heart Listening allows you to acknowledge the underlying emotion and de-escalate the situation in order to have a conversation about what's really happening.

- **Level 5: Open Listening.** Another option for how you might respond: "Honey, I hear your *anger* [emotion] and understand that this is a big deal. I also know that *equality* and *fairness* [values] are really important to you. Can you tell me what happened that seems unfair?"

Your daughter will probably exclaim, "Yes, exactly! When you go to John's soccer games every Saturday, it seems like you love him more than me."

If you listen on this level, you'll be able to identify and articulate the values that are fueling her behavior. Open Listening gives you a comprehensive picture by acknowledging the root of what's motivating another person's behavior.

When communication is challenging, it's easy to shut down and shift into a lower level of listening. (Hint: When the same issue resurfaces over and over, it's likely *not about the words that are being said.*) But this is exactly the moment where you have an opportunity to transform the entire experience. If you shift into a higher level of listening, one that seeks to recognize emotions and values, you have the potential to create a bridge of understanding rather than a divide. Believe me, you will be elated when your expanded perspective has the power to create connection in a relationship and break longstanding destructive patterns.

Many people take listening for granted—but not you any-more! You've been introduced to the power of deep levels of listening. So, from this point forward, it's time to pay attention to *how* you're listening. Are you closed to hearing others (level 1: Closed)? Are you primarily listening to yourself (level 2: Head)? Or are you actually L-I-S-T-E-N-I-N-G to others (levels 3: Ears, 4: Heart, and 5: Open)? Now that you are familiar with the i-Five Levels of Listening, it's time to reassess what level of listener you are most of the time. Is it the same number you picked at the beginning of the chapter? Or has it changed? This awareness will help you shift your thinking, expand your perspective, get curious about the stories you're making up, and become accountable about your part in what's happening. Different levels of listening influence whether you connect with or disconnect from the person you're communicating with. This, my friend, changes everything.

◆ ◆ ◆ ◆ ◆

TALKRx TOOLKIT

Level 1: Closed Listening (distracted/already know/don't care)

Level 2: Head Listening (Planner/Hijacker/One-Two Punch)

Level 3: Ear Listening (words only)

Level 4: Heart Listening (words + emotions)

Level 5: Open Listening (words + emotions + values)

YOUR 1-FIVE MOMENT

- To expand your listening skills and help strengthen your relationships, answer the questions in Chapter 10 of your *TalkRx Journal* (DoctorNehaTalkRx.com).

- Share what relationship you would like to transform through using a higher level of listening with the TalkRx Community. And if you're feeling especially courageous, we'd also love to hear about the times you find yourself using level 1 and 2 listening.

INTERPRETING YOUR EMOTIONS

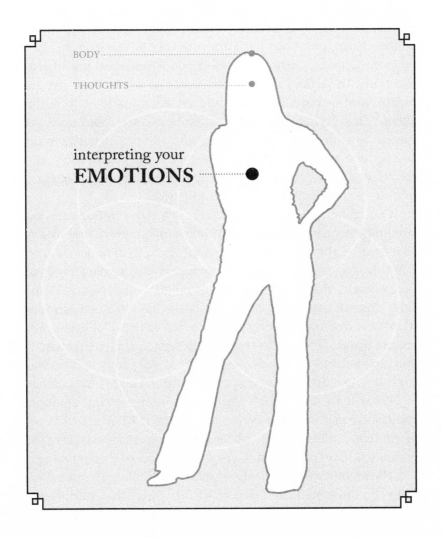

BODY

THOUGHTS

interpreting your
EMOTIONS

Have you ever heard comments like these made in the presence of strong emotion?

- "Suck it up."
- "Pull yourself together."
- "Dude, lighten up. I was just kidding."
- "C'mon, don't be such a baby."
- "You deserve an Oscar for that performance."

Let's face it. Some emotions can be awkward, uncomfortable, and messy. They take up time you don't have. And even if you do address them, emotions have a funny way of showing up again . . . and again . . . and again. In relationships we tiptoe around emotions. In professional environments we avoid them like the plague. And we even teach our children to control them by telling them, "Stop crying, and don't come out of your room until you have a smile on your face." We make up all sorts of stories in our heads, such as *a public display of emotion is inappropriate* or *out of control* or *a glaring sign of weakness.* Emotions are often thought of as unimportant, unnecessary, or in the way.

Our endless struggle to contain or sidestep emotions and our simultaneous frustration around their ambiguous nature lead us to minimize their importance or want them to disappear. Part of this thinking is derived from our culture. For example, in the corporate world, managing emotions is politely dismissed as a "soft skill." Yet ask any employee why he or she has left a company and it's usually due to not feeling appreciated or valued. Our data-driven culture demands proof. Researchers, academics, and skeptics say, "If you can't measure it, it doesn't exist." But as any parent knows, emotions are often the primary obstacle to putting kids to bed on time.

What if I told you that learning to interpret your emotions could solve many of your everyday dilemmas? Knowing what you are feeling can help you defuse awkward conversations, get off an emotional roller coaster, and, yes, even get out of the doghouse.

The inability to effectively manage emotionally charged situations can cause high stress in your life. On top of that, minimizing the importance of addressing unresolved emotions leads to disconnection, isolation, and broken relationships—and a decline in your physical health.

Most people try to avoid hard conversations, but what I've found is that if you lean into and experience your emotions, you are actually able to move through them and heal.

So how is it that we've managed to avoid recognizing the value of human emotions until now? Well, let's take a look at how we're schooled. By the time you graduate from high school, you've invested 12+ years in formal education to prepare for success in your adult life. Yet do you recall taking Emotions 101? Chances are you learned to navigate emotions informally by observing your family dynamics, modeling your caregivers' behavior, interacting with your community, and following societal norms.

We experience strong emotions on a regular basis, and they greatly influence our ability to interact with others and successfully navigate the world. Emotions can cause discomfort, pain, and vulnerability. So it's no wonder that you may have learned to resist, ignore, control, numb, or avoid them altogether. And without a formal education on how best to deal with emotions, you likely relied on your instincts and primal reflexes in combination with learned behaviors to protect yourself during emotionally charged situations.

What if we've got it all wrong? What if emotions aren't something to be avoided, but in fact are the key to healing ourselves and knowing what we want? The fact that we *have* emotions isn't what's getting in the way. What's keeping us from getting what we want is that we *don't know how to navigate* emotions. Stay with me. That's all about to change.

CHAPTER 11

THE ELEPHANT IN THE ROOM

I always loved making rounds on the cardiac unit. More often than not, the patients were improving. Their physical crises had taught them they could no longer use sheer determination and stamina to override the limits of their physical bodies.

Often my job was to stand in as their minister, priest, or rabbi as they confessed: "I swear, from now on I'm gonna drink less alcohol, eat better, and exercise every day. No more smoking. I'm gonna work less and love more." They had each been given a second chance, and what mattered most to them had come into sharp focus.

One day, amid the familiar beeping of heart monitors, I went to check on my 74-year-old patient Juan, who was on his third day of hospitalization. His white hair was in a buzz cut. He had horizontal lines across his forehead and a deep vertical line between his brows. Juan's eyes were dark and soulful, and his stony expression would have made him an excellent poker player.

I pulled up a chair, but before I could even speak, he began, "The food here sucks. When can I get out of here?"

"Fortunately, you're doing well," I answered. "I'll be ready to discharge you in the morning. Is there someone who can be here at nine to pick you up? We also need to discuss your discharge plan and how to best transition you home."

He gave me a slightly bewildered look, and I remembered being told that in the hospital he'd had only one visitor—a man in a uniform. "I can probably arrange something," he said halfheartedly.

"I'd also like to offer you an opportunity," I said. "I have five questions I ask my patients to contemplate before they go home. I call these questions the Awareness Prescription. Are you interested in hearing them?"

Juan nodded.

"First of all, why do you think it was a heart attack that brought you to the hospital? And why do you think it happened now, at this particular time in your life? What signals might you have missed along the way? Is there anything else in your life that needs to heal? And last of all, if you spoke from your heart, what would you say?

"I'd like you to think about these questions, and we can talk about them in the morning," I continued as I handed him the prescription. But Juan didn't need time to contemplate. It was as if he'd just been waiting for me to ask.

"You know, Doc, I don't remember ever crying. Not when my children were born. Not when my parents died. My whole life I've felt isolated and alone. I was close to my kids when they were young but not so much anymore. Things changed after my wife and I split. It's been a lonely road."

Tears welled up in his eyes as he continued. "I'm a Vietnam vet, and for years I've mocked others who expressed their emotions. This is nuts, but I haven't stopped crying for the past two days. After the war, I shut down. It was just too painful. I wanted to be strong and put the past behind me. You know, I thought I could leave it all in Vietnam. I can't believe it took a heart attack for me to feel the sadness I've been carrying around all these years.

"If I spoke from the heart, I would say that it's felt really good to let it all out."

I put my hand on Juan's shoulder. "As painful and scary as this experience has been, you sound relieved to discover that you didn't leave your heart in Vietnam after all. On the battlefield, you needed an immense amount of courage and armor to protect yourself. It sounds like you even built Fort Knox around your own heart. Now, in order to heal, you'll need to use a different kind of bravery—the kind that breaks down those walls and is bold enough to love with an undefended heart.

"As you know, the heart is the driving force delivering oxygen to every other organ in the body. When an artery that supplies oxygen to the heart itself gets blocked, that's what causes a heart attack. And even though it may sound strange, I've noticed a pattern with many of my other patients: they don't just have a blocked artery—they also have a parallel emotional block in their lives.

"Studies show that patients who have had a heart attack and become depressed are four times more likely to have another heart attack within six months. Since you're already on an antidepressant, having a strong support system now is not just a good idea; it's critical for your healing."[12]

I leaned over and gave him a hug. "So keep your heart open, Juan. It's exactly how you'll build strong relationships and lasting connection. I already know you're good at it—you're doing it with me right now."

As I looked into his eyes, I couldn't help but think how ironic it was that expressing his emotions, the very act that Juan mocked in others, held the key to exactly what he longed for—genuine human connection.

FROM A DOCTOR TO A HEALER

As a physician, I could relate to Juan's lifelong aversion to expressing his emotions. The very strategy that protected him as a soldier and allowed him to survive the war and its aftereffects was what caused him to feel disconnected and isolated from the people he loved. And just as in the military, in health care we are taught to focus on the physical aspects of our jobs. Our training emphasizes our analytical, logical, left-brain thinking. As we guide our patients through life-changing diagnoses, we are taught to keep a safe emotional distance. The impact of being emotionally distant is that these pivotal moments often turn into awkward and impersonal exchanges.

My medical training taught me this: The goal of med school and residency was to master the science of medicine, stay up-to-date on the research and the latest drugs, and be able to cite double-blind placebo-controlled trials to back up my decisions. The key to being a successful physician? *Don't get too attached!* Getting too close to your patients will drain you. Stay focused on their physical health. Leave the mental and emotional issues to a psychiatrist because they take too much time and can get messy.

My patients have taught me this: It's the *art* of medicine—not just the science—that transforms a doctor into a healer. If I focus only on treating symptoms and dispensing drugs, the root of the problem is often left unaddressed and my work becomes mechanical and repetitive. In order to engage patients to change their lifestyle, I must impact them on more than a physical level. It is the deep, emotional connection between us that empowers patient healing and brings meaning to my work.

Six months after Juan was released from the hospital, he stopped by to thank me for the work we had done together. Over a cup of tea I learned that he had changed his diet, reconnected with his children, and joined a support group for military veterans recovering from post-traumatic stress disorder. He had finally begun to heal from his experiences in Vietnam.

"Oh, and I almost forgot," he added. "I've been able to get off my antidepressants. And my cardiologist said my echocardiogram shows that my heart is stronger than ever!"

WELCOME TO EMOTIONS 101

emo·tion: a conscious mental reaction subjectively experienced as strong feeling, or the affective aspect of consciousness

Whaaaat? I don't know about you, but I had to read that definition three times, and I'm still not sure I got it.

I like to describe emotion as energy-in-motion. Emotion is a feeling or mood state, and it changes depending on how you are responding to your body, your thoughts, and your experiences.

Think about it. What happens when a child wants a toy in the store and his parent says no? His emotion bubbles up and moves through his body: his face gets red, a waterfall of tears emerges out of nowhere, he throws himself facedown on the floor and pounds his fists as he screams bloody murder! Within a few minutes his feelings will likely transform into another emotion. Who knows? If he sees another child happily playing with bubbles, he can be easily distracted and soon will transition into joy and play.

Toddlers are such a great example of energy-in-motion. They have not yet developed numbing strategies, so they experience and express their emotions in real time. It's like a wave that moves through them—and once fully expressed, just like that, it's over.

A lot changes as we grow up. The people in our lives have rules about how we "should" express our emotions, so as we get older, we learn to control or avoid our feelings in order to fit in. Sometimes even without our conscious awareness, we move from expressing our emotions to silencing them.

Juan's story clearly demonstrates the consequences of tightly packing away emotions. He thought not only that he could mentally talk himself out of feeling the devastation of war, but that it was possible to leave his suitcase of emotional trauma in Vietnam when he left.

So what happens to those painful, unexpressed, stuffed, or unacknowledged feelings? Many of us hope they will disappear. The problem is that they don't go anywhere. They're patient. They just wait, latent, for another opportunity to express themselves. In fact, they usually grow bigger and more intense—and then they either unexpectedly erupt in our interactions with others or remain stagnant and make us sick. Either way, not expressing emotion will cause stress in your life.

GOOD OR BAD?

First, let's start with what we think about what we feel. Often emotions are labeled "good" or "bad." Bring to mind three emotions that feel comfortable in your body, ones you would put in the "good" category. For me, those would be playful, connected, and loved.

Now, think of three emotions that you would rather not deal with, ones you would put in the "bad" category. These emotions typically feel uncomfortable in your body. For example, mine would be sad, frustrated, and lonely.

It's easy to see how certain emotions become your favorites while others get a bad rap.

Guess what? Emotions are neither good nor bad; instead, they are a powerful indicator of *how you are connecting to the experience of your life in this moment.*

You're probably thinking, *Whoa, wait a minute. It's not that simple.* And you're right. It's not. But it's important to understand how to navigate this sometimes murky experience of treading near your own heart. This will help you speak from a place of truth.

ONE WORD

Emotions can typically be described in one word. Think about it. *Happy, mad, sad,* and *glad* are simple, clear expressions of how people feel about themselves or toward others. Let's look at a simple example of how emotions can be named with single words.

Imagine your partner recently ended your relationship, and you haven't quite finished licking your wounds. You've been going to the gym because it's the one place you can "accidentally" run into him. Today you're sweating it out on the treadmill in order to shed the five pounds you gained lying on the couch feeling sorry for yourself. Across the gym, you see him conversing with a long-legged beauty who glistens with every move. As you reach to text your best friend, one simple word—*jealousy*—can describe your complex emotional response to an awkward situation.

When my childhood playmates bestowed colorful nicknames on me, I remember feeling *embarrassed.* What some would call beautiful natural curls were, from their point of view, a "fuzzball," "crazy hair," and "turd braids."

Bring back the memory of someone telling you that something about you was not okay. What emotion did you experience in that moment? Whenever others used to make fun of me, I felt *disappointed, humiliated,* and *ashamed.*

Even if you're not comfortable with emotions, you probably have at least a few words to describe how you feel in any given moment. In fact, you may use *only* those few words to describe a wide range of experiences. You know, kind of like your favorite songs. You download them, make a playlist, and put them on repeat.

Most people do the same with their emotional vocabulary. If you generalize and use only emotions like *happy, mad, sad,* and *glad,* you might miss what's really happening.

Before I understood Emotions 101, depending on the given situation, my repeat button was stuck on five familiar emotions: *excited, disappointed, stressed, upset,* and *grateful.*

In reality, there are dozens upon dozens of emotions. The benefit of clearly articulating them is that it will help you (and others) get clear about what's actually happening. But if you can't name what emotions you're experiencing, it can result in *frustration* and ultimately a communication breakdown.

When you are ambiguous about what you feel, others fill in the blanks with their own stories about what's going on for you. Then you make up stories about their stories, which in turn leads to their making more stories . . . and you can see how easily this can get out of hand!

Having a variety of words to better describe your emotional state will allow you to be clearer in your communication and to listen to others in a way that deepens your connection and saves you time.

NAME THAT EMOTION

So here's the deal. The sooner you expand your emotional vocabulary, the easier time you'll have navigating both everyday and emotionally charged situations, within yourself and with others. (Bonus: Expanding your emotional vocabulary will also help you with level 4, Heart Listening.)

Take a look at the emotional vocabulary list and notice which emotions you find most familiar and which ones you have the most aversion to. By no means is this list all-inclusive. You may want to add a few of your own.

Emotional Vocabulary List

Happy
Joyous
Proud
Elated
Peaceful
Surprised
Ecstatic
Generous
Grateful
Playful
Energetic
Relieved
Hopeful
Glad

Anxious
Irritated
Nervous
Stressed
Overwhelmed
Impatient

Curious
Intrigued
Concerned
Awed
Confused
Puzzled

Mad
Angry
Annoyed
Edgy
Irate
Resistant
Frustrated
Betrayed
Hurt

Fearful
Scared
Apprehensive
Panicked
Shocked
Horrified
Reluctant
Guilty

Connected
Adored
Loved
Grounded
Moved
Touched
Open
Nurturing
Trusting

Sad
Depressed
Lonely
Lost
Unloved
Disrespected
Tired
Exhausted

Disappointed
Bored
Disgusted
Dejected
Uncomfortable
Skeptical
Hopeless

Powerful
Comfortable
Confident
Eager
Energetic
Fulfilled
Empowered
Inspired
Engaged

I feel:

_____

(insert emotion)

In the introduction to Emotions 101, we thought of six emotions, three that we experience as comfortable and categorize as "good," and three that we experience as uncomfortable and categorize as "bad."

One of mine was *playful*. Three additional ways I could describe *playful* are *flirtatious, joyous,* and *energetic.* Another one of my emotions was *frustrated.* Some other ways I could describe feelings of frustration would be *annoyed, overwhelmed,* and *upset.*

Now it's your turn. Recall two of those one-word feelings you commonly experience. Then choose three different ways to describe each of them. You can refer to the list on the previous page.

See how easy that was! If you pay attention, it will get easier and easier to come up with alternative ways to describe your emotions and expand your emotional vocabulary. This is the first step to getting cozy with emotions. (I suppose that's why they got labeled touchy-feely.)

A Four-Letter Word

When I ask people to differentiate between expressing their thoughts and expressing their emotions, they often get thrown off. But these are actually quite different.

When you say, "I feel," it doesn't always mean you're expressing your emotions. You have to pay attention to what comes next. One four-letter word makes a big difference—the word *like*. When you say "I feel like [+ a string of words]," you are expressing a thought, not an emotion. On the other hand, when you say "I feel" and follow it with a one-word emotion (elated, angry, irritated, peaceful), then you're describing how you feel.

Look at the equations below to see the distinction:

- Thoughts = "I feel *like*" + a string of words including, but not limited to, an explanation, an opinion, a judgment, or a story.

- Emotions = "I feel" + one-word emotion (elated, angry, irritated, peaceful).

Identify which statements below are thoughts disguised as emotions, and which statements are clearly expressed emotions:

- I feel like you're a really good person.

- I feel connected.
- I feel disappointed.
- I feel like you shouldn't have done that.
- I feel like I want to leave now.

In the above examples, only *I feel connected* and *I feel disappointed* are clearly expressed emotions. The simple word *like* innocently inserted after the word *feel* is a warning signal that you're leaving your heart (emotions) and heading back up into your head (thoughts).

Begin to pay attention to the difference between thoughts and emotions. Notice how you speak to others and whether you express your emotions or your thoughts more often.

IT'S ALL CONNECTED

While emotions can be named easily—with that one word—what makes them complex is that they are inextricably linked to the physical sensations in your body, sensations that can sometimes make you squirm. Yep, I'm talking about the heart-racing, stomach-turning, face-flushing experiences that can literally make you want to run! Different combinations of physical signals from your body help you identify what emotion you are experiencing.

As a child, I saw these physical sensations represented in cartoons. Bugs Bunny was one of my favorites. I knew exactly when Elmer Fudd was upset and about to blow his top—he would turn red, and steam would literally come out of his ears.

What about you? How do you know when you're upset with someone? Do you have that experience of pressure building internally and feeling as if you're going to explode? Or do you have a quicksand-like sinking feeling in your stomach and legs? What is the combination of physical sensations that gives you an early warning, helping you identify what's happening?

You already know that your body is a finely tuned instrument picking up data from your external and internal worlds. In a split second you piece that information together in your mind to make sense of it. You make up a story. Which story you choose to believe will determine what emotion you feel. Yep! It's all connected.

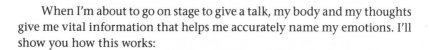

When I'm about to go on stage to give a talk, my body and my thoughts give me vital information that helps me accurately name my emotions. I'll show you how this works:

Scenario 1

Body:

- *External data:* There are 200 people seated facing the stage, one video camera, and six floodlights shining down from the ceiling. I am scheduled to speak at 2 P.M. It is now 1:58 P.M.
- *Internal data:* Armpits sweating + lower lip quivering

Thought: I wish there were a teleprompter. If I forget my lines, I'll look like a fool.

Emotion: Scared

Scenario 2

Body:

- *External data:* Same as scenario 1.
- *Internal data:* Relaxed muscles + slow, deep breathing

Thought: I have important information that will help people get more of what they want in their lives. I'm looking forward to sharing it with them.

Emotion: Peaceful

Your body's physiology is an early and obvious messenger giving you important information. Becoming curious about the stories in your head will help give you valuable clues about how you feel. Recognizing and identifying your emotions will help you move through them rather than get stuck in them. As you get clear about your own emotions, you'll also be able to listen at a deeper level to others. Listening beyond words shifts you into empathy, a feeling of connection to another person's experience. Let's build on what you learned in the last chapter about Heart Listening.

LEVEL 4: HEART LISTENING

It can sometimes be uncomfortable to be present with someone else's emotion. But Heart Listening will make all the difference in creating constructive conversations and building connection. You'll gain insight into the other person's emotions and understand his point of view. This gives you an excellent way to de-escalate an emotionally charged conversation and create an environment in which the other person is likely to be able to hear your point of view.

You might be thinking, *I'm only in Emotions 101, just learning how to handle my own feelings, and now you want me to take on someone else's?* Never fear. The empathy that comes from listening at a deeper level to someone else doesn't have to be overwhelming. And once you learn how to listen deeply, it's easy!

Think about an emotionally charged situation. What happens if you pay attention only to the words someone is saying and ignore his body language and tone? What happens if you listen only for content (level 3: Ear) and ignore the underlying emotions?

The answer is usually the same: you end up sleeping on the couch and getting a backache, not to mention the silent treatment as a bonus. If someone is expressing strong emotion, you can guarantee yourself a trip to the doghouse if you ignore that emotion and skip to speaking on a factual level or not at all.

If the other person doesn't feel heard, all sorts of chaos will ensue. Here are a few clues that indicate you need to hit your pause button and shift into Heart Listening:

- Her voice gets louder.
- She repeats herself.
- She storms out and yells that you never listen.

In general, most people don't repeat themselves if they feel heard. Instead, if you meet them where they are, you may be surprised to find that the intensity of their emotion dies down immediately.

Listening at level 4 will make communication smoother—and quicker, for those of you who value efficiency! Yes, I just said Heart Listening is a more effective way to build strong relationships *and* takes less time.

So, in conversation, how do you listen "beneath" the words someone is saying? Once you're paying attention to the other person's body language and tone in addition to the words, you'll be able to identify the emotion. Then you can express what you've picked up on in a simple phrase such as:

- "You seem _____ (insert emotion)."
- "You look _____ (insert emotion)."

Perhaps you aren't sure which emotion to name. Still, when someone is talking in an emotionally charged way, whatever it's about is clearly dear to her heart. So you could say:

"I can see how important this is to you."

Any of these phrases will help the person you're talking to feel heard and clarify how he or she is feeling.

Remember, emotions are neither good nor bad. They are simply the way in which someone is relating to a particular experience in his or her life. So when it comes to empathizing with someone else's emotions, keep three rules in mind to stay on track:

- **Rule 1:** Pay attention to the other person. If your gut reaction is to locate the nearest exit, notice your own discomfort, pause, then shift your focus toward being there for the other person.

- **Rule 2:** It is not your responsibility to fix or change someone else's emotions. Heart Listening allows you to provide a safe place for a person to express whatever is happening—and that is often all he or she needs.

- **Rule 3:** When you are naming someone else's emotion, you don't even have to get it right. (This one's my favorite.) The other person will let you know. And if she corrects you, it's okay. She knows best what she's feeling. What matters is that you are listening on that level. Your guess has probably helped her gain more clarity about what she is feeling. A simple response of "Okay, it sounds like you feel [restate the emotion they just expressed]" is sufficient.

How might a real interaction play out? Here's an example: At a dinner party, when my cousin Soni blurted out that my boyfriend and I had broken up, I whispered to my sister sitting next to me, "I can't believe she just announced that to everyone."

"You seem angry," my sister replied.

"No, I'm not angry, I'm surprised and embarrassed that she just told everyone we're not together anymore. I haven't made a public announcement."

"Oh, got it. I can see how that would be embarrassing."

Curiosity Cured the Cat

I hope you're starting to appreciate the immense value of curiosity. Not only is curiosity a part of listening, but it's also what builds a bridge to others. As you engage in Heart Listening, get curious about how you can best support the other person. The key here is that it's the other person's job to know what she needs. Ask—she usually knows. If she needs time, honor her request and give it to her. Whew! It takes all the pressure off you.

When someone else is experiencing a challenging emotion such as anger, shock, disappointment, or frustration, here are a few examples of how you can transform a potentially awkward situation:

1. A woman arrives home and sees her neighbor crying. One way to respond is: "You seem sad and disappointed. How can I help?"

2. A daughter notices that her normally talkative father is silent at the funeral of his brother. One way to respond is: "I know how important Uncle Joe was to you. Is there anything you need?"

3. You've just asked a question in a meeting, and your boss explodes at you in front of the others. One way to respond is: "I hear how upset you are about this. Can we discuss it privately immediately following the meeting?"

4. You've just prepared a new recipe and you serve it to your family. With a furrowed brow, your spouse comments in a disgruntled tone, "Is this all there is for dinner?" One way to respond is: "You sound disappointed. Was there something else you were hoping for?"

5. A friend was just diagnosed with a serious illness. She says, "I don't know how I'm going to make it through this." One way to respond is: "I'm so sorry. You sound devastated. How can I best support you?"

Watch the TalkRx video "It's No Laughing Matter" to see how Shaan, a start-up entrepreneur, discovers how to tackle the elephant in the room instead of deflecting it at DoctorNehaTalkRx.com.

See how easy (and quick) that is! Try it in your next conversation and see what happens. It's okay if listening and responding in this way feels a little mechanical at first, because trying anything new usually does. The upside is that when you bring empathy and curiosity together, you create trust, support, and connection.

Emotions drive every conversation, whether you're paying attention to them or not. Rather than resisting, if you make the counterintuitive move of acknowledging them and allowing them to move through you and others, the elephant in the room will no longer be so intimidating. Yes, there may be a few moments of physical discomfort. But in the longer term, as you lower stress and open the lines of communication, you'll build a deep sense of connection between you and another. With Emotions 101 under your belt, you're ready to navigate energy-in-motion in everyday situations.

Now it's time to turn up the heat.

◆ ◆ ◆ ◆ ◆

TALKRx TOOLKIT

Level 4: Heart Listening = empathy + curiosity

In emotionally charged situations, it's important to listen below the words being said. Listen for both: (1) content and (2) emotion.

Respond with:

- "You seem _____ (insert emotion). How can I help?"

- "You look _____ (insert emotion). How can I best support you?"

- "I can see how important this is to you."

TalkRx Video: Watch "It's No Laughing Matter" to see how to tackle the elephant in the room at DoctorNehaTalkRx.com.

YOUR i-FIVE MOMENT

- To expand your emotional vocabulary and level 4 listening in order to strengthen your relationships, complete the quick and easy exercises in Chapter 11 of your *TalkRx Journal* (DoctorNehaTalkRx.com).

- Share any i-Five moments, discoveries, or questions with the TalkRx Community.

CHAPTER 12

A Family
of Emotions

Emotions are social, but don't be fooled—they're not always as polite as your body's signals. They like company and tend to bring uninvited guests. Just like at a good dinner party, each one contributes to the quality of conversation and deserves a seat at the table.

Yes, seemingly opposite emotions can coexist.

The next level of interpreting your emotions involves real-life scenarios in which you may be experiencing several feelings at once. While you know that naming emotions is simpler than experiencing them, we rarely experience one at time. But you can still use the practical tools you've learned in Emotions 101 to sort them out and communicate clearly.

How does this show up in real life? For example, before giving a presentation, I have felt excited, petrified, and overwhelmed all at the same time. During the talk, I have felt confident, amazed, and irritated (when an audiovisual feature didn't work). And when it was all over and I heard the audience's applause, I have experienced a combination of relief, inspiration, and pride.

To help you understand how a family of emotions can exist inside you, let's look at how we generalize our feelings rather than expressing them with clarity.

The Emotional Dumping Ground

Have you ever said, "I'm stressed"? Of course you have. I bet it's one of the most commonly used statements in our society today. It encompasses so much, yet if you think about it, it says so little. "I'm stressed." On a deeper level, a variety of thoughts and emotions are behind these two simple words.

Take a hardworking single father who says, "I'm stressed." On what level do you understand his experience? Since stress can encompass a wide range of emotions, he could express himself more clearly by saying, "I feel *guilty* for not spending enough time with my son, and I'm *exhausted* from working two jobs." In addition, suppose he has just received a voice-mail message from the principal saying that his son has been assigned to after-school detention for throwing spitballs in class. He may feel *disappointed* in his son and *worried* about the impact of his divorce on the child's behavior in school. By expanding his emotional vocabulary, he can express his experience more accurately. For him:

"I'm stressed" = *guilty* + *exhausted* + *disappointed* + *worried*

Let's say this ambitious dad happens to be throwing a slumber party for his son's tenth birthday, with ten boys staying overnight at his house for the first time. Now his stress could manifest very differently. He may be *excited* to meet everyone his son has mentioned during the car rides home from soccer. As a lawyer, Dad feels at home in the courtroom, yet he finds himself feeling *awkward* being in charge of a social event for a bunch of boys. He is *nervous* that ten young stallions could wreak havoc in his home. And he may also feel *nostalgic* as he remembers how fun and carefree it was for him to be ten years old. In this situation, *"I'm stressed"* = *excited* + *awkward* + *nervous* + *nostalgic*.

Once you get curious, you can see how one emotion can represent a whole family of emotions.

It's your turn. Bring to mind a recent situation in which you felt stressed, and ask yourself if you could break it down more clearly. How many other emotions were you simultaneously experiencing? Did some of them seem to be opposing emotions? It's okay if they were.

When you have the ability to call out multiple emotions, you get a more complete picture of what's really happening. Getting to know the family of emotions that are present in any given situation provides you with clues and insight that, coupled with curiosity, will help you pave a path to your own heart and to those around you.

Why Smart People Do Dumb Things

Even with your emotional education, you may find yourself stumped by outbursts of emotion in yourself or in others. Have you ever been surprised by the intensity of someone's response to a seemingly innocent question or comment? It's biological. No, really, it is! I'm about to reveal the scientific secret behind it.

I had been living in San Francisco for seven years. One day I received a call from Ritu. She had been living in Michigan but was ready to explore an entrepreneurial life on the West Coast. She was calling to see if she could live with me.

It had been nearly 15 years since we shared living space back in college, so I knew it would be an interesting dynamic, to say the least. My older sister moving to my city and into my home? It sounded like either an opportunity to use my new communication tools or a recipe for disaster—I wasn't sure which. Despite my initial fears, deep down I was thrilled. I had built a life on the West Coast that I dreamed of sharing with my family, and of course, part of me still wanted the love and attention of my older sister. Some habits die hard.

When Ritu arrived, she settled in on the lower level of my two-story Victorian home. I was surprised by how much we had matured and how splendidly we got along as adults. Despite our years apart, somehow we had grown in the same direction. We had taken different paths, but our love of nature, healing, health, and community had us sharing much common ground. Ritu was respectful of my home, and I was reminded of how much I missed having family in close proximity.

Shortly after her arrival, she landed a job and our life together was in full swing. We even spent time in an adult version of Smart School, as she updated me on the latest happenings in the world of media, politics, and pop culture. I was once again impressed by her love of reading, her social skills, and her brilliant wit.

Ritu's contribution to household chores was to take out the garbage on Monday nights. This entailed rolling the garbage, recycling, and compost bins 100 feet from the back of my house to the front and then returning the empty bins to their original location the following morning.

At 8 A.M. one Monday, as she was heading to work through the garage on the lower level, Ritu yelled with a sense of urgency, "Naaayyyyy-haaaa!" I came running to the top of the stairs. I saw her messenger bag around her shoulder as she stood with one foot out the door.

"What's wrong?" I asked in a panic.

With an annoyed tone she began, "Neha, do you think you could maybe lift a finger around here?"

I reacted to her irritated tone by matching it myself. "What do you mean?"

"I mean, you could, maybe, take the garbage out once in a while? I mean, I'm the only one who does anything around here."

"That's ridiculous!" I exclaimed. "What are you talking about?"

"It's Monday. You know exactly what I'm talking about. Just take out the garbage, and don't be such a baby." And without giving me a chance for rebuttal, she slammed the door behind her and I heard the noise of the garage door opening.

I sprinted up the narrow hallway, flung open the front door, and ran onto the porch. With both fists clenched above my head and my voice raw and louder than I've ever heard it before, I screamed into the silent morning air, "I AM NOT A BAAAAAABBYYYYY!!"

Ten steps below me at street level, Ritu paused in bewilderment. The whites of her eyeballs doubled as she looked up and remarked, "No, you're *not* a baby. You're actually somebody's doctor." And with that she turned and headed off to work.

I was left standing on the front porch completely dumbfounded and alone. I had no idea what had come over me, but it had felt like an explosive volcano swelling from the bottom of my feet all the way out the top of my head.

As a 38-year-old woman, had I really just screamed at the top of my lungs in public that I was "not a baby"? Did I disrupt my peacefully sleeping neighbors with a cry that had obviously been suppressed for 35 years?

This was what I had read about so many times in psychology and neuroscience literature. I had just been hijacked—amygdala-hijacked, that is.

WHAT'S THE HIJACK?

CROSS SECTION OF THE BRAIN

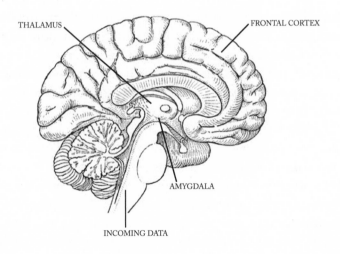

THALAMUS

FRONTAL CORTEX

AMYGDALA

INCOMING DATA

Biologically, your brain is hardwired to seek pleasure and avoid pain, so your natural reflex is to escape feelings of discomfort. This reflex is created by the amygdala, an almond-shaped mass deep inside the brain. Here's how it works:

You are continuously taking in information externally and internally. Incoming data pass through the thalamus, which you can think of as a central processing station for your brain. It's the hub—kind of like Chicago is for United Airlines. All planes land there first, and then they are routed to their next destination. The thalamus sorts information and sends incoming data to your frontal cortex (the thinking part of the brain), where you make sense of it. This is where your critical thinking skills lead to *the stories in your head*. Then the information travels to your amygdala, which is your emotional center. A special section of the amygdala stores memories of your past, including all of your emotional trauma. The amygdala compares the present experience with past experiences and identifies similar patterns.

It is not by chance that your amygdala sits next door to your thalamus and eavesdrops on incoming information. If information flows through the normal routes dictated by the thalamus, you will process your thoughts and emotions clearly. On the other hand, if the information coming in resembles a past traumatic experience, this communication loop can be short-circuited by the amygdala. The amygdala hijacks the information from the thalamus and doesn't let it go to the thinking part of your brain (cortex). Yes, the amygdala hijacks the incoming data, taking your emotions and response as hostage. It doesn't allow the cortex to make sense of it before responding.

An amygdala hijack results in an out-of-proportion response to what's happening in the present moment. So it's easy to recognize when you or someone else has been hijacked.

Let's play make-believe. Suppose when you were two years old, you were bitten by the black poodle that lived next door. You were small, and the dog looked big. It scared you silly, and you cried and cried. You might have even bled. Now, fast-forward 40 years. You go to a new friend's house. When he opens the door holding a black poodle, you let out an abrupt, "Oh my gosh!" as you jump back and brace yourself.

Your new friend would certainly be confused at the strength of your reaction when he was just expecting a hello. He's not the only one who might be taken aback. You might be, too, especially if you don't consciously remember the childhood incident with the dog. But even if you don't remember, I promise you, your amygdala does!

This explains why I woke up my neighbors yelling, "I am not a baby!" When Ritu called me a baby, it triggered my amygdala with the memory of my desperately vying for my sister's love and attention, an effort that was repeatedly thwarted by one simple statement: *"Babies aren't allowed to play with big kids."* For years I had wanted to stand up to my sister, and now it all came up, like verbal vomit.

The wounds of our past that remain unhealed lurk in our subconscious. They get triggered when we face similar experiences later in life. Eckhart Tolle refers to these unhealed wounds as invisible pain bodies. I think of unhealed emotional wounds as pain that we have experienced but never expressed or resolved. This is why acknowledging and getting curious about your emotions is so important. It allows you to articulate them—no matter how many you are feeling simultaneously—and thereby facilitate your ability to heal.

The Fuel That Lights the Fire

Emotions drive communication. So it's easy to see how quickly conversations can get confusing if, while articulating your message, you're trying to sort through a family feud of emotions or getting hijacked by your amygdala. At that point, it probably seems impossible to carry on an effective dialogue. To top it off, it's not just your own emotions that can cause a strong physiological response; it can also be hard to be in the presence of someone else experiencing these sensations. No wonder you might want to avoid them.

Stick with me, though. You're not going to believe how the stories you've been making up have been playing with your emotions!

Over the past decade, I've heard my patients and clients struggle with sadness, anger, and anxiety. We often misinterpret the physical sensations that result from stress and emotions as health issues that require medical treatment. It's true that some-times physiological or biochemical causes underlie these intense emotions. And in those situations, medication is appropriate. But often the same physical sensations are simply emotional clues to unresolved conflicts that need your attention.

I find it curious that an entire pharmaceutical industry has flourished as health care professionals prescribe pills to numb the physical sensations associated with anxiety, depression, insomnia, and countless other ailments. While this approach can be bene-ficial in the short term, it raises the question "What's your long-term strategy to address and heal the underlying cause of these symptoms?"

Witnessing uncomfortable emotions expressed by others often triggers an experience in the observer that reflects those emotions, thanks to "mirror neurons" that make emotions feel "contagious" because these brain cells pick up on behaviors in others and mimic them.[13] That's why many people have difficulty dealing with tears, anger, or anxiety in others—they begin to feel tearful, angry, or anxious themselves.

This is where using your pause button and Heart Listening will come in handy. If you can shift how you relate to emotions, you will lower your blood pressure and heart rate while strength-ening your relationships.

People deal with uncomfortable emotions in one of two ways: either they express them as they arise and then move through them, or they suppress their feelings and hold on to them until they can no longer do so, and then they explode. We learn our patterns for dealing with emotions early in life. One pattern could be to explode in the moment if something upsets us. Another pat-tern could be to cry. But more commonly, people begin by *not* expressing emotion.

When you experience discomfort in your body and a strong reaction to what's happening, and yet you choose not to express your emotions, you've probably convinced yourself of one of these myths to justify your choice:

- Myth 1: The other person can't handle it. (Yes she can. It's that you think *you* can't handle being in the presence of her emotional reaction.)

- Myth 2: It's not the "right" time to bring this up. (Ask yourself: Is the time really not right, or is it just that you feel uncomfortable?)

- Myth 3: It will make the situation worse. (Short term or long term? In the short term, some conflict may arise. In the long term, you'll move closer to honest conversations and feel empowered.)

- Myth 4: The other person might not like you anymore. (If she likes you because you don't speak your truth, it's not *you* she really likes.)

- Myth 5: If you ignore the issue, it will go away. (Left unaddressed, the conflict will likely grow in intensity.)

These myths lead people to justify stuffing their emotions. This is like trying to hold a beach ball under water. How long can you do it? After a while the burning sensation builds up in your muscles, fatigue sets in, and the ball comes flying upward, uncontrolled. This is exactly what happens with emotions. If you suppress them, they will boldly express themselves at the most inopportune moment.

Now that you can name your family of emotions, you'll be able to clearly articulate what you're experiencing. Plus you also know why you can sometimes have an out-of-proportion response to a seemingly trivial comment or experience. In the next few chapters we'll dive into what you may have struggled to handle gracefully in yourself or others—tears, anger, and anxiety.

◆ ◆ ◆ ◆ ◆

TALKRX TOOLKIT

When you feel conflicted in a situation, make sure you acknowledge the whole family of emotions at the table:

Emotions you like + emotions you don't like = your family of emotions

Amygdala hijack *(an out-of-proportion response to what's happening)* = thalamus *(the hub for incoming data)* – frontal cortex *(ability to make sense of it)*

The Hijack Recovery Tool

When you get hijacked, what do you do then?

- Hit your pause button.
- Get curious, not furious!
- Ask yourself:
    - What does this experience remind me of?
    - When have I felt similarly?

YOUR 1-FIVE MOMENT

- To recognize your emotions and how to avoid a hijack, complete the exercises and questions in Chapter 12 of your *TalkRx Journal* (DoctorNehaTalkRx.com).
- Share with the TalkRx Community about a time when you got amygdala-hijacked. Do tell.

CHAPTER 13

Raining Down

When you feel a raindrop, you probably run for cover. Do you react the same way at the first sign of a teardrop?

Sometimes tears create an awkward silence. Sometimes tears create an element of surprise that causes a cascade of additional emotions—embarrassment, humiliation, or shame, to name a few. The person tearing up often has a strong desire to do or say anything that would stop the overflow of emotion that's rapidly becoming visible to others. All of a sudden, everyone is frantically searching for a box of tissues so they can do something about it.

The most common judgment I've heard about tears is that they are a sign of weakness. All the way back to our days on the playground, children make fun of other children by calling them "crybabies." As an adult I've heard a more complicated reaction to tears: "Oh, she's just crying to manipulate the situation."

Just as we have with everything else, it seems we have developed a strong set of stories defining when it's okay to cry. It goes something like this: Tears are warranted for extreme celebration, such as the birth of a child or a wedding. They are also appropriate for the loss of a loved one, such as at a funeral. Anything in between—not so much.

The Universal Discomfort of Tears

My travels to the Middle East expanded my understanding about the universal discomfort of tears. For seven days I was in Saudi Arabia speaking at a conference with Dr. Paul Rosch (the man who sent the e-mail in all capital letters). I had just finished packing when the hotel phone rang. It was Dr. Abdullah, the chairman of the conference, a charismatic pediatric cardiologist. Dr. Abdullah was a man whose mere presence commanded respect. He was married to a gracious and beautiful woman and together they had several children.

"Neha, if you're packed, why don't you come with the gentlemen? We're going to Prince Abdul Aziz's palace, and we can take you to the airport from there."

"Of course. I'll be down in five minutes," I said.

Three men from the conference and I joined Dr. Abdullah. As we drove away from the hotel, the sun was shining and the desert sand extended as far as my eye could see. After a few minutes, the conversation died down. In that moment, Dr. Abdullah glanced back at me and inquired, "Neha, we still have fifteen minutes before we arrive. Would it be okay to consult you about something that has been weighing heavy on my heart?"

"Sure," I replied, intrigued. "But are you sure now is a good time to talk about it?" I asked as I glanced around the car at the company we shared.

"Sure, it's no problem. It's about one of my children."

He continued, "You remind me of one of my daughters. You're compassionate, hardworking, and intelligent. What makes you different from her is that you are strong. You travel to international conferences and speak for large audiences. You're brave.

"The problem is that when my daughter faces a challenge, she becomes weak. Can you help her?"

"I hear your concern," I replied. "I'm curious—what makes you think that your daughter is weak?"

"Because any time something is difficult or challenging, she cries. My fear is that she isn't going to survive in the world. Can you help her?"

All of a sudden, I had a flashback of my own father getting angry and trying to stop me from crying. I quickly returned to the conversation at hand.

"I hear how important this is to you. What if I don't think this has to do with your daughter?"

"Well, then who does it have to do with?" he answered in a bewildered tone.

"I have been in your country for a week and watched you orchestrate an international conference with ease. I've heard how highly your colleagues and your patients speak about you. I've even spent time with your wife and children. They, too, revere you. I know how much you love your daughter, so I wonder if, when she cries, it's one of the rare times you experience not being in control. It seems like that's the experience you're asking me to help you change, not your daughter's tears."

The longest 60 seconds of silence followed. I could feel my heart beating out of my chest and my palms sweating as I awaited his response. The other three men kept their gaze forward and didn't move a muscle.

"This is absolutely correct," he finally replied. "Thank you, my friend. I have much to learn about communication."

I was stunned. I thought that, due to our cultural differences, he might resist taking ownership for his part in the interactions with his daughter. Instead, he reinforced that his personal power matched his positional power in the world. I was awed by his grace and humility and especially his willingness to lean into discomfort with curiosity.

His profound love for his daughter led him to feel unbearably uncomfortable when she cried. He could fix most things in the world—even the abnormal electrical rhythm of a baby's heart. What he couldn't control, fix, or change was the vulnerability and raw emotion moving through his own heart when he witnessed his beloved daughter's tears.

The Healing Power of Tears

Did you know that scientifically there are different types of tears? Research from William Frey, a biochemist, has shown that there are, in fact, three different types of tears, released for different reasons by your lacrimal ducts:

1. **Continuous tears** keep your eyes moist and functioning throughout the day. They have an antibacterial agent called lysozyme that prevents

infections and dryness in your eyes as well as your nasal passages.

2. **Reflexive tears** arise in response to a foreign object, such as dust or the chemical released by a cut onion. These tears, which are 98 percent water, help the eye flush out irritants. This is what happens when you first put in your contact lenses and your eyes begin to water.

3. **Emotional tears** have stress hormones in them. Who knew the body actually uses tears as a physical mechanism to rid itself of stress and toxic chemicals in order to heal? After a good cry, the body also releases endorphins, the same "feel good" hormone secreted when you exercise. Your breathing rate and heart rate will decrease after crying, too. So cry away—you're probably going to feel a lot better![14]

Now that you understand the physiology of tears (Interpreting Your Body), it's time to get curious about the stories you make up about them (Interpreting Your Thoughts). As you saw in the story with Dr. Abdullah, he had created limiting beliefs that resulted in disconnection from his daughter.

Somewhere along the way, tears have become associated with weakness or with inappropriate or overly emotional behavior. But if you are able to listen deeply and get curious in order to expand your perspective, you'll find that tears can be not only informative, but also healing.

◆◆◆

Do you remember sitting on the couch as a child, watching a TV program with your family, and just when you were hoping no one would notice you were tearing up, one of your siblings busts out with "Hey! Are you crying?"

Think back to what you learned from your family growing up. What did you observe in your household? Have you ever seen your parents shed tears? What about your siblings?

Was it okay to cry if:

- You got yelled at?
- You felt disappointed?
- You skinned your knee?
- You had a bad dream?
- Your pet died?

━━━━━━━━━━━━━━◆━◆━◆━━━━━━━━━━━━━━

When I was a child and felt disappointed about not getting a blue ribbon at the science fair, I expressed my disappointment through tears. I remember someone commenting, "Oh no, here comes Neha's big crocodile tears . . ." The story I made up was that my tears were not acceptable and it was probably safer to keep them inside. So I put all my energy and effort into hiding them as I ran to my room and hid under the covers. My disappointment about not winning the science fair rapidly turned to shame about how I had expressed myself. It took me several decades to shift my perspective and make peace with tears.

Here's what I've learned as a physician working with patients during pivotal moments in their lives: Tears aren't just tears. And the stories we make up about them are often not true. Tears represent a number of emotions, and letting those emotions move through us is a big part of what heals us—physically, mentally, and emotionally.

For instance, saying good-bye to a loved one at the airport can result in tears of sadness. Receiving a medical test result confirming that a child does not have a genetic abnormality may bring on tears of relief. Taking ownership of behavior that hurt someone may generate tears of guilt. Poking yourself in the eye (oops!), now that's a different kind of tears. (Remember, those aren't emotional tears. Those are reflexive tears.)

Working as a hospital physician, tears became a normal and accepted part of my practice. When I delivered news to patients that they had cancer, I expected tears of shock. I expected tears of pain in the emergency room when someone had broken a bone or was in the midst of a crushing heart attack. After a broken hip or a stroke, when patients realized their ability to function had radically declined, tears of loss were common.

Since we're making up stories, why not make up some different ones? After witnessing these experiences and studying the physiology beneath tears, the story I make up is that *the tenderness that comes with tears is one way to connect to the experience of our lives in a particular moment.* When tears are triggered, one thing is for sure, the topic is important to the person shedding them.

When you're feeling tearful, it doesn't have to hinder your communication. It can actually help. If you're confused, ask yourself: *If my tears could talk, what would they say?* All you have to do is verbalize what's happening behind your tears, and it doesn't require more than a few words:

1. Identify the emotion(s).

2. Name what triggered the emotion.

3. State what you need, if anything (time, space, support . . . a hug!).

Let's take a look at a few examples.

- If your tears are tears of sadness, grief, or hurt, your response may be:

  - "I feel hurt, and I'm not sure why. I need some time."

  - "I'm sad. I'm missing home. I'd love some company."

  - "I feel lonely in this time of transition. Let's do something fun."

- If they are tears of joy, your response may sound something like this (and you may not need to ask for support):

  - "Wow, I am so happy! This means a lot to me."

  - "I'm grateful for the care you show my children. Thank you."

  - "I'm touched that you planned such a relaxing weekend. Let's do it again soon."

- If they are tears of relief, your response could be:

- "I'm relieved. At least now I know the truth. I need time to make some decisions."

- "I feel peaceful. Thank goodness it's over. Let's celebrate."

- "I'm glad you're okay. Next time, please text me if you're going to be late."

Since sometimes tears may be overwhelming, you may not be able to tie them to a specific emotion in the moment. That's okay. This three-step approach works when you feel confused as well. Simply say, "I'm overwhelmed by this new information," and then ask for what you need, such as: "I need a few moments, please." Or you can say, "I'll call you back," "I need to go for a walk," or "I'll sleep on it"—whatever is true for you.

When you're tearful and you tell someone what's happening, it allows you to express yourself and lets them know how to best support you. And when you are on the receiving end of someone else's tears, you already know what to do. Listen deeply using level 4, Heart Listening (from Chapters 10 and 11), that combines empathy and curiosity.

Let 'em Roll

Rather than running from my tears, I now view sharing my tears with another person as an act of courage. It's a moment when I trust myself—and trust someone else enough to allow them close to my heart.

This shift in my ability to navigate tears effectively is what gave me the courage to ask my patients those five key questions as a part of their treatment plan. This is what Juan, the Vietnam veteran, experienced when he showed the bravery and strength to express his sadness through tears. His willingness to be vulnerable created the connection that he so deeply longed for. It was not the fact that Juan had a heart attack that was memorable; the awakening of his heart is what's blazed in my memory.

My willingness to sit in the emotional discomfort with patients has led to some of the most enlightening and meaningful experiences of my professional life.

❖ ❖ ❖ ❖ ❖

TALK R$_X$ TOOLKIT

Navigating Tears

Express Your Tears Tool

1. Identify the emotion(s) underneath the tears.

2. Name what triggered the emotion.

3. State what you need—if anything (time, space, support . . . a hug!).

Here are some ways to respond:

- "I feel hurt, and I'm not sure why. I need some time."

- "Wow! I am so happy. This means a lot to me. We should celebrate."

- "I'm relieved. At least now I know the truth. I need time to make a decision."

Responding to Tears Tool

1. Hit your pause button (breathe).

2. Acknowledge his emotion.

3. Get curious about what he needs.

Here are some ways to respond:

- "I see how important this is to you. How can I help?"

- "I hear your pain. How can I best support you?"

- "I hear how deeply this has touched you. Is there any way I can be of assistance?"

If you aren't sure how to express *yourself* in a tearful moment, ask yourself:

- "If my tears could talk, what would they say?"

If *someone else* hasn't expressed what's causing his tears, you can ask:

- "If your tears could talk, what would they say?"

YOUR 1-FIVE MOMENT

- To see how comfortable you are with the discomfort of tears, answer the questions in Chapter 13 of your *TalkRx Journal* (DoctorNehaTalkRx.com).

- Share with the TalkRx Community your perspective on tears—and if it's changed, we'd love to hear the before and after.

CHAPTER 14

TAMING THE VOLCANO WITHIN

Do you have an issue with anger? Most people do.

The day has come to define your lifelong relationship with anger because it can dramatically affect how you communicate with others. Yes, you've been in a committed partnership with anger, with or without your knowledge.

You've likely been:

- Running away and avoiding anger in yourself or others

- Dancing with anger when it shows up and using it effectively when necessary

- Expressing it a little too frequently at the expense of your personal and professional relationships

Anger is strong displeasure related to a feeling of having been offended, mistreated, or wronged. Anger can evoke the desire to defend oneself or a loved one.

Anger is an instinctive and natural emotion that almost everyone feels at some point. But how you relate to anger often depends on your past experience. Let's explore how anger physically shows up, your thoughts about anger, and the hidden emotions underneath it. Understanding anger from a physical, mental, and emotional angle will give you an edge when you encounter this oh-so-common reaction.

Let's Get Physical

If anger bubbles up when you're communicating, you may notice the pace of your speech quickening, the volume of your voice rising, and your tone changing. You may find yourself stomping your feet or slamming doors. Instead of using affectionate nicknames, you may revert to formal names, as in "Edward William Haskel, get down here *now!*"

On the other hand, your anger may show up more subtly. For example, instead of participating in dinner conversation, you may take an undeclared oath of silence and not say a word all the way through the meal. Another approach to suppressing the rumblings of anger within is to retaliate with sarcasm. Or you may choose the passive-aggressive route, dig your heels in, and make life more difficult for the person or people who upset you. You know what I'm talking about: payback.

While tears and anger may seem like polar opposites, research has shown that they can, in fact, overlap. While men tend to use a more aggressive or physical manner to display their anger in public, women often feel ashamed or hesitant to express themselves in this fashion and instead express their anger through tears with a friend or spouse in private.[15] However you manage anger, it's often a familiar response that you have seen modeled in your life. Or it can be how you learned to protect yourself in the face of intimidating situations. Whether you explode in the moment, use sarcasm as a defense, take an oath of silence, or cry yourself to sleep, you've got a strategy that gets you by.

Anger is expressed in varying intensities and forms, from minor irritation to frustration to full-blown rage. As anger shows up physically in your body, your heart may start racing, your muscles may tighten, your face and ears might flush, and you may experience warmth or pressure building in your head or chest. Some people describe feeling superhuman strength; others describe weakness in the knees. Whatever the combination of physical signals, pay attention, because your body is talking to you.

When you get angry, it means your thoughts (in response to something you've observed) have triggered a fight-or-flight response in your sympathetic nervous system. This has an impact on your physiology and causes a series of biochemical reactions including the release of hormones, most notably adrenaline and cortisol. Your heart rate and blood pressure rise, along with your blood sugar and cholesterol levels. This process readies you to handle a looming threat.

Your body's biological ability to shift into fight-or-flight mode is likely what allowed your ancestors to survive in the wild. When they found themselves in life-threatening situations, this biological readiness allowed them to fight or run away from danger. The key is that it happened only once in a while and lasted for only a few minutes.

In more recent history, anger has been used constructively to facilitate change. "Without any anger, slaves might never rebel, workers might not stand up for their rights, you might never express your distress about being mistreated," Dr. David Sobel and Robert Ornstein have written. "The key is how often and how much we get angry and what we do then."[16]

In today's high-stress, fast-paced society, we trigger this series of biological reactions for everyday events such as bumper-to-bumper traffic or an unanswered e-mail or text message. The catch is our bodies aren't meant to be in a state of high alert for an extended period of time.

As a physician, almost daily I witness the physical effects of poorly managed anger, which may show up as sleep difficulties, high blood pressure, and digestive issues, to name a few. And more alarming, research has shown that chronic anger is directly linked to an increased risk of heart disease and strokes.[17]

SECONDHAND ANGER

Anger doesn't only affect the person who's getting angry. It can also cause a cascade of biochemical reactions in the body of a person witnessing anger. Merely being in the presence of anger can elicit the stress response.

My dad's anger didn't just raise his own blood pressure; it had a ripple effect in our family that impacted each of us in unique ways.

I remember my mother lying on our 1970s yellow polyester couch with her elbow bent and her forearm resting over her eyes. She suffered from paralyzing and frequent migraines. Initially her doctor tested her for sinus and allergy issues and had her using a neti pot. When that didn't work, he ruled out more serious causes such as a tumor. Finally, he put her on strong pain medications to alleviate the symptoms. The narcotics, however, made her nauseated. When my mother complained that the pain pills were making her sick, her doctor said it was time to explore an emotional cause of the headaches.

So she set up several appointments with a psychologist. After six sessions, he said to her, "Do you think your husband would cooperate if I requested that he join us for your next session?"

"Sure, if you think it will help," she replied.

At the next session, the doctor explained to my dad that two causes led to my mom's migraines. First, my mom didn't know how to express her own anger. Second, repeatedly experiencing my dad's temper triggered an emotional landslide in her that she didn't know what to do with. So she absorbed the emotional stress and manifested it physically through her intense headaches.

Aside from recommending that both of them learn to communicate more effectively, the doctor requested that my father allow my mother the opportunity to show her anger. The psychologist told my father, "Your job is to encourage your wife to express her frustration without getting upset at her." My father agreed. Then the doctor turned to my mother and said, "Your assignment is to state when you are upset and stand up for yourself. When this interaction happens, pay attention to how you feel afterward."

Subsequently, my mother began to express her feelings more clearly. She told my father how it often upset her when he made decisions without talking to her first. Later, when he lost his temper, she began to ask for what she needed. "I feel myself shutting down," she would tell him, "and I need to take a nap. When I'm ready to talk I'll let you know."

True to his word, my father allowed her to express these feelings without retaliating or stopping her.

My mom later told me, "It was like a lightbulb switched on when I made the connection between my headaches and your father's temper, and I never had another migraine after that joint session with the psychologist."

When my mom shared this experience, I felt immense respect for and gratitude toward her physician for being able to distinguish when her symptoms had an emotional cause rather than a physical one. If you remember, at the beginning of this section, I described emotions as energy-in-motion. When an emotional response is not being acknowledged or expressed, such as my mother's anger, that energy gets stuck and often reveals itself physically.

You're a Loose Cannon

Just like your stories about tears, the stories you make up about anger depend on your past experiences. Why is this important? Because your judgments about anger—the stories you make up—will determine how you express your own anger and how you react or respond in the face of someone else's.

Have you ever caught yourself thinking or saying a comment like one of these about someone else's anger?

- He's out of control.
- She's irrational—no, she's just plain crazy.
- Who does he think he is?
- There she goes again, flying off the handle!
- Boy, he sure does need to get a grip!

Or in contrast, have you ever had thoughts like these about expressing your own anger?

- It's okay that I got angry because I was provoked.
- It's not polite to raise my voice.
- Anger is the only way I can get people to listen.

- Anger is okay if it results in positive change.

- When I feel strong emotion, anger is a powerful way to express it.

None of these thoughts is right or wrong. Remember, these are stories in your head based on what's happening in the external world. For example, if someone raises his voice and starts swearing at you and you think it means you're being attacked, you may get upset and become quiet. Or you may try to defend yourself. Or you may go into attack mode yourself and attempt to yell louder than the other person.

Your response to anger is also determined by the situation in which it arises. Suppose someone bumps into you and spills wine on your pants. You won't necessarily get angry in response. It may depend on whether it happened in a professional or a personal setting, whether it was your favorite pair of pants or a tattered pair of jeans, whether the person was a stranger or your two-year-old toddler, what you interpreted as his intent, and how he responded to your discomfort.

Let's look at another example to see how three similar situations could provoke different emotional responses, depending on the circumstances and the story you make up.

In the mall parking lot, suppose someone was backing out and hit your car. You might be angry if you thought the other driver could have avoided it. You might even get out and yell, "You idiot, why weren't you paying attention?"

On the other hand, if you were parked in the mall parking lot during a windstorm and a tree fell and hit your car, you might feel sad instead of angry, because—other than Mother Nature—there was no one to blame.

Or suppose instead that you were fumbling with your phone as you began backing out of a parking space and ran into someone else's car. In this case, you might feel anger toward yourself because of your own carelessness.

So the circumstances surrounding a situation often play a big part in whether you get angry, and at whom. In other words, it's not the fact that you have wine spilled on your pants or that you have a dent in your car. What matters are your beliefs surrounding how or why the incident occurred and if there's any way you can control what happens next.

ANGER IS NOT REALLY ANGER

Anger is often rooted in other emotions—mainly the ones that make us feel vulnerable, such as hurt or fear. For example, Juan was afraid to show his heart, so he shut down, and in defense of his vulnerability, he mocked people who showed their tears.

Anger is a mask. When people feel hurt, it can be from many causes, such as they felt betrayed, disrespected, or abandoned. What matters is that anger is how they protect themselves. Think back to what I described at the beginning of this book, when, as a new physician, I was getting bullied by a colleague. I was most surprised to learn that underneath all that pomp and circumstance, Tyler had a very tender heart that hadn't healed from a painful experience. He felt humiliated and hurt by his patient's telling him he wasn't credible as a physician because he was overweight. He used his anger and bullying behavior as a strategy to protect himself from experiencing similar pain and ridicule.

Anger can also show up in response to fear—fear of losing something or someone you love, fear of losing control, fear of not getting what you want. When I got into Smart School and heard Ritu crying and screaming that she hated me, I can see in retrospect that her anger was based on her fear of not being loved and recognized by others.

In these examples, anger served as a protective defense and allowed Tyler and Ritu to create an image of strength and power, even if it was short-lived.

Remember, though, that anger in itself is neither good nor bad. Sometimes anger can motivate change and promote justice. It's when you ignore anger or overuse it that it causes problems and adversely impacts your health. Experiencing anger is a warning sign that you need to pay attention, because something has changed.

How My Dad Got Curious

Confronting and working through our ideas about anger and our emotional responses to it are not easy tasks, but the rewards are great.

I experienced this firsthand when I spoke to my father about his anger. Remember, at the start of this journey, I had a very difficult time facing my father's anger. After my experiences with my patients, and once I'd developed a better understanding of emotions and the i-Five Conversation, I decided to shift into curiosity about my dad's anger. As you read about our conversation, notice how enlightening, transformative, and healing it was for both of us to share our experiences and deconstruct the stories we had made up.

I began by asking him, "When do you first remember experiencing a temper in yourself or others?"

"My mother had a huge temper, and both of my parents yelled whenever they were upset. They yelled at us. They yelled at each other. Yelling seemed like a normal way of communicating. As a result of that, I think a couple of us kids developed quick tempers—especially me and my youngest sister. Ever since, if I think something is going to hurt me or someone I love, or if I perceive that something is wrong or unfair, the anger automatically flares up."

He continued, "Growing up, we didn't have much money. With five kids in the house, my parents could barely make ends meet. When I was maybe eight years old, my father promised to take me somewhere. I don't remember where it was, but he didn't fulfill the promise. I was so mad that I took a pair of shears to a new blanket and cut it into pieces. That shows how much of a temper I had, even as a kid.

"Your mother used to tell me that my temper wasn't normal. Now that I'm thinking about it, even my grandfather had a big temper. I wonder how much of this is in the genes?" he asked.

"I'm sure genetics have some influence, Dad. And there are other variables at play—the environment you grew up in, the amount of stress you're under, and the level of threat you perceive."

"Then I guess what you're saying is I can't blame it all on my parents," he said, sighing.

I chuckled. "No, Dad. Not unless you'd like me to blame everything I don't like about my behavior on you. So tell me, what exactly do you want when you're yelling?"

"I guess I just want my point to be clear. And obviously it's not."

"You want to be heard."

"Yes, I want to be heard."

"It's funny," I replied. "When you lose your temper and want to be heard, the effect is the opposite. I shut down and can't hear your message. It sounds like you're attempting to maintain control. But you can't be in control of a situation if you aren't even in control of yourself, right?"

"Very true, Neha beti. But to solve a problem," he said sincerely, "you have to deal with it head-on."

"The problem is that you're not really dealing with it," I said. "You're just getting angry and pushing everybody away."

My father and I then turned the conversation back to his parents. "I've been angry at myself for leaving my family back in India and never returning," he admitted. "It's like I abandoned them. Somehow I always felt I owed them something for educating me. I think I took out my anger on your mom and you girls."

"Dad, I remember your sending money to India periodically. But maybe it wasn't as much as you had wanted to. So the real question is, now that your parents have passed away, what's it going to take for you to have compassion and forgiveness for yourself?"

He replied, "Yes. This is the difficult question. How exactly does one forgive?"

I could hear the analytical left brain in him, the part that made him such a great engineer, requesting the *formula for forgiveness*.

PUTTING OUT THE FIRE

It's no secret that we all make mistakes. The question is, what do we do once we realize we've made one?

If you view an unhealthy experience of anger as an opportunity to learn, then you become wiser for it. If you don't learn from it, you will get another chance to do so, as the anger will likely show up in another relationship, job, or situation.

Suppose something happens that would normally trigger your anger. Rather than reacting, notice your body's physical signals and hit the pause button in order to manage yourself first. Don't underestimate the power of three soft, deep belly breaths in this moment. Then, once your physical signals have subsided, it's time to get curious about the underlying emotions fueling your anger. The ability to pause and be curious before you take action changes everything—and opens the door to move through your anger.

The keys to resolving anger are compassion and forgiveness. Compassion is the ability to listen with empathy to yourself or someone else. There are many paths to forgiveness; here's one:

1. Notice the physical sensations that tell you something needs to be healed.

2. Take a deep breath, and thank your body for communicating with you.

3. Are you ready to give up all hope of a better past? If yes, proceed. If no, you're not ready.

4. Think of the person you are trying to connect to after experiencing anger, and in a journal or notebook, complete the following prompts.

- To work through anger *with another*:

    - The impact of this relationship on me has been . . .

    - What I wanted from you that I didn't get was . . .

    - What I've always wanted to tell you is . . .

    - The ways I've held back are . . .

    - If I believed you *did the best you could with what you knew at the time* and treated you with compassion and forgiveness, I would . . .

- To work through *self-directed* anger:

  - The impact of getting angry with myself has been . . .
  - What I wanted for myself that I didn't get was . . .
  - I've wrongly blamed myself for . . .
  - If I apologized to myself, I would say . . .
  - If I acknowledged that I *did the best I knew how with what I knew at the time* and treated myself with compassion and forgiveness, I would . . .

5. Express out loud to yourself or to another what you discovered in step 4. If you don't have access to the other person, ask a close friend to stand in for this person and listen deeply.

As you get used to exploring and releasing anger, you'll notice your heart opening up, almost as if there is more space in your chest cavity. Many clients have described it as being able to breathe more easily. What does it feel like in your body?

If you can't seem to let go, don't worry. It just means there's more you need to say. Ask yourself: *What else do I need to express?* You may not know yet. You may need to dig deeper to articulate your underlying pain or fear. It's okay. Have compassion for yourself in the process.

> Go to DoctorNehaTalkRx.com to watch the video "How to Manage Yourself in the Face of Anger."

COMPASSION AND FORGIVENESS

In the conversation with my dad, I realized that the forgiveness formula could give us an opportunity to transform the dynamic in our relationship.

"Dad, how about if you and I experience a forgiveness exercise together?" I asked. "It will mean bringing up issues from my childhood that I haven't had the courage to talk to you about. Is that okay?"

"Sure," he replied.

"Wow. I didn't expect you to say yes. I can feel myself tearing up already," I said.

I took a few deep breaths and began, "I'm going to use four prompt lines and then fill them in with what I need to say to you. All you need to do is listen deeply. Please don't interrupt. It'll only take five minutes. After I'm finished, I'm open to hearing what the impact was on you. Does that work?"

"I'll do my best," he replied.

"*Dad, living with you was* . . . sometimes scary and unpredictable. I used to try and figure out what mood you were in so I'd know if it was a good time to talk or not. I used to feel scared when you and mom would fight because I thought you might get divorced. When you used to yell or get angry, I used to get a stomachache and cry myself to sleep.

"I focused on academics and tennis to vie for your love. While I loved playing tennis with you, I wish you'd been a little easier on me. I think I've taken on your voice, and I'm pretty hard on myself when you're not around. I'm working on having more compassion for myself.

"*Dad, living without you was* . . . hard. I wished that you didn't work so much. You got so much recognition at work, though. I heard how much your team admired you when I met them.

"*Dad, what I wanted from you that I didn't get was* . . . your love and compassion when I cried. Whenever I would express tears, you used to raise your voice and yell at me.

"*Dad, what I've wanted to tell you is* . . . I'm so grateful that you and Mom came to America and stayed, that you valued education and instilled this in me. I appreciate how hard you work and that you have been a steady and consistent provider all these years. Thanks for waking me up with chai each morning. Thanks for teaching me to be affectionate and for how much you love doing housework and taking care of the cars. I'm definitely spoiled!

"I've been too scared to even bring this up. I had no idea how open and willing you would be to discussing it. I love you, and I've worked my whole life to make you proud. When you tell me you love me, I know that it's true, but I've so desperately longed to hear you say you're proud of me. Are you proud of me? And most important, I forgive you. That's all, Dad."

My dad was silent.

Then he began, "I love you so much. I'm sorry for the ways I've hurt you. Yes, I'm proud of you, Neha beti. And it is awfully hard for a dad to hear his daughter cry. Sometimes I don't tell you enough, but please know that I love you and I hope that my actions show you that I would do anything for you. What can I do to make it right?"

"Thanks for listening. That's exactly what I needed you to do. I feel so much better now."

"You're welcome," he said softly, "but it's too late for me. I can't do what you just did because my parents are gone."

"Sure you can, Dad. The important part is that you express it and get it out of you."

"Okay, I'll think about what I want to say to them. One more question, beti. How does one forgive oneself?"

"That's a great question, Dad. It's similar to the way you forgive another. You just may need to do it more often. The best explanation I've ever heard about forgiveness is that *it's giving up all hope of a better past*. That requires a huge amount of acceptance—both for yourself and for your parents.

"The way you forgive yourself is by asking, did you do the best you knew how with the knowledge and awareness that you had at the time?"

"Yes, beti, I did," my father replied.

"And when you knew better, did you do better?"

"Yes. That's what I'm doing with you now, right?"

"Exactly, Dad."

Through this experience, I realized how much potential exists when people are open to transforming their relationships. I used to physically remove myself if I thought there was even a possibility of witnessing anger. Now I had chosen to stay engaged with compassion and forgiveness instead of being fearful. This choice changed the connection with my dad from logistical exchanges of data to deep and personal conversations. The doors to healing were now wide open.

Remember, anger must first be acknowledged and heard before it can be soothed because it often serves to shield fear or pain. Recognizing the physical signs of anger early, treating them as valuable information, and then cultivating compassion and forgiveness transform an unwieldy emotion into an opportunity for healing. Once you have a healthy relationship with anger, experiences that once seemed scary or uncomfortable will serve as opportunities to create understanding and connection.

◆ ◆ ◆ ◆ ◆

TALKRX TOOLKIT

Navigating Anger

Express Your Anger Tool

- State what you observe (if something has physically changed).
- Name the underlying emotion.
- Get curious.

Examples of how to articulate this are:

- "I can see how upset you are. How can I best support you?"
- "I hear your frustration. What happened?"
- "Your tone has changed and you've gotten quiet. Are you angry?"

Responding to Anger Tool

- State what's happening.
- Then ask for what you need.

Examples of how to articulate this are:

- "I feel myself reacting; I'd like to talk about it."

- "I can feel myself shutting down. I need to go for a run."
- "I'm not in the right frame of mind to continue this conversation. I need time."

Self-Forgiveness Tool

Are you ready to give up all hope of a better past? If yes, proceed. If no, you're not ready.

1. Acknowledge the physical sensations telling you something needs to be healed.

2. Take a deep breath and thank your body for communicating with you.

3. Ask yourself:
   - "Did I do the best I knew how with the knowledge and awareness I had at the time?"
   - "When I knew better, did I do better?"

4. In your journal, write the answers to the statements that apply:
   - The impact of getting angry with myself has been . . .
   - What I wanted for myself that I didn't get was . . .
   - I've wrongly blamed myself for . . .
   - If I apologized to myself, I would say . . .
   - If I acknowledged that I did the best I knew how with what I knew at the time and treated myself with compassion and forgiveness, I would . . .

5. Express:
   - What you wanted to say (or apologize for) to yourself.
   - What will be different moving forward.

Forgiving Another Tool

1. Become aware of your body's signals telling you something needs to be healed.

2. Take a deep breath and thank your body for communicating with you.

3. Ask yourself:

   • "Did this person do the best they knew how with the knowledge and awareness they had at the time?"

4. In your journal, answer the statements that apply:

   • The impact of this relationship on me has been . . .

   • What I wanted from you that I didn't get was . . .

   • What I've always wanted to tell you is . . .

   • The ways I've held back are . . .

   • If I believed *you did the best you could with what you knew at the time* and treated you with compassion and forgiveness, I would . . .

5. Express:

   • What you need to say to the person directly, or

   • Have a friend stand in for this person and listen deeply.

TalkRx Video: Go to DoctorNehaTalkRx.com to watch "How to Manage Yourself in the Face of Anger."

Your 1-Five Moment

• To better understand your relationship to anger—in yourself and in others—answer the questions in Chapter 14 of your *TalkRx Journal* (DoctorNehaTalkRx.com).

• Share one of your answers with the TalkRx Community. Go ahead, pick one.

CHAPTER 15

THE SKY IS NOT FALLING

Chicken Little was way ahead of his time. His worry and fear about the sky falling would have been so much more timely in our current society of amped-up anxiety. We're moving at a breakneck pace, and we're maxed out, overcommitted, and exhausted. And survival is often our top priority.

In our personal lives, we're managing our energy with caffeinated and carbonated drinks just to get through the day. And at work, we're laser focused on the next deadline. Efficiency is king. We want immediate results. We rarely pause long enough to realize that in the name of efficiency we've sacrificed effectiveness. And quite frankly, if we did slow down, we'd probably start worrying about the time we were wasting.

At the pace we're moving, it's no wonder that one in eight Americans ages 18 and older suffers from an anxiety disorder, and that the rates of Xanax and Valium use have skyrocketed in the past decade.[18] Not to mention the increase in prescriptions for insomnia medications. "I'm not dependent on Ambien, I just use a little bit at night if I can't sleep," a patient once said to me.[19] As a nation, we are worrying ourselves sick.

Chicken Little had so many good things to worry about. And so do we. They usually start with the words *what if* followed by some sort of catastrophic thinking:

- *What if the deal doesn't go through?*
- *What if I get sick?*

- *What if I can't get it all done?*
- *What if it's too stressful?*
- *What if I fail?*

This isn't the only way we scare ourselves silly. What about the other fears that haunt millions of Americans, such as spiders, heights, dogs, flying, the dark, crowds, needles, public speaking, and death? After reading that the fear of public speaking trumps the fear of death for most Americans, comedian Jerry Seinfeld joked, "If you have to go to a funeral, you're better off in the casket than doing the eulogy."[20]

WHAT IS ANXIETY?

Just like anger, anxiety is rooted in other emotions; in this case, it's fear. Though we are born with only two natural fears—the fear of falling and of loud noises—we sometimes learn fear as an adaptive behavior to protect ourselves from danger.[21] So it's normal to feel anxious at times. While guilt and regret are about past behavior, anxiety is an attempt to control the future.

Anxiety can be motivating and lead you to take action—for instance, to meet a rapidly approaching deadline. Anxiety can fuel you to pull an all-nighter to solve a problem, double-check your work to avoid errors, or deep-clean your house to prepare for a peaceful visit with your in-laws. On the other hand, anxiety may have you treading water. Some people repeatedly think through the endless scenarios that could happen in hopes of outsmarting an undesirable outcome. Then, if what they're anxious about actually does happen, maybe it won't be as bad, because they think they will have already prepared themselves. They can say, "I already thought of that" or "I *knew* that was going to happen."

But pay attention if you find yourself preoccupied with what-ifs and worst-case scenarios. Even if you have a compartmentalized fear, say only about losing your money, your youth, your job, or your relationships, this anxiety can unravel your health and happiness. Chronic anxiety repeatedly triggers the stress response and drains your emotional and physical energy. Excessive anxiety shuts down the cortical thinking part of your brain that helps you problem-solve and come up with creative options. Eventually, it will undermine your ability to communicate and function day-to-day.

To make it easy, think of anxiety in three categories:

1. **Generalized anxiety** is a state of worry that lasts for at least six months and is usually focused on one or two specific areas of your life (your health, your finances, your work, etc.). People with generalized anxiety tend to feel on edge and have difficulty sleeping, relaxing, and enjoying life.

2. **Phobias** are intense fears of a specific object or situation—such as taking an elevator, being bitten by a dog, or using a public toilet—that tend to be out of proportion to any real risk. Sometimes, a past traumatic experience, like being locked in a closet by a sibling, can trigger an ongoing fear of being stuck in a closed space (claustrophobia). People with phobias often worry continuously about whether the situation they fear is going to occur. (Extreme trauma, such as surviving a serious injury or fighting in war, can alter the adrenaline response and several areas of the brain, leading to post-traumatic stress disorder, or PTSD.)

3. **Panic attacks** are intense feelings of being overwhelmed, accompanied by the fear of losing control, going crazy, or dying, even without any evidence to support those fears.

In whatever form anxiety takes, it triggers your nervous system. When adrenaline is released, it causes a flood of physical sensations, such as a racing heart, sweating, and tightened muscles. This makes it challenging to slow down and listen deeply. When you're anxious, you *react* rather than respond. Fear and panic interfere with your brain's critical thinking and hinder your ability to communicate effectively.

So why all the worry? Underlying anxiety is a lack of self-trust to handle uncertainty. When experiencing a loss of control, anxiety is often an attempt to create order out of perceived chaos. Except there's one small problem: it doesn't work. You've probably heard people say, "Worrying doesn't take away tomorrow's troubles; it only takes away today's peace."

THE QUICK FIX

If you have recurring anxious thoughts that increase in frequency and intensity, they will eventually take on a physical manifestation. Surprise, surprise! If you've been missing the early signs, your body will likely be the messenger that no longer allows you to ignore your anxiety. You may feel helpless and be willing to do almost anything to restore sanity to your life.

Anxiety can bring on everything from mild physical discomfort to the palpitations, shortness of breath, and dizziness of a full-blown panic attack. It can cause sleepless nights for executives, public speakers' repetitive finger tapping, nail-biting for parents who are concerned about their children, and tummy aches for little kids who have been bullied or neglected. I've seen dozens of physical ailments result from prolonged anxiety: hives, headaches, irritable bowel syndrome, asthma attacks, and abnormal heart rhythms, to name a few. By the way, now would be a good time to check in: Has merely reading this list provoked some anxious thoughts or feelings in you?

Once anxiety sends clear physical signals, people will often turn to physical strategies, such as prescription drugs, to alleviate them. Since they don't know what to do with their worrisome thoughts or fearful emotions, it can seem easier to control their physical bodies instead. And often people become dependent on these short-term reprieves. The irony is that anxiety has a mental and emotional basis. Physical strategies serve to get you through the moment, but they won't solve your problem.

When I see patients who are suffering from anxiety, they've usually already found a coping method, or several, to temporarily alleviate the physical symptoms. Some people turn to smoking, others work long hours, and still others numb themselves with food, alcohol, or drugs in order to function. When these behaviors go on too long, they can lead to health problems, burnout, or addiction.

And then there are the folks who use yoga or running as a strategy to relieve their discomfort. The interesting part is that focusing on your physical body *alone* relieves two things, the muscle tension and the need to be in control—but it only works until the next time you feel anxious. This is complex because society rewards people for this type of strategy. Your friends may be impressed, but you haven't gotten rid of your anxiety. It's fueling your healthy coping mechanism, which is a good short-term strategy.

Let's see how this might play out: If you have a new boss who keeps close tabs on your work, this may cause you to have a glass of wine (or three) to "take the edge off" your day. Your anxiety may even lessen after a few drinks, but tomorrow, it will be time to head back to work and nothing will have changed. You're just getting by.

On the other hand, if you choose to manage your anxiety by running a few miles after work each night, you will probably feel stronger and in better shape. That's a good thing. After a few months, you might even get compliments from your friends and colleagues about your stellar physique. Except your relationship with your micromanaging boss will still be the same each morning, as if it were Groundhog Day.

Both of the above scenarios demonstrate that coping strategies can have a beneficial impact in the short run—and to some degree, even longer-term, as in the running example. However, the takeaway is that neither of these strategies solves the underlying problem: your relationship with your boss. Until you commit to having an honest conversation, your anxiety will continue.

When you experience anxiety, use your pause button, just like you've learned to do with tears and anger. Once you've managed your physical symptoms, pay attention to the internal conversation driving your fear. Then it's time to get curious and challenge those beliefs in order to create new possibilities. Slowing down may seem counterintuitive, but actually it's the fastest way to get back on track.

SCARED TO DEATH

At 27 years old, Carly, a good friend of my younger sister, Sarika, had just been diagnosed with cancer that had spread throughout her body. Sarika was blindsided by the news. She and Carly had so much in common. They were both independent, strong women who had excelled in school, were committed to environmental causes, ran marathons, worked hard, loved cooking healthy and delicious meals, and were changing the world.

That summer while receiving treatment, Carly moved home from New York City to surround herself with the love and support of her family. Sarika, willing to do anything to help her friend, offered to sublet Carly's apartment.

The very day that she moved in, Sarika noticed herself burping and tasting acid in the back of her throat. She saw multiple physicians who scoped her throat and her colon, looking for the physical culprit. The end result was the same. "Everything looks normal, Sarika. You're doing great. We're not sure why you have this intractable reflux, but we can give you a medication to cut the amount of acid your stomach produces. Hopefully, that will take care of your symptoms."

Even though the doctors agreed on the treatment for reflux, Sarika wasn't convinced. It was then that she called me to relate her story and her diagnosis. It was clear the physical exploration of her reflux was not yielding results. So I got curious about her mental and emotional stress response to moving into Carly's apartment.

She burst into tears. "This isn't fair! Carly is such an amazing woman, and I thought I would be helping her financially by moving in. But it's like I can't get away from my fear. I'm surrounded by it—everywhere I go, I'm reminded of Carly. What if she doesn't make it?"

"I'm so sorry, Sarika," I responded. "I hear how devastated you are. You sound like you're paralyzed with fear. Do you think your anxiety could be contributing to your symptoms?"

"Maybe. I think about it all the time. She's so young. It completely freaks me out that someone with such a positive outlook on life who focused on her health could get cancer," she replied.

"Are you, by any chance, afraid that you might get sick, too? Are you anxious about losing control?"

Sarika was silent for a few moments, but I could hear her short, shallow breaths and her sniffling over the phone. "Rationally, I know I can't catch cancer from being here, but why did this have to happen to her? I feel like an awful friend. In comparison with what Carly's going through, my fears seem insignificant. I'm battling, wanting to support Carly while dealing with my own fear. If it can happen to her, why can't it happen to me?"

"It's perfectly understandable why you'd be afraid," I told her. "You're worried about the future and what might happen. And as a doctor, I'm concerned because your symptoms have been going on for over a year now. Aside from your reflux, is there anything else wrong?"

"No, except that I keep thinking about what might happen. Neha, what if—"

I interrupted her. "Sarika, take a nice, deep breath. Soften your belly, let your shoulders relax and just feel your bottom on the chair. You're way out in the future, trying to control something that hasn't even happened yet. I think I know what's going on, but before I can partner with you to heal your body, you have to get back in the present moment and become aware of the thoughts and emotions that are undermining you."

Together we took three slow, deep breaths as Sarika shifted her focus from her racing thoughts to her body.

"Okay, I'm better. I can listen now, so tell me what's happening," she said.

"From what you've shared, it sounds like you're brokenhearted about Carly. That in itself is an emotional tidal wave of stress that can overwhelm your body.

"You said your reflux symptoms started the day you moved into Carly's apartment. You've checked it out with your doctor, and the results are normal. But stress can often cause a breakdown in your gut, and this affects your sensitivity to the food you're eating and how you feel. There are so many nerves in your GI tract that anxiety commonly shows up as a stomachache, diarrhea, constipation, or even reflux.

"Short-term, you can take the acid blockers to relieve your physical symptoms. The problem is that your stomach needs a low pH in order to digest your food and absorb key nutrients. So if you take acid blockers as a long-term solution, it will eventually affect your absorption and soon we'll have other issues to deal with. So let's get to the root of what's causing your stress—the paralyzing thoughts, intense fear, and devastation around your and Carly's health. Then maybe you won't need the medications anymore."

THE CURE

I bet you can relate to my sister's anxiety or know someone who has had a similar experience. Since Sarika's anxiety manifested as reflux, she was searching for a physical remedy. She didn't realize that her thoughts and emotions were the real culprits. Her inability to express herself to Carly led to feeling trapped and more anxious—which made her reflux even worse.

No matter how strong your confidence in certain arenas, there may be other areas that, in Sarika's words, "totally freak you out." While I feel at ease in the midst of a medical crisis, I completely freak out when swimming in deep water, even if I can see the bottom. My anxiety began after I saw the movie *Jaws*. No, I'm serious.

I've worked through anxiety with myself, Sarika, and hundreds of patients to resolve their physical symptoms and help them express themselves. Here are the steps I use.

1. Get present. When you notice you're having worrisome thoughts about the future, a quick way to interrupt that pattern is to focus on your body.

First, identify the unique physical signals your body is giving you (tense muscles, throat constriction, racing heart, trembling hands, etc.), and when they occur, hit the pause button. To do this, use grounding and soft belly breathing to focus on your body right now. Just be sure to use the proper techniques outlined on page 52 in Chapter 4.

It might sound too simple, but when you're present in your body, you are focused on the here and now—and therefore, you can't be in the future.

2. Name that fear. The monster under your bed loses its power when you turn on the light and all you find is an extended family of dust bunnies.

Begin by acknowledging the stories in your head. Name your fears about the person, place, or situation you're confronting.

Start by writing down the phrase "What I'm afraid of is . . ." Then finish the sentence. For example, when Sarika and I went through this exercise, she said:

What I'm afraid of is . . .

- I'm sick—and it's really, really bad.
- Carly might die, and I can't imagine life without her.
- I won't be able to handle it.
- If Carly can get stage 4 cancer, so can I.

Keep writing until there is absolutely nothing left to write. And remember, this is all about you. If you're worried about someone else, gently bring the focus back to yourself by asking, "What if this is about me?"

Sarika thought her greatest fear was about Carly. But what she discovered was that the underlying trigger for her anxiety was a deep-rooted fear about her own health.

3. Expand your perspective. It's time to challenge your anxious thoughts by identifying how they limit your beliefs. You're a pro at future-thinking. The only problem is that no matter how hard you try, you can't control the future. So just as we did with your body, it's time to get your thoughts into the present moment.

Go back to your list of fears, and after each one, write the following statement: "Right here, right now, what I know for sure is that . . ." Then end each statement with the facts you know about what you're afraid of—not the stories in your head.

For example, when we examined Sarika's fears about the future, she gained a completely different perspective about what was actually true versus the stories she was making up in her head.

- Right now, my tests are normal.

- Right now, Carly is alive, receiving treatment, and living with her family.

- Right now, I have been aware of Carly's condition for some time and have been dealing with it day by day.

- Right now, I am cancer free. And I know that cancer is not contagious.

4. Reprogram your thinking. Once your body, thoughts, and emotions are in the present moment, you can access the creative part of your brain to build new patterns of thinking. I suggest using this rediscovered part of your brain to create affirmations—"I am" statements—that replace fearful thoughts. This will rewire your brain to engage in expanded thinking whenever anxiety strikes.

Sarika's affirmation naturally emerged. "I am whole, healthy, and well," she proudly stated. And she began saying it out loud to herself whenever anxiety about her health arose.

5. Trust yourself. Ask yourself one simple question: *What would self-trust and courage do now?*

Listen to the answer and allow it to guide you. (And in case you were wondering, there are no wrong answers.)

Sarika's answer was "Self-trust and courage would communicate directly with Carly."

In response, Sarika found her favorite stationery and pen and wrote Carly a letter expressing how much she admired and loved her.

After mailing it, Sarika felt lighter and free. And over the following weeks her reflux subsided. Isn't that interesting? She hadn't gained any control over how Carly's illness would progress, nor had she been able to secure any guarantees about her own future health. Instead she had gained something much more valuable. She had become acutely aware of how stuffing her emotions caused them to show up physically. She was able to come off her acid-blocking medications as well. She recognized the power of her thoughts and how she could turn them around to face her fears head-on. By trusting that she could handle whatever came next, she discovered courage and inner calm.

In this example, Sarika wrote Carly a letter. It felt like the best way to communicate. For you it might be something different. You may want to express your fears by having a conversation with someone. Or you may want to write down your fears in a journal and then do some sort of ritual to release them from your life. Most important, listen to the answer that comes after you ask yourself: *What would self-trust and courage do now?* That's the right one.

DISMANTLING THE TIME MACHINE

Even if you think through all the what-ifs, it's possible that you might not think of the one that actually happens. What a waste of time and energy. And, to top it off, you've missed what's happening *now*! Trying to control something that hasn't happened yet can be a mind trip. Left unchecked, anxiety can wreak havoc on your health and your happiness.

Paying attention to your body, thoughts, and emotions will help you discern whether anxiety is a paralyzing influence in your life. If it is, allow it to move through you and use it as an opportunity to bring yourself into the present moment. The more courageous you are about facing your fears head-on, the more self-trust you'll build. You'll see that as the future unfolds, you have everything inside you to handle what comes next. You'll shift from trying to survive to learning how to thrive—right now.

Welcome back from the future.

THE WAY HOME

Like the weather, challenging emotions can be unpredictable and shift unexpectedly. You can't wish them away. When they do show up, if you choose not to deal with them, they will just wait for another opportunity to express themselves. Ignoring, suppressing, or storing your emotions has an effect opposite what you're hoping for: you drift farther and farther away from your heart and the people you love.

When a situation or conflict introduces fear or self-doubt, if you deal with it head-on, it will likely resolve. At the very least, you'll learn something so you can avoid a similar experience in the future. If you use a numbing strategy (physical or mental) instead, you'll temporarily avoid the situation, but the same issue will recur in other relationships and settings.

For example, your hurt can turn into blame. And suppose your blame is unresolved. It can evolve into anger and eventually, if unaddressed, progress to resentment. It may seem as if you're targeting another person, but resentment is the equivalent of drinking a glass of poison you intended for someone else.[22] It makes you feel awful, and it corrodes your health. How effective is that? Resentment is one of the most damaging emotions—to you.

Another example would be fear or self-doubt in a relationship. If unaddressed, it may progress to frustration or apathy. While apathy may seem benign, don't be fooled. When it sets in, this is the precise moment when people check out of their jobs or their committed relationships and turn to full-blown numbing strategies. Yes, I'm talking about when affairs and addiction become prevalent. These emotions can potentially transform into feeling trapped or hopeless. When people get to this point and feel there's no way out, they may find themselves severely depressed and even suicidal. If this is you, please seek professional help.

If you aren't sure how to handle your own emotional storms, you put your health and your relationships at risk. When you're ready to listen to your uncomfortable emotions, they will inform you of the path back to your heart.

EMOTIONAL FREEDOM

Now I hope you can see why it's important to navigate emotions—even challenging ones—both in yourself and in others. By stating what's happening on an emotional level, you can defuse an awkward situation with ease. And when you find yourself stuck on a roller coaster of intense emotions, don't forget to use your pause button and name that emotion, so you can begin to explore how it's showing up in your body and how to help it shift. As you begin to expand your emotional vocabulary and pick up on emotions sooner, you will recognize them and communicate earlier. Addressing issues proactively will save you precious energy and time.

Don't underestimate the power of expressing your emotions. You can write in a journal, speak, or type about the experience to explore what emotions you're feeling and what thoughts are tied to them. If you prefer, you could draw or paint what your internal experience feels like and then express what you see in words. Research has shown that when patients with asthma or arthritis journaled about a traumatic event for 20 minutes per day for four days, not only did they feel better, but their symptoms decreased while their immune systems got stronger. And that was from only four days of writing—imagine if you made it a daily practice![23]

For those of you dumbfounded because you ended up in the doghouse again, you hold the key to getting out. All you need to do is master Emotions 101 and practice using your expanded vocabulary with Heart Listening to acknowledge the other person's emotions. (An apology goes a long way, too.)

Emotions are powerful, aren't they? But they're not nearly as scary as you might have once thought. Emotions are the invisible bridges that connect our hearts. Your ability to manage yourself effectively, even during tender or difficult times, allows you to engage and build strong relationships. When you let energy-in-motion move through you, identify what's happening, and know how to clearly express yourself, you have developed a powerful partnership with your heart.

◆ ◆ ◆ ◆ ◆

TALKR$_X$ TOOLKIT

Navigating Anxiety

Back from the Future Tool

1. Get present (soft belly breathing + grounding your body).

2. Name that fearful story in your head.

   - What I'm most afraid of is . . .

   - What if . . . (your fears)

3. Expand your perspective.

   - Ask yourself: Is what I'm afraid of really true in this moment?

   - Right here, right now, what I know for sure is . . .

4. Reprogram your thinking.

   - Turn your fear around. Ask yourself: What is the opposite of this?

   - Create an "I am" statement that supports an ideal outcome (see pages 87–89).

5. Trust yourself by asking:

   - What would self-trust and courage do now?

Express Your Anxiety Tool

- State what you observe.

- Name the emotion.

- Ask for what you need.

- Ask yourself: what would self-trust and courage do now?

Here are some ways to respond:

- "I'm going to miss my flight. I'm worried. Give me a few minutes to calm down and I'll figure out what's next."

- "My heart is racing. I'm scared the package won't arrive on time. So we have a backup plan, can you please send a second copy of the materials to my home address as well?"

- "I'm anxious about what other people are going to think. I need to stay focused on myself. I'm trusting that I will do my best."

Responding to Anxiety Tool

- Breathe and ground yourself.

- Shift into level 4: Heart Listening.

- Name the other person's emotion.

- Get curious.

Here are some ways to respond:

- "I hear how concerned you are. How can I help?"

- "I see how worried you are. What do you need?"

- "I can tell this is anxiety-provoking. How can I be of support?"

YOUR 1-FIVE MOMENT

- To explore your personal relationship with anxiety, complete the questions in Chapter 15 of your *TalkRx Journal* (DoctorNehaTalkRx.com).

- Share with the TalkRx Community whether anxiety plays a motivating or paralyzing role in your life.

INTERPRETING YOUR DESIRES

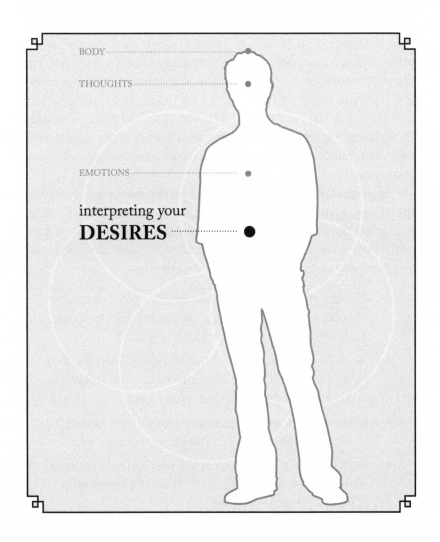

In the last section, you didn't invest all that energy-in-motion for nothing. Yes, it's true, the quality of your communication depends on your ability to interpret your emotions. And you probably won't be surprised to hear that your body, thoughts, and emotions will all serve as the framework for you to interpret your desires. When you know how to navigate these four aspects of communication, it will lead you to less stress, ease in communication, and clarity about what is most important to you.

In this section, *desire* and *want* will be used interchangeably. The important distinction to make is that just knowing what you desire or want is different from being able to interpret your desires. Interpreting your desires is based on both knowing what you want and understanding the motivation beneath it—what you value. Knowing both what you want and what you value provides the clarity to make decisions with ease in everyday conversations and gives you the confidence to take bold action when necessary. In addition, you'll be able to listen for others' values in conversation, which will allow you to identify common ground and create connection.

In general, most of us think we know what we want—whether it's in our relationships, in our jobs, or with our families. When I've asked people about their desires, depending on what decade of life they were in, a pattern emerged that usually indicated what was most important to them. If they were:

- Under ten, they said: "I want another piece of candy." "I don't want to go to sleep." Or, as my four-year old niece exclaimed, "I want to be a unicorn!"

- From 10 to 20, they said: "I want the kids at school to think I'm cool." "I don't want to follow the rules." "I don't want people to tell me what to do."

- In their 20s, it progressed to: "I want to fall in love." "I want to make money." "I want my team to win."

- From 30 to 40, they often responded with: "I want to raise a happy, healthy family." "I want a promotion." "I want a job that pays well."

- In their 40s and 50s, people replied: "I want to be recognized for my expertise." "I want my children to be successful and happy." "I want to reconnect to my hobbies and friends."

- Above 60, most answered along the lines of: "I want to be strong in my body." "I want to retire with ease." "I don't want my traditions to get lost with the next generation."

In general, up to a certain age, people usually expressed short-term desires for themselves. As their age increased, however, I noticed that their wants seemed to be a mixture of what they wanted for themselves and what they wanted for their loved ones. There was also a shift toward longer-term desires, such as leaving a legacy or leaving the world a better place.

Patients who had health issues or had gone through a crisis were in a contemplative place—open and curious about life's big questions—no matter what their age. Time and time again, I wondered why it took a jarring experience, a trip to the hospital, or a challenging life situation for my patients to get clear on their deepest values. I've often daydreamed about how different the world might be if, early on, we had all learned the importance of getting clear about what mattered most to us. So let's get started.

Think of the first four aspects of the i-Five Conversation—your body, thoughts, emotions, and desires—as a navigation system directing you toward clear, direct, and concise communication. When you know what you value, it's easy to navigate obstacles and detours in conversation in order to stay on track.

CHAPTER 16

THE CONSEQUENCES OF NOT KNOWING

After reviewing my patient Mary's latest tests and reports, I walked toward her room. As I entered, I glanced at a stunning photo of Mary, her husband, and her three sons that sat on her nightstand.

Unfortunately, the woman lying in the hospital bed bore little resemblance to the happy, smiling woman in the photo. Mary's stage 4 breast cancer had spread to her brain and bones, so she was undergoing another arduous round of chemotherapy. A gorgeous, jewel-toned scarf was draped around her head where wavy brown hair with blonde highlights once sat, and she now had more IVs, shunts, and ports going in and out of her than any human should have to endure.

Mary's chemo had weakened her immune system so much that she had developed an infection in her blood. Due to the emotional and physical trauma she'd had to endure, she was on both an antidepressant and antianxiety medication. During this latest hospital stay, Mary's infection had slowly subsided and her immune system had regained momentum. She had finally gone 24 hours without a fever, so it looked like I might be able to discharge her in the morning.

"Mary," I began, "we've known each other for five days now, and you've been in this isolation room with a lot of time to think and reflect. So I'd like to ask you a few questions that often help my patients gain insight about their next steps in healing. Would you like to hear them?"

"Of course," she replied.

I pulled out my prescription pad and began jotting down the five questions as I spoke. "Why do you think it was breast cancer that brought you here, and why now? Were there any signals you might have missed? Is there anything else in your life that needs to be healed? And if you spoke from your heart, what would you say?

"Take your time to think about these, and maybe write down whatever comes to you. Remember, there are no wrong answers. We can talk in the morning about what you've discovered. How does that sound?"

"It sounds great," she said. "It'll give me something productive to do instead of worrying."

The next morning I asked Mary if she had thought about the Awareness Prescription.

"Yes. I thought a lot. The truth is that I've been angry at my mother as far back as I can remember," she began. "She lives at a nursing home in Florida now, and my brother is the one taking care of her. I haven't visited her and she doesn't even know I have cancer.

"I never felt like I belonged in my family—it seemed almost like I was a stepchild. I felt like she never really loved me. She always seemed to favor my brother. We haven't spoken since I went away to college almost thirty-five years ago.

"Last night as I was journaling, the craziest thoughts started pouring onto the page. What if I got cancer because of all the hatred I've harbored for her? I have no idea why I've held on to it for so long. I've just always felt this emptiness inside, and now that emptiness is filled with cancer."

"That sounds like a painful and lonely experience," I said. "You've definitely given a lot of thought to these questions. Let's take a few deep breaths together, and then we'll explore what you've discovered."

As soon as we finished our breaths, I asked, "So what was it that you wanted from your mom? What did you need?"

"That's a good question," Mary replied. "She was always busy with parties or with my brother's baseball games. She would always tell him how proud she was of him. Maybe it was her love and attention that I desperately craved. I don't actually know. I just know that whatever it was, I wasn't getting it. But you asked me what else I need to heal? I need to talk to her, but how will I ever forgive her?"

"Exactly what is it that you want to forgive your mother for?" I asked.

"Forgive her for not knowing what I needed . . . even though, as a child, I couldn't articulate it myself," Mary said. "Do you think there's any relation to my cancer?"

"Let me make sure I understand," I said. "You aren't sure exactly what you needed as a child, but you felt a deep sense of emptiness. You heard her praise your brother more than you and thought she somehow loved you less. You felt hurt, so you stopped communicating with her after you left the house. You've never had a conversation with her about how you felt. So there's a chance she's not even aware of why you two have grown apart. And you're wondering if this resentment is the reason you have cancer. Is that what you're asking me?"

"Yes," she replied, as she began to cry.

I took Mary's hand in mine. "I'm afraid there's not a straightforward yes or no answer to your question. There are so many factors involved. What I can tell you is that genetics can play a role, and so can stress—physical, mental, and emotional. Over time, chronic stress can break down your immune system and make your body susceptible to all sorts of illnesses.

"I'm a firm believer in listening to your heart and letting it guide you. And from what I'm hearing, you're ready to mend your relationship with your mother and begin healing, and you want to know how to do that. There are many paths you can take. Let's help you get clearer on what you want and value so you can have a meaningful conversation with her."

"That would be great. It's about time." Mary sighed and gently smiled.

"Tell me what you wish your mom had done differently when you were young."

"I wish she had spent more time with me and been interested in who I was. I'm not even sure if she loved me," Mary said. "My dad was always working, so he wasn't around much, either."

I paused. Then I responded, "My initial thought is to focus on what you can change. Start by practicing on yourself. Is there anything you need to forgive yourself for?"

"It's only now, when I see my boys getting unruly and rebellious, that I realize I'm not a very good communicator. I haven't known how to talk to my sons about my illness. And boys, they speak even less than girls. Until I encountered this challenge, I'd never thought about what my mother must have been struggling with all those years. I focused only on what I wasn't getting.

"Last night I realized that instead of feeling guilty that I may be leaving my boys someday soon, I want to ask them how they feel about everything that's happening with me. I want to create videos that they can play at important milestones like their birthdays, graduations, and wedding days. I need to express my love now, so that when I'm gone they'll have memories, and they can heal from losing their mother. Mostly, I need to hug them more and tell them that I love them.

"I've been so afraid about my illness that I think I've stopped communicating. I just leave it up to my husband to do it. But the truth is, communication has never been his forte. He takes care of the bills, the cars, and the house. I want to tell my husband what an amazing man he is. I want to make the most of the time I have left."

"Wow," I said, "what a great place to start—by reaching out and letting your family know you love them. It sounds like you want to get curious and ask your sons what they're experiencing during your illness, and you want to leave behind a legacy of your presence in videos for the special milestones in their lives. And you want to make certain your husband knows how much you love him, and how grateful you are for who he is and everything he does for you and your children. It also sounds like you're experiencing some grace and compassion for how your mother might have struggled."

With tears streaming down our faces, we fumbled to see who could get the other one a tissue first.

"Yes, that's right," Mary said. "I guess it's time to stop blaming other people and figure out how I want to spend the precious time I have left."

A SIGH OF RELIEF

Mary hadn't known what she wanted, but one thing was for sure: she was upset she wasn't getting it. Mary hadn't even known how to express her feelings of disappointment and rejection. She withdrew, became silent, and stewed until her blame turned into resentment. And we all know how toxic that can be. She expected her mom to give her the love and attention she needed, even though Mary herself had no clue how she could best receive it.

Mary had made up stories about her mom's intentions: her mother never loved her; her mother cared only about Mary's brother. The problem was Mary never got curious. Instead, she held these stories as truth and stuffed her emotions until she was corroding her insides with resentment.

Through an honest conversation coupled with curiosity, Mary got crystal clear about what she wanted. It was time to mend her relationship with her mother and express herself authentically to her husband and sons. Most important, it was time to quit playing the blame game with her mother and be accountable for how she was showing up (or refusing to). By taking ownership of her actions, she not only realized her part in how the situation had gone astray, but also expanded her perspective in a way that allowed her to see new possibilities in her relationships.

After we talked through the conversations Mary needed to have with her mother, her husband, and her sons, she was soon taking actions that were consistent with her deepest desires and values. She acknowledged what she needed to clean up from her past. She figured out how she wanted to show up in the present for her family. And she knew how she wanted to create a meaningful legacy.

Nearly 12 months later, Mary died. Her husband told me that during her last few months, Mary had a renewed sense of hope. She no longer needed her antianxiety medication. She reconnected with her mother and had a few healing conversations with her. Her sons started spending afternoons talking with their mom and got comfortable expressing their love and sadness. And one of the last activities he did with her was to make videos for their sons. It was shortly after they completed them that Mary passed away, peacefully, as he held her hand.

I thanked him for sharing all of this with me.

"Mary made me promise," he said. "She wanted me to thank you and to be sure you knew how much the questions you asked her, and the conversations the two of you had, changed her life."

Do Versus Don't

How many of you can relate to Mary blaming another person for not getting what she wanted?

When you have unfulfilled desires, your initial reflex might be to insist your unhappiness is someone else's fault. Though these accusations may temporarily leave you feeling justified and empowered, I promise you that your sense of righteousness and superiority will be short-lived. Blame only pushes you farther away from others and from getting what you desire most.

Remember, when you experience something painful, scary, or uncomfortable, your brain (amygdala) has built-in memory to alert you if whatever is happening resembles a past challenging experience. This is a protective mechanism that can serve good purpose: if the last time you smelled smoke your house was on fire, you would want to remember that the next time you smell smoke.

But this built-in warning system can work against you as well, when the memory of painful or frightening experiences has fear driving your actions.

This is why many of us make the mistake of getting clear about what we *don't* want, rather than what we *do* want. There are so many don'ts in our language that we program our world with exactly what we don't want:

- I don't want to lose my cool.
- I don't want to get sick.
- I don't want to go to the wedding alone.
- I don't want to say yes.
- I don't want to see your family.

Pay attention to what's motivating your desires. If it's fear, self-doubt, or self-protection, you will find yourself shying away from situations you perceive as emotional or challenging. (Of course, by now you know what I would say about that: leaning into short-term discomfort is an opportunity to turn it all around.) It's true that knowing what you don't want can steer you away from discomfort. It's just that it doesn't move you toward your deepest desires. Only love, courage, and self-trust will allow you to risk reaching for what you really want. So you get to decide—will it be fear or love that motivates your desires?

Sports commentators frequently talk about how winning is a "mental game." That's why athletes are taught to focus on precisely what they want. An Olympic diver, for example, wants to nail three perfect 10s in order to be the world champion and take home the gold medal. It's no wonder that successful divers aren't wasting time and energy focusing on what could go wrong or on hoping someone else messes up. Instead, they focus on themselves and guide their mental experience toward what it looks and feels like to create a perfect dive and enter the water with such control that they barely make a splash. They envision this over and over again until they create it. That's why it's so important to get clear about what you want—because what you think about occupies precious mental real estate.

Let's see how easy it is to take what you *don't want* and transform it into what you *do want,* using the previous statements as an example.

DON'T WANT	Becomes	DO WANT
"I don't want to lose my cool."	→	"I want to express my disappointment effectively."
"I don't want to get sick."	→	"I want to be healthy."
"I don't want to go alone to the wedding."	→	"I want a date for the wedding."
"I don't want to say yes."	→	"I want to decline."
"I don't want to see your family."	→	"I want to stay home."

When you don't know what you want, you will be left guessing. Without realizing it, you'll set yourself up for another round of disappointment. *I want* statements are the direct route to fulfilling your desires.

IT'S AN INSIDE JOB

Another way your desires can be misdirected is when you project them onto others.

"I wish you'd be more considerate."

"Stop making me mad!"

"If only he would show some respect."

We often think it's easier to control our outside environment than to deal with our ambiguous internal world of stories, emotions, and unspoken expectations. Problems are a lot simpler—or at least a lot easier to complain about—when they're someone else's fault. Putting the focus on ourselves forces us to take owner-ship for our part in the situation.

When you have a lot of energy and momentum directed to-ward changing someone else (unless it's a toddler with a stinky diaper), this is a flashing danger sign. But most people miss it and continue in an endless loop of what I refer to as *wanting for another.*

Here's where most people get stuck: to get clear about what you want, you can't be busy *wanting for another.* You have to focus on yourself. Yes, you can wish another well, but if you are want-ing for someone else and you believe their behavior determines whether you can have what you want, then "Houston, we've got a problem."

Think about my situation with my dad's anger. While I des-perately wanted my dad's temper to go away, how many lifetimes do you think I'd have been waiting for that to happen? It might have happened. It might not have happened. I could express my desire to him, but when push came to shove, his behavior was solely under his control.

As soon as you notice that you're focusing on someone else, it's a good time to pause and reassess what's happening. Ask yourself:

- What am I trying to achieve?

- What am I trying to protect myself from?

- What am I trying to change so that I can be more comfortable, happy, peaceful (or whatever your desire is)?

Remember when Dr. Abdullah didn't want his daughter to cry? He told me exactly what he didn't want for someone else. Although his desire for his daughter to be strong sounded noble—and it was—Dr. Abdullah's external environment was triggering an emo-tional response inside him that he was uncertain how to handle.

When he changed the story in his head, it became clear that the real issue was seeing someone he loved in pain and feeling powerless to fix it. When he shifted the focus onto himself, what he wanted changed. Instead of wanting to stop his daughter's tears, he got curious and expanded his perspective about how he could manage himself more effectively in the face of those tears. Once he got clear about what he wanted (even if nothing changed for his daughter), he could change how he showed up for her.

So how do you stop wanting for another and shift to wanting for yourself? You gain the awareness that your own desires are the only ones you have the power to change.

If you're still wanting for another, ask yourself: *If nothing changes for this other person, what do I want for myself in this situation?*

Yes, it will take some practice. But knowing how to communicate your desires in any situation will put you on the fast track to getting what you want.

FROM SELFISH TO SELF-FULL

As you're figuring out what you want, you might be thinking, *Hey, wait a minute. Everybody else has wants, too. Focusing on myself is selfish!*

Pause for a minute. Where do you think that story came from? Because it's definitely a story you've made up or adopted from someone else.

Don't worry; knowing what you want won't lead you down a treacherous path to greed and selfishness. It will actually lead you to what I call being self-full. Being self-full means you first know what you want and then you're able to communicate it clearly. Being self-full brings much-needed order and balance to your relationships—a win-win for everyone. And the benefits of harmony with others are less stress, better health, and a deep sense of connection and belonging.

Getting clear about what you want is essential to creating solid relationships. Most important, notice that I didn't say, "Think only of yourself." I said the first step is getting clear about what you want. This simply makes you part of the equation. Once you're clear about yourself, then you can use levels 4 and 5 listening to consider other people's needs as well. Your own clarity is merely preparation to engage in meaningful interactions with others.

It is sometimes difficult to distinguish the difference between what other people want for us and what we want for ourselves, because looking for outside approval is a natural instinct.

In childhood, we were helpless and dependent on others to feed, bathe, and care for us. So we learned in infancy how to tune in to our external environment to make sure those who took care of us were pleased with us. We paid attention to what made them laugh. We paid attention to what resulted in a hug and a kiss. We paid attention to how and when we got what we wanted. And then we did more of those behaviors. This is how we first learned to navigate relationships. Our survival depended on it.

As adults, our journey transitioned into a dance of knowing what we ourselves wanted and becoming aware of the needs and desires of those around us. Wanting for ourselves, while simultaneously wanting to belong with others, is a balancing act. Both are important, but guess which one should come first? You have to be self-full before you can give to others.

ANYWHERE BUT HERE

Did you notice what else was holding Mary back from getting clear about what she wanted? She was hung up on the past while attempting to control the future. How did I know? Come on, you know the answer—it's level 4 and level 5 listening. Let me explain.

I saw a family photo on Mary's nightstand. She talked about her relationships with her mother, her brothers, her husband, and her sons.

I heard her say:

- "I have been angry at my mother as far back as I can remember."

- "I never felt like I belonged in my family—it seemed almost like I was a stepchild."

- "You asked me what else I need to heal? I need to talk to her."

Heart Listening led me to hear her feelings of rejection, guilt, resentment, love, and hope. (Here's proof that an unlikely family of emotions can coexist!) When someone feels guilty or resentful, they are most often stuck in the past. Guilt is about feeling regret about one's own behavior. Blame is focusing on another's behavior—and if you let it continue for too long, that blame transforms into resentment. On the other hand, when people are uncertain about the future—whether it's regarding their health, finances, relationships, an impending crisis, etc.— they often attempt to control it. But all they end up with is a Chicken Little mentality.

So it's easy to see how challenging it must have been for Mary to answer my questions and move forward. Until that conversation, her resentment, guilt, and anxiety were blocking her openness to new possibilities. Focusing on past disappointments or future worries created barriers to knowing what she really wanted. I had witnessed this predicament all too often with my patients, so my first job was to bring Mary into the present moment and simultaneously listen at level 5 to discover what was most important to her: belonging, connection, family, and health.

When she focused on the here and now, she was open and receptive enough to create what she truly wanted. By the end of our conversation, she felt at ease and empowered.

As I witnessed Mary's transformation, I couldn't help doing some of my own self-reflection. I realized how ironic it would be if I needed a crisis to hit before I got clear about my own desires. As I left her room, I found a quiet place to capture the thoughts and emotions that were bubbling up inside me. What did I want—especially as a physician caring for hospitalized patients? Of course, I wanted to help cure them and alleviate their physical suffering. But I wanted much more than that.

I wanted to be profoundly curious about what their bodies and souls needed. I wanted to partner with them and ask thought-provoking questions. In addition, I wanted to create an opportunity for them to become aware of how their thoughts and feelings influence their physiology. I wanted to listen deeply to what was most important to them. I wanted not only to see them but also to hear them. Most of all, I wanted to be a healer who met them at a milestone in their lives and bravely walked beside them and inspired them to take accountability for their own self-care.

Yes, that was exactly what I wanted.

This kind of deep dive into your own desires is important to help you understand yourself and your motivations better. With this knowledge, you'll be able to get more of what you want as you create more effective communication. This is my hope for you. By identifying your values and knowing what you want, you will be ready to navigate your desires and your relationships.

◆ ◆ ◆ ◆ ◆

TALKRx TOOLKIT

Get What You Want Tool

To figure out your desires, ask yourself the following questions:

1. What is it that I *do* want (not what I *don't* want)?

2. Am I coming from a place of fear or love?

3. Am I focusing on myself or on another? If you are focusing on yourself, then continue to question 4. If not, answer the following:

    • What am I trying to achieve?

    • What am I trying to protect myself from?

    • What am I trying to change so I can be more comfortable, happy, peaceful (or whatever your desire is)?

    • Assuming the other person's behavior or circumstance remains the same, what do I want for myself in this situation?

4. If I get what I want, how will I feel?

5. If I get what I want, what will it give me?

Your 1-Five Moment

- To continue your journey from selfish to self-full, complete the exercises and questions in Chapter 16 of your *TalkRx Journal* (DoctorNehaTalkRx.com).

- Share your experience of turning a *don't* want into a *do* want with the TalkRx Community.

CHAPTER 17

20/20 VISION

There's a reason your best friend is your best friend. I'd venture to guess it's because in that person's presence, you feel heard and valued.

Everyone wants to feel loved and appreciated. When I'm talking to an individual, I ask, "What makes you feel most appreciated by your partner?" In the corporate world, I ask this same question a different way. I ask, "Is it important for you to feel recognized by your peers or by your leaders?" Yet when those very people show up as vulnerable patients trembling in paper-thin gowns, all pretenses are stripped away. It no longer matters if they are high-powered CEOs from Silicon Valley or stay-at-home moms; they speak of what matters most. It comes down to one word: *love*—specifically, how well they love and whether they feel loved in return.

What Matters Most to You

While we all want to feel loved and appreciated, each of us also has unique personal values that fuel our desires. What we value is often based on our family of origin, our education, our culture, our experiences, and our environment. As we grow up and gain independence, these values evolve. They become more clear as we begin to notice what brings us joy or pain. If we experience joy, it fuels us and we want more of it. If we experience pain, we develop clarity about what we don't want. We learn to adjust our desires accordingly.

Being able to identify these personal values is extremely important in communication in order to get what you want. Though values can be challenging to recognize initially, we can look at them similarly to how we looked at emotions: they can often be simplified into one word (okay, maybe two). Values are what you regard highly. What you value is worth your time, energy, and money.

Sometimes, it takes losing something important in order to recognize that you value it. Once my patients were admitted to the hospital, they would have given anything for flannel pajamas, a hot shower, and a home-cooked meal. It didn't take long for them to gain 20/20 vision on what was truly important: health, comfort, and nourishment.

Not many people can name their top five values. Just as with emotions, in order to communicate effectively, you'll need to expand your values vocabulary. Here's a partial list of common values. (Feel free to add your own.)

Values Vocabulary List

Ability	Beauty	Control
Abundance	Belonging	Cooperation
Acceptance	Caring	Cost-Consciousness
Accountability	Challenge	Courage
Achievement	Change/Variety	Creativity
Advancement	Collaboration	Decisiveness
Adventure	Command	Dedication
Aesthetics	Commitment	Democracy
Analysis	Communication	Determination
Appearance	Community	Diplomacy
Appreciation	Competence	Discipline
Authenticity	Competition	Diversity
Authority	Connection	Effectiveness
Autonomy	Continuous Improvement	Efficiency
Awareness	Contribution	Effort

Empowerment	Involvement	Risk-Taking
Ethics	Joy	Safety
Excellence	Justice	Satisfaction
Excitement	Knowledge	Security
Expertise	Leadership	Self-Acceptance
Fairness	Learning	Self-Control
Faith	Logic	Self-Respect
Fame	Love	Sensitivity
Family	Loyalty	Serenity
Forgiveness	Meaningful Work	Service
Friendship	Nature	Sophistication
Happiness	Objectivity	Spirit
Harmony	Openness	Spirituality
Health	Order/Neatness	Stability
Heart	Ownership	Status
Helping Others	Participation	Strategy
Honesty	Passion	Support
Honor	Peace	Tolerance
Independence	Performance	Tradition
Individualism	Perseverance	Trust
Influence	Personal Development	Truth
Innovation	Physical Challenge	Urgency
Integration	Play	Vision
Integrity	Reputation	Wealth
Intellectual Exchange	Respect	Wisdom
Intelligence	Responsibility	
Intimacy	Responsiveness	

Let's take this one step further. Just as with emotions, there are multiple words that can describe the same value. For example, I value honesty, wit, and generosity in others. Two additional ways I could describe each of these would be:

- Honesty
  - Truth
  - Integrity

- Wit
  - Humor
  - Play

- Generosity
  - Kindness
  - Compassion

And again, like emotions, multiple values can fuel a single desire. For example, suppose you want a promotion at work. More than one value could be motivating this desire. When you want something, it indicates that it will give you something meaningful—even though you may not even be consciously aware of what that is. Once you realize the value(s) that you're really after, that's when you start to gain clarity on what's motivating you. Let's break it down.

What do you desire?
I want to be promoted.

What will a promotion give you?
Prestige, money, and a title.

What's important about those results?

- Acknowledgment for how hard I work. (Potential underlying values: recognition, appreciation, respect)

- I'll have more power in decision-making. (Potential underlying values: influence, control)

- I won't worry about money. (Potential underlying values: freedom, financial security, comfort)

So, what would you say if I asked you to name your top values? No worries if you're a little stumped. A quick and easy way to get started is to bring to mind a close friend and name three qualities that you admire about him or her. You don't have to admire everything about this person, you just need to identify a few qualities you appreciate.

The characteristics of the friend you admire may seem to be about the other person—and they are. But the reason you admire those qualities is because they reflect what *you* hold dear. These are some of your highest values as well.

Now turn the focus back toward yourself and read through the Values Vocabulary List (pages 216–217). Notice what stands out as most important. Also, pay attention to where you spend your time, energy, and money. These clues will help you determine what it is that you value.

Some of my highest values include love, integrity, and service. Of course, many other values fit underneath each of these for me. Under love is strong relationships, honest communication, and courage. Under integrity is accountability, fairness, and loyalty. Service encompasses spirituality, kindness, and collaboration.

You may or may not be able to identify your top values right off the bat. Be patient and they will soon reveal themselves. Like me, you may find it easier to recognize values in others than to recognize them in yourself.

UNEXPECTED VALUES

As you decipher your values, you'll probably notice that some are harder to identify because you have strong judgments about them. I had this problem with the value of beauty. The story in my head was that if someone valued beauty, it meant they were superficial and externally focused. I noticed myself reacting strongly when someone else mentioned the importance of beauty, so I decided to explore what was triggering in me. I challenged myself to find as many forms of beauty as I could. What a shift in perspective! I began to see the beauty of the lemon tree on my front porch, the trees in Golden Gate Park, and the gentle, kind smile of the woman delivering my mail. Even my patients who hadn't showered in days and had been vomiting all night had inner beauty. It was everywhere. Then I realized how photos, images, and unique color combinations in fashion and design inspired my inner author. Most obviously, I realized that I invested a significant amount of time and money shopping for and taking care of my external self—all the while deeming it unimportant. I had to laugh at myself. Beauty was definitely high on my list. I just needed to shed my judgments about what I thought it meant about me.

The second value I resisted was play. I was raised to work hard, and I used it as a badge of honor. What would it mean about me if I valued play? Well, I had thought it would mean I was lazy or a slacker. So I got curious about the stories in my head. The truth was, my older sister, Ritu, makes no excuses about valuing play. She embraces her creativity and loves being social. Her playfulness has made our family holidays so much fun. She's the one who makes me laugh—and I mean belly laugh until it hurts. And curiously, I began to notice most of the men I had dated were witty and playful. I *love* being silly.

So if you notice some resistance toward certain values, pay close attention! There's hidden gold there. Then get curious and begin noticing how those values show up around you.

The Two-Step Decision-Making Tool

You have to know yourself to navigate this complex world. Values drive all communication, whether you're aware of them or not. But now that you've identified what's most important to you, you have what you need to make decisions that are in your best interest. With every decision that comes your way—especially the big ones—simply ask yourself these two questions:

1. Does this request, opportunity, or idea support my highest values? You've already identified these, so check to see if the incoming request aligns with them.

2. Do I want to do this? In other words, am I making this decision from a place of inspiration (energy-giving) or from a place of obligation (energy-draining)?

If you're unsure, spend a few days paying attention to:

- What people, interactions, tasks, and conversations *give* you energy.

- What people, interactions, tasks, and conversations *drain* you of energy.

Also note the signals coming from your body and pay attention to your thoughts.

When I feel passionate and inspired, my body often feels relaxed and open. When I'm inspired and receiving energy from an experience, I feel a wave of energy moving through me. I notice my thoughts are expansive and include words and phrases such as "I want to" or "I'm excited to . . ."

My body's physical signals and thoughts send me very different messages when I'm acting out of obligation. Physically, I experience throat constriction, muscle tightening, and jaw clenching. My body literally contracts to protect me—and then I feel drained of energy. I also hear myself using words and phrases such as "have to" or "should." That usually indicates I'm coming from an energy-draining place.

Here's how to translate your answers into a decision:

- **Say yes:** If an opportunity or request lines up with your values while also fueling you with energy, then it's a go! Say yes, and move confidently in the direction of your desires.

- **Say no:** If a request or opportunity does not align with your highest values, then you say thanks for the opportunity and politely decline.

- **Say maybe so:** If you say yes to question 1 (a request aligns with your highest values) but no to question

2 (it feels like an obligation), what do you do then? It requires a little more thought. Generally, it is okay to move forward with committing your time, energy, and money to an obligation as long as you are aware of the values it supports.

I'm not saying that everything you do has to be inspiring, but what I've noticed is how often people make decisions out of obligations that don't line up with their values. This leads to the paradox of being really busy while feeling disconnected and disengaged.

I keep track of what energizes or drains me, so it's easier to recognize where I'm taking action out of obligation versus acting out of inspiration. This process wakes me up to my current desires. Go ahead and try this new way to make decisions, and see how much simpler it is.

> To see how I use these steps, go to the video "Two-Step Decision Making Tool" at DoctorNehaTalkRx.com.

WHY 20/20 VISION MATTERS

Knowing how to articulate what you want and what you value is a huge advantage in communication—actually, it's a prerequisite to getting what you want.

Think about it. You make dozens of decisions every day. Decisions can range from simple (what to wear in the morning or what to eat) to complex (whether you've outgrown a relationship or a job). You probably feel confident about certain areas of your life. And at other times, you feel stuck in uncertainty. You may find yourself saying yes when you really mean no, missing key opportunities because you couldn't make up your mind, or staying in a relationship long after its expiration date. When you're stuck in situations like these, it's because you aren't clear about what you value, or you've made decisions more heavily weighted toward what someone else values. Knowing what you value and letting it guide you is the foundation for true connection and happiness in your life.

◆◆◆◆◆

TalkRx Toolkit

Notice your body, thoughts, and emotions that arise as you read the Values Vocabulary List in this chapter, paying attention to what's most important and taking note of any values you are resisting.

Value Discovery Tool

1. Bring to mind a close friend or public figure you admire.

2. Identify three qualities that you appreciate about him or her.

3. Describe how these qualities show what's important to you.

Two-Step Decision-Making Tool

Ask yourself:

1. Does a request, opportunity, or idea support my highest values?

2. Am I making this decision out of inspiration or obligation?

The answer:

- Yes—if it aligns with my values and inspires me.

- No—if it doesn't align with my values (even if I want to do it).

- Maybe So—if it aligns with my values, but feels like an obligation (pay close attention to how many decisions fall in this category).

TalkRx Video: To see how I use these steps, go to the "Two-Step Decision Making Tool" at DoctorNehaTalkRx.com.

YOUR I-FIVE MOMENT

- To get clear on what matters most to you, complete the exercises and questions in Chapter 17 of your *TalkRx Journal* (DoctorNehaTalkRx.com).

- Inquiring minds want to know—share your top three values with the TalkRx Community.

CHAPTER 18

LOVE AND GRATITUDE

How can we long for something and still not be able to receive it? My patient Mary was a classic example. It was obvious that she valued family. And, like most of us, she also valued love. But her inability to express that need to her mother left her frustrated and disconnected—in the very relationship where she desired love most. Mary made the common mistake of assuming her mother should have been able to read her mind.

You can know you want something but still not know how to effectively communicate that need to others. There are many avenues to receiving what you desire, yet even when people have the best of intentions, signals can get crossed. Once you align your body, thoughts, and emotions, you will have a much better chance of getting what you want.

THE DANCE OF OUR HEARTS

In *The 5 Love Languages*, Dr. Gary Chapman discusses the key to feeling appreciated, which is knowing how you receive love and letting others in on that secret. This means you have to tell others what you desire most and how you best receive it. And yes, I mean out loud.

Here's the rundown of Dr. Chapman's five love languages:[24]

1. **Words of affirmation:** Acknowledgment through spoken words or in writing, such as an e-mail or old-fashioned card.

2. **Quality time:** Shared experiences and making time for each other

3. **Gifts:** Items having monetary value, such as jewelry, or sentimental value, like a drawing from a child or fresh-picked wildflowers

4. **Acts of service:** Kind deeds, such as making meals, fixing the car, or cleaning the house

5. **Physical touch:** Holding hands, a gentle touch, a hug

It's important to identify how you feel most loved, appreciated, or valued and to understand that love and appreciation can be given and received in many ways. If you aren't sure where to begin, just go through the following steps:

1. Reflect on a time when you were deeply touched by someone else's gesture. How did that person give to you? What made his or her action feel special? This will help you figure out which aspects of caring mean most to you.

2. Acknowledge how other people in your life have been showing their love and appreciation to you.

3. Thank them.

4. If another way would work even better for you, muster the courage to tell them what it is.

5. Give to others in the way they receive. If you're unsure about the way another person best receives, pay attention to how they give to others and listen for what they value. (Or you can always make it easy on yourself and just ask!)

For example, suppose words of affirmation and quality time mean a lot to you. So when someone joins you for dinner and tells you how much they've missed you and how great it is to see you, you could reinforce that person's actions by saying, "I love spending time together and how expressive you are." And remember, this doesn't apply just to romantic relationships; it applies to all relationships.

Now be careful: If you have ever felt rejected, dismissed, or insecure, you may form stories in your head that it's unsafe or risky to open yourself to love and appreciation from others. In that case, even if someone gives you love in the form that you receive best, you may unknowingly block it. In fact, you may have a move that would work better on a football field than in a relationship. I refer to this move as a defensive lineman strategy. While blocking is valuable as a defense mechanism in sports against members of the opposing team, that same move will leave you disconnected and alone. Let me explain.

My love languages are words of affirmation and physical touch. Suppose I'm in a social setting and someone greets me with a hug and says, "Neha, I love that soft pink scarf. It's a great color on you!"

Although I take pride in my fashion sense, I may have stories in my head about what it means to accept a compliment. If I think it's arrogant or boastful, I may worry about what others will think of my response. Or suppose I worry that others will be upset or jealous if they hear the compliment and don't get one themselves. So, even if a person gives to me in the way I receive best, I may wave my hand dismissively and respond with, "Oh, this old thing? I got it on sale for ten bucks."

Big mistake! This creates two issues: It doesn't allow the person who has noticed my scarf to share her appreciation and connect with me. And it blocks me from getting what I desire most: to be connected to someone else. It's a double whammy!

Another common way to block what you want most is when someone says something kind to you, you proceed to tell them why it actually isn't true. For example:

"Neha, I love the way you led the workshop today. Thanks for doing such a great job."

"Oh, it wasn't me, it was you. We did it together."

"No, really, I appreciated the way you calmly handled that gentleman who got angry and how you addressed the discomfort in the group. And by the way—love your slides!"

"Listen, anybody could have done what I did. You would have, too. And about the slides, it's not me. I have this great graphic designer; she did it all. I can give you her contact information, and she can do your slides."

What a love and appreciation disaster! Even if my love language is words of affirmation, I can easily sabotage myself in relationships by feeling tension in my body, making up stories, feeling uncomfortable, and then blocking what I desire most.

When another person expresses love and appreciation, in order to make sure you're not blocking it, follow these simple steps:

1. Notice your physical sensations, thoughts, and emotions in response to the gesture.
2. Take a soft belly breath (or three).
3. Say, "Thank you."
4. Identify which love language this person is using.
5. Recognize and take in the gesture as an expression of love.

An Attitude of Gratitude

The simple act of both giving and receiving appreciation can create more space for what you want. The key to eliminating the defensive lineman strategy comes down to awareness and choosing your attitude. Your perspective makes all the difference. By shifting toward gratitude, you'll be able to find your way back to what matters most.

Just like your breath, gratitude is one of the most abundant, low-cost, effective ways to shift your internal state of being and your emotions so you can get what you truly want. Reflecting on a list of what you're grateful for will undoubtedly shift the focus from what you *don't* have to what you *do* have. Remember how Mary's experience changed when she refocused her attention from what her mother never gave her to the wonderful family she had created?

The twist is that the power of gratitude comes from inviting it in at the precise moment when it seems counterintuitive. It's one thing to feel thankful when there's money in the bank, you're celebrating your wedding, or you've just lost that last 15 pounds. But how do you feel when your bank account is overdrawn, your partner just left, or you've just received a devastating diagnosis?

Gratitude deserves a permanent seat at the table with your family of emotions—because it leads you back to your heart and what's most important.

Setting an intention of gratitude takes practice. A few years ago, each night I began writing three items, people, or experiences I was grateful for in my journal. I spent my days looking for the events, activities, people, and conversations I appreciated. I began looking forward to this sacred time each night. What surprised me was that I began dreaming about what I had written in my journal. I began to feel happier and more joyful just by expanding my perspective and recognizing the gifts in my life.

So when I encountered a cute little six-year-old struggling with conflicting desires, I remembered an exercise from my Mind-Body Medicine training and knew just the remedy!

THE GRATITUDE DANCE

While in transition between apartments, a friend and her daughter stayed with me for a few weeks to make it easier on their morning commute and weekend parent handoffs. The daughter, Shannon, was a typical six-year-old who loved sparkles, dresses, and anything related to magic and princesses. Over dinner each night, she would imitate her favorite characters, gab about first-grade drama, and school me on her latest accessories.

One evening, as she and her mom walked through the door, I innocently inquired, "How was your day?"

Her mother replied, "Shannon, why don't you tell Dr. Neha what's wrong? Mommy has a headache, and she's going to lie down."

Shannon shyly came over to where I was sitting on the couch. I could see the swelling, redness, and irritation of her eyes from what must have been an emotional struggle.

"What happened, princess?" I asked.

She said, "You guess."

"I have no idea," I said in a surprised tone. "Where were you just now?"

"Playing at my friend Suzie's house," she said as she looked down and away.

"Okay. My guess is that you wanted something of Suzie's and you couldn't have it, or you didn't want to leave and your mom made you."

She looked at me in utter disbelief. "How did you know?" she asked.

"Just a lucky guess. So, what's the problem?"

"I want everything Suzie has. I want her bed, her dolls, her toys . . . and I want her house, too!"

"Oh," I said. "It sounds like you want everything Suzie has instead of what you have."

"No!" she clarified. "I want everything I have—and I want everything Suzie has!"

Wow, I thought. You're clear about what you want. "It sounds to me like you're feeling yucky because you want Suzie's toys and you wish you lived in her home. Is that true?"

She nodded as big tears ran down both cheeks.

"Where does it feel yucky in your body?" I asked.

"Right here," she said as she pointed to the front of her chest and circled up to her neck and her jaw. "It feels like a bucket of snakes inside there. It's black and creepy. I just want it to go away."

"That sounds awful. What you're feeling is called envy. It's when you feel yucky when you want something that someone else has. Hmmm, I have an idea. Let's draw what it feels like inside you."

I pulled out a blank sheet of white paper and some crayons. After she drew a black ball in the center with a rainbow of colors surrounding it, she began to articulate what was really underlying her jealousy. She wished that her parents were still married, that she had siblings like Suzie, and that she could decorate and play make-believe in a room that was her very own. She sometimes felt lonely because she was often with adults and had to travel between houses. I told her I would help her express herself to her mom when she was ready.

"I have another idea to help you feel better right now. You want to try something?" I asked.

"Sure," she said.

We both stood up, and I turned on music that had a strong beat. "Follow me," I said as I began shaking my wrists. "Act like you're a rag doll—as if you have no bones. Now add in your elbows and your shoulders and let them make circles and other shapes in the air. Let your jaw hang loose, and let out any noise that's inside you."

"Uhhhhhhhhhhhhh," she moaned as her jaw hung open.

"Good job, Shannon. Keep going. Shake it up. Now add your hips, your legs and knees. Shake that envy right out of your body. Shake and dance!"

In a few minutes, the music ended and I continued. "Stand still and feel your body now. What do you feel?"

"Tingling in my chest and all the way to my fingers and toes!" she exclaimed.

"What happened to the yuck in your neck and chest?"

"It went away."[25]

"Good job. Now let's put on your favorite song and do a gratitude dance and fill your body back up with all that you're grateful for, okay?"

"Okay. I'm grateful for my mommy," she said, as she twirled around with her arms straight out, "and my daddy."

"Perfect. I'm grateful to have you as my dance partner."

"My turn!" she exclaimed. "I'm grateful for toys because some kids don't have them." She began to giggle.

"Shannon, do you know what we did just now?"

"We got all the yucky stuff out."

"Yep. We shook all the envy out of you and then we filled you back up with everything that makes you grateful!"

And just like that, she was on her way. I realized that while it worked with a six-year-old girl, it worked for me, too. I felt so much better myself. I started referring to this practice as the Gratitude Dance.

Dancing Your Way to Health and Happiness

The Gratitude Dance works for adults, too, because, remember, it's all connected. When you experience uncomfortable emotions, you can release energy-in-motion by moving your body.

––––––––––◆◆◆––––––––––

If you're up for trying the Gratitude Dance,* begin by finding a song with a steady beat. It's important to move your body in ways it normally doesn't move and not worry about doing it "right." No pressure. This is not dancing, really; it's shaking. Begin with your wrists, then progress to your elbows, shoulders, head, hips, and finally knees and ankles. When the song finishes, check in with your body and feel the difference. Pay attention to see if the tension or uneasiness in your body has shifted. If so, can you feel that it has left your body? (If not, no worries; you may need more physical movement to help you shake it out of your muscle memory. Just hit repeat.)

If your body has loosened up, put on some of your favorite inspirational music and let the music move you. Fill your mind and heart with all that you're grateful for. When you shift your thinking to gratitude, you have the power to change how you feel.

––––––

*Always first check with your health professional to make sure you can engage in this type of activity. If you have any pain or discomfort, stop immediately.

––––––––––◆◆◆––––––––––

What if you find yourself needing the Gratitude Dance over and over for the same concern? You may not be allowing yourself to address the underlying issues that are driving your discomfort.

In the short term, the dance shifts sensations in your body, allowing you to better deal with uncomfortable emotions that could be a result of unmet desires. To gain a deeper understanding of what's actually happening, you may want to work with a coach, a therapist, or another qualified professional.

Grounding your body is one way to make room for gratitude, but there are other avenues to open your heart to gratefulness and expand your perspective. You may find that being in service to others, prayer, meditation, or being in nature can also bring you back to your heart. It's important to find the experience that resonates most.

Gratitude highlights what is most important to you. Cultivating an attitude of gratitude changes your perspective and reconnects you to yourself as well as to others.

Expressions of love and gratitude are among the most powerful tools to build relationships and create a sense of feeling valued and appreciated.

The Beatles had it right when they called their hit song "All You Need Is Love." (And gratitude.)

◆ ◆ ◆ ◆ ◆

TALKRX TOOLKIT

Gary Chapman's Five Love Languages

1. Words of Affirmation
2. Quality Time
3. Gifts
4. Acts of Service
5. Physical Touch

Letting Love In Tool

1. Notice your physical sensations, thoughts, and emotions in response to the gesture.

2. Take a soft belly breath (or three).

3. Say, "Thank you."

4. Identify which love language this person is using.

5. Take in the gesture as an expression of love.

Gratitude Practices

1. Verbal expression (in person, phone calls, voice mail)

2. Written expression (cards, e-mails, tweets, emoticons)

3. Affirmation (reframing your thoughts)

4. Gratitude Journal (write three items, people, or experiences you're grateful for each night)

5. The Gratitude Dance

   • Find a song with a steady beat.

   • Move and shake your body for three minutes to release any stuck emotions.

   • When the music stops, check in with your body and notice any shifts.

   • Play an inspirational song next.

   • Allow yourself to move freely, and fill your mind and heart with all the reasons you're grateful.

YOUR 1-FIVE MOMENT

   • To get crystal clear on how you give and receive love, complete the exercises and questions in Chapter 18 of your *TalkRx Journal* (DoctorNeha TalkRx.com).

   • Share your favorite gratitude practices with the TalkRx Community.

CHAPTER 19

FINDING COMMON GROUND

Once you have 20/20 vision about your own values, you can expand your focus to include what matters to others. Just like you, most people want to feel loved and appreciated and they have their own sets of values.

One of my favorite lessons about getting what I want came through an exchange I had with Prince Abdul Aziz when I was in Saudi Arabia for the King of Organs Medical Conference. It was the last day of my trip, and our conversation shifted to our cultural differences.

The prince inquired, "Now that you have had a chance to spend time in Saudi Arabia, what have you learned from the media about our culture that you find to be true? And what have you learned from the media that you find not to be true?"

After a few seconds of contemplation, I answered, "Well, the separation of men and women at the conference and in society as a whole seems to be true.

"What I find not to be true are the warnings that as a woman, I wouldn't be safe and I'd be treated like a second-class citizen. This has not been the case. Everyone has treated me with honor and respect.

"Also, I didn't realize that some Middle Eastern women like wearing their burkas and abayas. Some of them told me they enjoy the anonymity and privacy they feel in public. They described feeling like protected precious jewels. I definitely didn't expect to hear that."

Our curiosity about each other's perspectives had surfaced, in combination with the courage to ask the real questions. I noticed that in the middle of the desert, insulated by the sand and sky, I felt connected in our common humanity, and my brave heart took over.

"Okay, it's my turn," I blurted. "I've broken rules that your moral police could send a woman to jail for: I don't typically cover myself from head to toe, I'm 38 years old and unmarried, I've shown affection toward men through handshakes and hugs. Despite these differences, why is it that you treat me with such honor and respect?"

He paused for a moment and said, "Okay, I cheated."

"What does that mean?" I asked.

"Well," he began, "when I found out you were going to speak in place of Dr. Gordon at the conference, I didn't know what to expect. We were unsure about your intentions in coming. So I asked someone to go to the airport and then report back. When I received word that you got off the plane dressed all in black with a scarf covering your head, I knew that you had come here with the intention to honor our culture. In that moment, I knew my job was not to make you a part of our culture; it was to honor the culture from which you come."

Something profoundly changed in me that day. With the act of placing a scarf over my head and being mindful of the Saudi culture, I had earned his respect. It seems that many times it's easier to demand the respect of another and try to make them more like us. And yet, I learned that in order to get what I want—I had to first give it away.

Watch a video showing how a client discovers "The Secret to Getting What You Want" at DoctorNehaTalkRx.com.

WHY THEIR VALUES MATTER

Ultimately, the goal of the i-Five Conversation is to help you easily navigate interactions with others. Since any conversation includes at least two parties, a successful outcome requires collaboration. So being able to understand another person's values is essential to:

- Building strong relationships
- Finding common ground in conflict
- Saving you time, energy, and needless stress

When you listen for others' values, you have a better chance to create a synergistic outcome that meets the desires of both of you. Listening deeply to another and paying attention to how that person feels loved and valued will build a bridge of connection. Sometimes, in dialogue, it's easier to recognize what divides us. But that only leads to disconnection and loneliness. The techniques in this chapter will show you how to get to a place of understanding, compassion, and openness in everyday conversations and even when interactions get off-track.

LOST IN TRANSLATION

You can dance alone, but the art of dancing with another takes communication to the next level. Partnership requires tuning in to your own values and desires while simultaneously paying attention to someone else's. Of course, it's easy to make assumptions that others understand our perspective or have the same priorities. So despite the best of intentions, we can find ourselves out of step and wondering how our message got lost in translation.

This was happening in my own backyard and I didn't even know it—until my parents attended a communication retreat that I was co-leading with my colleague Bev Foster. In December 2011, my family was coming to the West Coast to celebrate my father's 70th birthday. I invited my parents to extend their trip in order to attend our weeklong retreat in Hawaii.

Shortly after inviting them, I found myself up at night worrying about the prospect of leading both of my parents through a communication workshop. What if their communication concerns had to do with their middle daughter—me? What if they asked a question about their marriage? How awkward would that be?

So I decided to ask Bev, who had 40 years of experience leading groups, what she thought of my parents' joining us. She said, "I've taught both of your parents, and they're genuinely interested in their own growth and learning. If they're okay with it, I am, too. And if it gets to be too much, trust yourself. You can always defer to me." That was all I needed to hear.

For the most part during the workshops, my parents followed the guidelines for participants and stayed focused on their own learning. Of course there were moments when I had to steer them back to their part in a situation, but that was natural and I expected it. Then we began talking about the fundamental human need to be acknowledged and heard. And that's when things began to heat up.

I told the group, "Now I'd like you to journal about two experiences in your life when you felt most valued and heard."

After a few minutes, my mom raised her hand and blurted, "What if your husband never tells you he loves you and never spends time with you? It's really hard to feel loved and appreciated in a relationship with someone who works all the time. He's never home. And when he is, he's busy with other projects."

Just as I was about to answer, my father interrupted with an irritated tone. "What do you mean? That's not true. I've woken you up with chai every morning for forty years. I vacuum. I clean the dishes. I take care of the cars and the house. I spend a lot of time at home!"

By now, my mother's arms were crossed and my father was looking away.

I glanced at Bev and said, "I'm going to take this one, and if I get in trouble, you're on standby, okay?" She just smiled and nodded.

"Thank you both for your honesty," I said as I glanced first at my mom and then at my dad. "I can see how important being appreciated, being acknowledged, and feeling heard is to each of you. This is exactly what I was talking about earlier.

"Mom, let's start with you first. What I hear is that you value hearing Dad say, 'I love you' out loud. And that you want more quality time with him, but he has other projects that keep him occupied. Is that true?"

"Doesn't everybody want that?" she asked. "And by the way, the words don't always have to be said out loud. Every once in a while a card would be nice, too."

"Wow, I hear how frustrated you are, and that you may have said this in the past and not felt heard. It sounds like you feel appreciated when people express their love through words and when they spend quality time with you."

"Yes, this isn't the first time I've mentioned it. And yes, I've always enjoyed writing letters and reading. Come to think of it, that's how my best friend and I communicated for many years. We also spent summers together when I was in India."

"Now, Mom, let me talk through what Dad said and then I'll come back and help you understand why it feels so hard. Okay?"

She nodded.

I then turned toward my dad. "I hear how hard you work. I also hear that when you do housework and make chai in the morning, these are much more than chores to you. They are, in fact, acts of love. Is that true?"

"Absolutely, beti. This is an unfair comment by your mother because I have always worked very hard, both at work and at home, to show my love. I'm not good at poems or saying, 'I love you.' It's just not how I was raised."

"I hear you, Dad. One way you have been in service is by providing for the family, cleaning the house, and maintaining the cars. Speaking from personal experience, one way I feel loved and appreciated is through your affection. I love your hugs."

His shoulders relaxed, and a gentle smile came to his face.

"So here's the deal. You're both right, and the problem is you're just not speaking each other's love languages."

My parents had been married for nearly half a century. In the workshop, it became clear that the way they were conveying their appreciation to one another was not matching the way the other person received love. It was like they were ships passing in the night. They both wanted to feel valued, yet they were unaware that how they communicated mattered on the receiving end. All it took was awareness and curiosity about their love languages combined with the ability to listen deeply in order to turn this around.

When you're feeling challenged in a relationship, it's important to identify the ways someone else is already showing love and appreciation—even if it's different from how you receive it. This acknowledges the other person's efforts and creates common ground. Then you can share with him or her your favorite love languages. Make sure you do more than hint; tell the other person out loud. While it may seem awkward initially, you'll give the other person key information that will strengthen your relationship.

◆ ◆ ◆ ◆ ◆

TalkRx Toolkit

The Secret

If you want something, first give it away.

Deciphering the Language of Love

To give and receive appreciation:

1. Identify two ways in which you feel most appreciated. (Let the people close to you know what they are.)

2. Notice the ways in which other people give love.

3. Give to others in the way they receive—not the way you do!

TalkRx Video: Watch how a client discovers "The Secret to Getting What You Want" at DoctorNehaTalkRx.com.

YOUR I-FIVE MOMENT

- To get clear on what matters most to you, complete the exercises and questions in Chapter 19 of your *TalkRx Journal* (DoctorNehaTalkRx.com).
- Share any insights, discoveries, or questions that occurred as you read the chapter with the TalkRx Community.

CHAPTER 20

THE
COMMUNICATION
TANGO

Do you like to dance? I hope so, because there's a dance you've been doing your whole life. I call it the Communication Tango. Who knew that when toes got stepped on and elephants entered the room, it was all part of the choreography? If you learn the communication rules, rehearse the steps, and pick the right partners, you'll be dancing your way toward health and happiness.

Every chapter you've read so far has been providing the steps for the Communication Tango. Now that you've been practicing new ways to interpret your body, thoughts, emotions, and desires, you're ready to learn even more about the fifth and final level of listening.

LEVEL 5: OPEN LISTENING

When you tune in to not only the words and emotions, but also to what someone values, you set the stage for meaningful connection. When you are able to hear why something is important to the person speaking, you're listening at level 5. Just as you can pick up underlying emotions by noticing the tone and body language someone uses to express his or her thoughts, you can pick up underlying values by paying attention to what someone wants and getting curious.

The big question is, how do you do that?

The best way to do this is to become familiar with the Values Vocabulary List on pages 216–217. With your expanded awareness, you'll hear not only what other people are saying and how they're saying it, but also the underlying values that are motivating their desires. So let's look at some examples:

Comment: "I love it when Cinderella finally gets her Prince Charming!"
Possible values: romance, love, and fairytale endings

Comment: "My goal is to be CEO by the time I'm 50."
Possible values: success, leadership, influence, and power

Comment: "I want to travel the world."
Possible values: adventure, exploration, and cultural diversity

Comment: "I love volunteering at orphanages. I want to adopt one of those cuties someday."
Possible values: family, service, and hope

So rehearse listening for and stating values in day-to-day conversations, and pay attention to how others respond. Just as with emotions, you don't have to be exactly right in naming values. People will correct you and then clarify what is motivating their desires. What matters is that you're listening on a deep level. The other person will likely feel heard and valued. Once you're confident using Open Listening (level 5) in everyday conversations, you'll be able to use it to bridge to another in conflict.

For example, you ask your brother to take a trip with you and he says, "I can't be that far away from my wife and kids. Not to mention, you always stay in five-star hotels when you travel." One option is to convince your brother that his wife won't care, or to defend your spending habits. If you choose Open Listening instead, you might respond, "I hear that you want to be near your kids and that you value saving money."

Your brother may reply, "Yeah, I miss the days when we could go on adventures together. It's just that it's a tough time financially right now, with two toddlers."

Practicing Open Listening with someone else will help you start developing the skills to identify values, but you can also practice this solo. If you're on your own, recall a peak experience, milestone, or fond memory and write a description of the experience. Then, once you're done, read what you've written with the Values Vocabulary List in front of you, and choose three values that underlie your story.

Ask a friend to tell you about a meaningful experience in his or her life. Set a timer for three minutes (that's not a long time—although it may seem like it). Have your Values Vocabulary List next to you to refer to. As you focus your attention on the other person, let her speak. Your job is to listen deeply in silence. (No interrupting, no clarifying questions, and no "uh-huh's" or "hmm's" allowed. Just pure, uninterrupted, level 5 listening.) When the timer goes off, use the Values Vocabulary List to tell the other person what you heard that she values. Make sure to get curious about whether what you said resonates with her, and whether there were other values she expressed that you didn't mention.

Then switch. This exercise can also be useful to help you identify your own values.

WHAT'S NOT BEING SAID

The key to picking up on what another person values requires that you also pay attention to what is *not* being said: not only moments of silence, but changes in tone and body language as well. These subtle messages often occur when someone has a reaction in the middle of a conversation. For example, someone suddenly becomes quiet, holds back on a response, or shifts from being engaged to crossing her arms and mentally checking out of the conversation—or she physically gets up and leaves. Because it can be confusing and tricky to navigate, often people ignore these dynamic changes or pretend they didn't happen and find themselves out of sync with others.

Remember learning about the Curiosity Tool in Chapter 1:

External data + curiosity = clarity

State what you observed and get curious. It could sound something like this:

- "After I asked about going to Mexico, you got quiet. What happened?"
- "When Dad said we needed to take separate cars, I saw you get up and leave the room. Is everything okay?"

Remember that every interaction is co-created. Even though I've been doing this for years, I don't always get it right. What makes that okay is that I name what I observe and get curious. So don't worry so much about perfection, as long as you have genuine curiosity in your back pocket.

RULES OF THE DANCE

Now that you know what you value, and you know that listening to and working with the values of another will help create authentic connection and strong relationships, here are a few simple rules that will ensure your success and help you avoid common missteps in the Communication Tango.

Rule 1: Determine your desires.

Knowing what you want and what's motivating you (what you value) before you engage in a conversation is as important as knowing what kind of dance you want to do before you step out on the dance floor.

Watch the video "Is Love Taking You for a Ride?" to see how critical it is to understand your desires and values before you can effectively engage in partnership with someone else (DoctorNehaTalkRx.com).

Rule 2: Choose your internal state of being.

It's important to set the stage by choosing an attitude that honors your values. You get to choose whether you come to a conversation with honesty, clarity, and openness or with an attitude of anger, blame, and resentment. What are the qualities that will help create the outcome you hope for? Are you going to show up with courage and self-trust? Do you want to be open and flexible? Do you want to be a good listener? You get to choose your internal state of being, and it's up to you to create the atmosphere in which you would like to interact with someone else.

For example, let's say I want to improve my relationship with my sister, but I realize I've been showing up with defensiveness and impatience each time we speak. I will need to first take ownership for my behavior in our conversations. Suppose, instead of defensiveness, I choose curiosity and love. My body language, tone, and words of love and curiosity will send a message very different from the ones that come from defensiveness.

For any interaction, base your attitude or internal state of being on your highest values. Then you will be set up to move smoothly through the communication dance and be proud of how you did it.

Rule 3: Shift to an "and" mind-set.

This means changing your thinking to expanding thoughts rather than limiting ones. Rather than using the words *but* or *or*, try using *and*. Here's what I mean:

Instead of saying:	Shift to saying:
"We can do this or that."	"We can do this and that."
"We can do this but not that."	"How can we do this and that?"

The *and* mind-set opens the door to new possibilities that allow both people to get what they want and often results in a synergistic and creative outcome. This way of thinking will allow you to enter any interaction with curiosity and a collaborative mind. For example, if your partner wants to play tennis and you want to go for a run, rather than saying, "We can play tennis *or* go for a run," try saying, "We can play tennis at the courts across town *and* jog there and back."

Rule 4: Ask for anything you want.

If you can find the courage, you can *ask* for what you want. If you don't, unspoken expectations often lead to awkwardness, tension, and blame.

Many of us fear that someone might say no or might reject us, so we don't say anything at all. But silence only ensures that we don't get what we're seeking. So if you find yourself repeatedly disappointed (which is often the emotion that accompanies unmet desires), ask yourself whether you have communicated those desires.

Once you're clear about what you want and you've set your intention, then it's essential that you communicate your desires out loud, whether with your best friend, your family, or your boss—and especially in romantic relationships.

You know how this plays out: You hope your significant other has mental telepathy or knows you so well that he or she is already aware of what you want, especially when it comes to celebrations, gifts, and surprises. For some reason, it's easy to think that telling your partner what you want (e.g., "I like pink roses better than yellow ones") makes a gift not as special. My first question when I hear this complaint is "Have you asked for what you want?" People often say, "Well, he definitely overheard me talking about it on the phone with my sister. I gave a huge hint when we passed the flower shop—I said how awesome the flowers smelled."

I just smile and say, "I mean out loud, directly to your partner." I am often met with a look of utter disbelief. "Out loud?

Directly? What a crazy thought. Are you serious? That takes all the fun out of it, and then it doesn't count anymore."

I've got news for you: it still counts.

The reason is that if you speak up, your partner gets the opportunity to make you happy, and you'll have a better chance of getting what you want. So I say, throw your partner a bone!

Of course, just because you ask for something doesn't mean someone else has to give it to you. What do you do then? You may feel disappointed; that's the risk of being open and honest. The bigger risk is withholding what you really want and hoping others figure it out on their own. If you express your desires, you'll know you've been clear and have shown up in a way that lines up with what you value.

Rule 5: Others can ask for anything they want.

It doesn't mean you have to give it to them. Say a friend asks for something and your first reaction is: *That request is outrageous. How dare he ask for that?* Watch out. Don't rush to say yes or no right away. When you get really upset or feel even slightly put off in reaction to a request, it's not because your friend shouldn't have asked; it's because you feel uncomfortable or torn about your response. This is when it's time to hit your pause button, take a few deep breaths, and notice the discomfort in your body. Ask yourself what stories you're making up about the request. What emotions are you experiencing? Then it's time to get curious. Are you hesitating to speak what is true for you?

Instead of saying *yes* when you mean *no* or stuffing your emotions in a suitcase for a rainy day, shift your focus onto the other person so you can listen deeply for the motivation and values driving his request. Just be present in the moment for him. If you need to, ask for time to think through how the request would impact you. This way, whether you agree or politely decline, you have created an opportunity to connect with the person in front of you. Ta-da! Time for a bow. You can't hear me, but I'm applauding.

I have often focused on other people's desires without having a clue as to what I wanted. This resulted in an endless, exhaustive effort to make others happy, while I was left feeling lonely and resentful. As a recovering people-pleaser, the most important lesson I've learned is that I need to know what *I* want first. Then I need to muster the courage to articulate those desires to others in order to build a solid connection between us.

❖ ❖ ❖ ❖

TalkRx Toolkit

Level 5: Open Listening = words + emotions + values

Open Listening Exercise with a Partner

1. Set a timer for three minutes and have your Values Vocabulary List (pages 216–217) open.

2. Ask a friend to tell you about a meaningful experience. (Let that person speak uninterrupted.)

3. Tell him what you heard that he values.

4. Get curious to see if your answers resonate with him.

5. Ask if there were other values he expressed that you didn't mention.

Opening Listening Exercise On Your Own

1. Recall a peak experience, milestone, or fond memory.

2. Write a description of the experience.

3. Reread what you've written with the Values Vocabulary List in front of you.

4. Choose three values that underlie your story.

5. Share your values with someone else.

Rules for the Communication Tango

1. Determine your desires.

2. Set your internal state of being.

3. Shift to an *and* mind-set.

4. Ask for anything you want.

5. Others can ask for anything they want—it doesn't mean you have to give it to them.

TalkRx Video: Watch "Is Love Taking You for a Ride?" to see how critical it is to understand your desires and values before you can effectively engage in partnership with someone else (DoctorNehaTalkRx.com).

YOUR 1-FIVE MOMENT

- To create connection with even the most challenging personalities in your life, complete the exercises and questions in Chapter 20 of your *TalkRx Journal* (DoctorNehaTalkRx.com).

- Promote collaboration with the TalkRx Community by sharing how an *and* mind-set has turned around your *either-or* thinking. We'd also love to know your favorite dance move.

STEP 5

INTEGRATING INTO ACTION

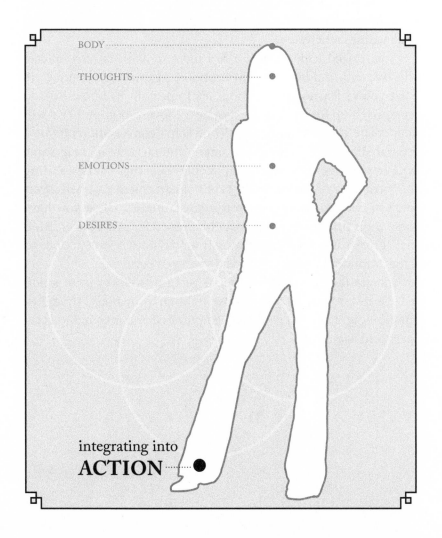

BODY

THOUGHTS

EMOTIONS

DESIRES

integrating into
ACTION

Doesn't it feel good to have 20/20 vision about what's most important to you? It should. That's an important step toward attaining health and happiness. However, even if you notice what's going on in your body, expand your thoughts, experience your emotions, and know what you desire, unless you integrate those four areas of the i-Five Conversation into action, you'll remain in an endless state of longing.

You need the navigation system—your body, thoughts, emotions, and desires—in order to move forward in communication and relationships. Remember, it takes only one person to change the outcome of any conversation, and that person is you—and you're almost there!

You'll need to learn just a few more tools in order to create effective and empowering conversations. As you begin to integrate what you've learned into action, it's important to know how to set yourself up for success. Setting up a conversation properly will help create the best outcome. While some conversations involve general sharing of experiences, many interactions include some type of agreement between the people speaking. Understanding the intricacies of the different types of agreement can help avert some of the most common misunderstandings. Once you have these tools under your belt, you'll be ready for any conversation that comes your way—everything from day-to-day interactions to tense emotional discussions—and yes, even conflict.

Integrating the steps of the i-Five Conversation into action will be rewarding. As you choose to align your body, thoughts, emotions, and desires, you'll feel empowered and inspired to act—again and again.

CHAPTER 21

HE SAID, SHE SAID

Have you ever been flaked on? You know, when you make plans with somebody and they're a no-show? How often have you been frustrated because you thought you had an agreement and the other person didn't have the same understanding?

As you already know, we all walk around with our own set of wants, desires, values, and expectations. It would be a lot easier if we had them posted on our foreheads, but unfortunately we don't. So unless we make agreements with people (and yes, I mean out loud), we can wind up disappointed and surrounded by conflict, even over something as simple as meeting for tea. In three seconds flat, missed expectations, assumptions, and unspoken agreements can undo all that we've done to create clarity and trust in our relationships.

Agreements seem simple once you understand them, but the catch is that almost every challenging relationship scenario has to do with some sort of agreement, whether it's verbalized or not. Agreements that you don't verbalize are unspoken expectations. If you keep your expectations to yourself, it will likely result in disappointment, as you learned in the previous chapter.

THE FIVE LEVELS OF AGREEMENT

We make agreements all the time. I'm not talking about the big agreements—those that are enforced by law—but the everyday ones: informal arrangements, understandings, plans, and negotiations between people about various aspects of life, such as who will pay the check at dinner, who will take out the trash, how long visitors will be staying with you, or the status of a relationship. Informal agreements happen as we make requests and statements as simple as:

- "I'll see you at six."
- "On your way home, will you buy milk?"
- "Can I borrow the car?"
- "Let's split the check."
- "Are we exclusive?"

The problem is that assumptions, competing intentions, and unspoken desires can lead to unmet desires and ultimately conflict. This is where "he said, she said" arguments and disagreements often originate.

While some agreements have a date, place, and time, others are more ambiguous. It's important to examine the level of agreement you think you have versus the one you actually have.

A classic example occurred when I was teaching communication skills to an operating-room (OR) team of more than 100 surgeons, anesthesiologists, nurses, and staff. The morning of our second session, I opened the floor to questions. One of the anesthesiologists, a thin man with dark hair and glasses, stood up and said, "Yeah, I've got a question. How are the communication tools we're learning going to make the staff around here more competent? Because when I ask for something in the OR, it's never there."

I could see eyes popping and faces flushing in the audience. I faced him and said, "I hear your frustration. Can you give me an example of what you're talking about?"

"It's not brain surgery. When I say, 'I need two units of blood, stat!'—you aren't going to believe this—but twenty minutes later there's still no blood in the operating room. That's egregious! In fact, it's totally unacceptable as far as I'm concerned. A patient could die if we don't get the blood in time."

It was a perfectly awkward moment. Without saying a word, everyone began making eye contact with one another and scoping out potential culprits. No doubt, people were silently personalizing, projecting, and blaming. It was what I call a great opportunity. So I asked the anesthesiologist if he would be willing to help me teach the group about agreements.

"Sure," he said, confidently joining me at the front of the room.

"Thank you for asking your question and being brave enough to speak honestly in front of everyone else. So, before we answer your question about why there's a breakdown in communication happening in the OR, it would be helpful to understand a general framework about how agreements are made. Let's start on the simpler end of the spectrum, with something much less emotional, like making an agreement to go to the movies with a friend. Then we can come back to your specific question, which is a bit more complex. Does that work?"

He nodded.

"The way you can help me teach the room about agreements is by asking me the exact same question five times. Will you do that?"

"Sure, that sounds easy enough," he said. "You'll tell me what to ask, right?"

"Yes. Ask me if I'd like to go and see the new James Bond movie. And I'm going to respond differently to that same question five times. After each unique response, you and the audience are going to tell me if we have an agreement. Okay?"

Take 1: "Hey, Neha, do you want to see the new James Bond movie this weekend?" he asked.

"Ooooh, James Bond? I didn't know it was out already," I replied. "Okay, do we have an agreement?"

"Uhhhh, it doesn't sound like it."

"You're right to be skeptical, because all I've done is acknowledge that you spoke. This is a level one agreement—when someone merely acknowledges you."

Take 2: "Hey, Neha, want to see the new James Bond movie this weekend?"

"Sounds like fun. I have been dying to see it ever since we saw the advertisement for it last fall.

"Okay, this time let's ask the audience to help you if you're unsure. Do we have an agreement?"

"I think so, but . . ." he replied as he looked out at his peers who were equally confused, some nodding yes, some shaking their heads no, and others shrugging their shoulders.

"Well, the good news is that you're at a level two agreement. You got more than an acknowledgment; you got feedback that I was interested in seeing the movie. So in a level two agreement, the other person not only acknowledges you but also shows positive interest."

Take 3: "Hey, Neha, do you want to go to the movies this weekend?"

"Sure! As long as I get my house clean and my taxes done, we're on," I responded. "So, do we have an agreement?"

"Definitely yes!" he replied. Everyone in the group was nodding in agreement this time.

"Okay, it looks like you guys got tricked by the *sure*. This is a level three agreement, a qualified yes—or what I refer to as a 'California yes.' In California, the weather is so nice and there are always plenty of fun options, people often don't want to limit themselves. They tend to say yes, but they qualify it with several exit strategies to keep their options open.

"By the way, this person is going to flake on you. This is the person who will call or text you ten minutes before the show and tell you she didn't finish cleaning or didn't get her taxes done, so go ahead without her."

"Oops, I think I do that sometimes," the anesthesiologist mumbled under his breath.

Take 4: "Hey, Neha—movies? You comin' or not?" he said as he playfully winked.

The audience started laughing. I smiled, made eye contact, and spoke with clarity and confidence. I said, "Sure, I'd love to go."

He asked, "That's a clear yes, isn't it? We're going to the movies. You said yes, and it sounded like you meant it."

"Be careful. We're at a level four agreement. You're right, I said yes, but who knows when? The weekend could slip away because we haven't figured out the details yet."

Take 5: "Want to see James Bond this weekend?"

"Yes. Let's meet at the Embarcadero theater on Saturday for the 1 P.M. show. I'll buy our tickets online, and you get the popcorn. Deal?" I paused. "Do we have an agreement?"

"Absolutely—and a plan!" he replied. The room erupted with applause. I'm not sure if it was out of relief for him or because they finally got it. Either way, at least everyone was more relaxed and at ease.

"Okay," I said, "now it's time to go back to your original question with the team. When you said, 'I need two units of blood, stat!' and were frustrated at the staff's incompetence, can you tell me what level of agreement you had?"

"Well . . . um, I guess I had no . . . I guess I didn't. I thought Betty, the circulating nurse, was going to get it, but come to think of it, she didn't say anything out loud. I just assumed she would get it because she always does. So just because I call out an order and make it stat, it doesn't mean that I have an agreement?"

"If no one acknowledged your request, that would be a level zero agreement—no one agreed to anything. For that matter, we don't even know if anyone heard you. Perhaps someone heard but assumed that someone else was going to take care of it. There are so many ways miscommunication about agreements can play out. Blaming someone else is a surefire way to get into trouble.

"When something is very important, make sure you have a level five agreement on it. So how would you request the blood now?" I asked.

He paused, then said, "Betty, I need two units of A-negative blood from the blood bank. Can you call and make sure it's ready and have it here within fifteen minutes?"

"That's perfect!" I replied. "Now you need to make sure she acknowledges what you've said, shows positive interest, and agrees to the time frame. If not, that's where the negotiation begins. Depending on how badly you need the blood, you may need to ask someone else to get it. You may need to wait a little longer. But at least you know who is agreeing to help you, when the blood is coming, and what level of agreement you've got."

AGREE TO AGREE

What's important about agreements is that you know what level you want and recognize what the other person is committing to. This demystifies unspoken expectations and simplifies your interactions with others. This is essential in everyday interactions as well as in difficult conversations. Once you know what level of agreement each of you is willing to commit to, it will guide you to the questions you need to ask next, if any. Understanding the levels of agreement will give you options when it seems as if you've come to a stalemate.

So here's a recap. Notice the progression in clarity of the commitment.

Level 1: Acknowledgment

Level 2: Positive interest

Level 3: Qualified yes

Level 4: Clear yes (no details)

Level 5: Yes + details confirmed

When there is a discrepancy between levels of agreement, the lowest level wins. That's the level you've both been able to say yes to. It's important to adjust your expectations so that no matter how much you want something, you can hear someone else's *actual* commitment level. So, for example, when you find yourself in what I call "deep like" and desperately want to take someone on a date, his or her winking and smiling at you doesn't mean you have a level 5 agreement. Don't start making dinner reservations quite yet. You've only been acknowledged, and we aren't even sure for what, so I'd call that somewhere between level 0 and level 1 (closer to a 1, since you're actually being acknowledged).

A note for all you overachievers and perfectionists out there: level 5 is not the best or most appropriate option every time. Each level of agreement is valid—but just know that levels 1 through 4 are still in negotiation. Too often, we make someone else "wrong" or "bad" for only being willing to commit to a lower level of agreement than we would like. That is where agreements often fall apart and we wind up disconnected. It's not so important for both people to be at level 5. What matters most is that two people are at the same level of agreement—whatever that is.

Here's an example: Two people who are acquainted through a mutual friend run into each other at the grocery store. One says to the other, "The weather is getting nice. Do you want to go hiking sometime?" The other replies, "Sounds like a good idea," and then they continue on their merry ways.

What level of agreement do they have? Each acknowledged the other and showed positive interest. The good news is, they both seem to be at level 2. Whether they actually follow through or not, there likely won't be any hurt feelings or disappointment. Neither sounds very committed. If either of them wants to raise the level of agreement, that person has to take the initiative to work out the details. If not, neither of them will likely think about it until they meet again at their mutual friend's birthday party.

Look at the areas in which you've been successful at creating what you want. Those are typically arenas where you have clarity and are able to turn your desires into action. Think about the areas of your life in which you have been less successful at creating what you want. I would guess that's where you have had the most difficulty creating level 5 agreements with others. Does that ring true?

Watch what happens when a young woman realizes the impact of not making clear agreements in the video "Have You Ever Been Flaked On?" Go to DoctorNehaTalkRx.com.

SAYING YES TO YOU

When it comes to taking bigger action in your life, there's another agreement that matters most: the one you make with yourself. Now that you've gotten clear about what you really want, there's no excuse to bail out on yourself. If you find yourself saying yes when you really mean no, you're not actually saying yes to someone else, you're saying no to you.

It's easy to point out how others don't keep their agreements. When this happens, it causes drama and conflict that may even end a relationship. But when you don't keep agreements with yourself, there's a much bigger price to pay. The misalignment erodes your self-esteem and sends you into a perpetual cycle of believing you're "not good enough." That's how you wind up making choices that only account for what others value while dishonoring what *you* value—and you end up living someone else's life.

So what's it going to take to say yes—to you?

◆ ◆ ◆ ◆

TALKRX TOOLKIT

The Five Levels of Agreement

Level 1 – Acknowledgment

Level 2 – Positive interest

Level 3 – Qualified yes

Level 4 – Clear yes (no details)

Level 5 – Yes + details confirmed

TalkRx Video: Watch what happens when a young woman realizes the impact of not making clear agreements in "Have You Ever Been Flaked On?" Go to DoctorNehaTalkRx.com.

Your 1-Five Moment

- To help you avoid disappointment and make
  sure you're never flaked on again, answer the
  questions in Chapter 21 of your *TalkRx Journal*
  (DoctorNehaTalkRx.com).

- Share your thoughts about the video "Have You Ever
  Been Flaked On?" with the TalkRx Community.

CHAPTER 22

Prep for Success

It's time to talk. And yes, I mean out loud.

Now that you've interpreted the first four steps of the i-Five Conversation and understand agreements, it's time to lay out exactly how to step into clear, direct communication with others. Most of the time, you will use your knowledge in everyday conversations, but occasionally it will be for more challenging communication that may require bold action.

You may be thinking, *I don't want to be that annoying person who is always sitting people down and asking, "Can we talk?" How do I know when it's the right time to initiate this type of conversation?*

I'll let you in on a little secret. I choose whether or not to have a conversation by using something I call the Three-Time Rule. Often the first time I experience a situation that seems "off," I hit my pause button and check in. When I notice my body reacting, I pay attention to physical signals, like throat constriction or a racing heart. I take a few soft belly breaths and notice if I'm making up stories that are affecting how I feel. Then I get clear about what I want.

The second time this situation occurs (or some version of it), I store it in my mental filing cabinet for future reference. This is my clue that a pattern might be developing, and it will likely be important to address.

The third time it happens, it's time to talk. I now know that I'm having a consistent reaction and there's something for me to learn here. I ask for a conversation with the other person, and when I speak to him or her, I can give three specific examples to describe what I'm talking about. (That's a lot of data.)

Another tool I use to decide whether it's time to have an important conversation is what I call the Sunrise Rule. If I wake up thinking about a situation (in the morning or the middle of the night), then I know it is occupying precious mental real estate and it's time for action. (Warning: Knocking yourself out with NyQuil or Ambien interferes with the effectiveness of this rule.)

THE 1-FIVE SETUP

Once you're ready to have a dialogue, it's essential to set up your conversation for success. This begins with your being clear about what you'd like to discuss and how you'd like to discuss it. Make sure you've thought about each of the five topics below. This may seem simple, but don't underestimate the value of a few minutes of planning.

1. **Topic:** What do you want to discuss?

2. **Time:** How long will it take? If you are uncertain, give it your best guess and add a few extra minutes.

3. **Attention:** When would be a good time for the other person?

    Yes, you read that right. You might be wondering why you should focus on the other person. Ask yourself, "When I have something important to convey, is it in my best interest that the person listening be able to give me his or her full attention?" I bet you said yes. You wouldn't want to start talking about an important topic when your audience is preoccupied, distracted, or only physically available but not mentally and emotionally present. If you miss this step, you may find yourself frustrated and back in the blame game.

4. **How:** In Chapter 5 (page 61) you learned how to match the method of communication with the level of importance. Here's the key: make sure you also consider how the other person best receives

communication. Most people have a preferred method of receiving information. Some like the time-tested personal handshake or talking on the phone or corresponding through e-mail. Others prefer the convenience of texting. We tend to communicate with others in the medium that we prefer. This is a rookie mistake.

You communicate with many people—your family, your colleagues, your friends, your boss, your partner—so pay attention to how each of them best gives and receives communication, and combine it with the appropriate method of delivery.

5. **Where:** Make sure you choose the best setting for the conversation. If you're speaking in person, be mindful of your surroundings. The sensitivity of the topic (for either of you) should determine whether you talk in public or in private.

(Note: Unless it's their birthday or a special occasion, most people don't like surprises. So as you shift your behavior, some people may question the change, especially if they've known you for a long time. If you encounter resistance or skepticism with this new way of setting up a conversation, just let the other person know you've learned some new tools that you're hoping will make you a better communicator in your relationship with them.)

MAKING THE REQUEST

Once you're clear, it's time to make your request. How you articulate that request is important. Do this by using "I" statements of accountability rather than "you" statements of blame. This will create a feeling of openness and keep people from becoming defensive before the conversation even starts.

It's also good to mention how long will be needed for the conversation and to suggest a time. Or you can just ask the other person when would work best for him or her.

Instead of: "You said something rude yesterday. We need to talk."
Try: "I had a reaction to what I heard in yesterday's meeting and was curious about it. Can we talk for fifteen minutes tomorrow before our next meeting?"

Instead of: "You didn't let me share my thoughts."
Try: "I didn't have time to speak up during our meeting yesterday, and I wanted to give you my input. It will take approximately fifteen minutes. When's a good time to meet?"

Instead of: "You misunderstood me."
Try: "I could have communicated more clearly. I'd like to clarify what I meant during our conversation over the holidays. When do you have an hour to talk?"

Once you make a request for someone's time, he or she may respond in a variety of ways. It doesn't have to throw you off track.

If someone replies with "I'm busy," make sure not to fall into the trap of trying to figure out their schedule ("What about 3:30 P.M.? Or tomorrow morning?"). Don't take it personally; just say, "It sounds like right now is not good. When would be a better time?" Put the ball back in their court. Allow them to manage their own schedule. Slow down, pause, and get curious.

If someone responds with "That was a long time ago," you can say: "It's true that it happened six days ago (six months ago, six years ago, or when we were six), and I noticed that it's crossed my mind a few times recently. I think it will be helpful for me to share what I've discovered. When would be a good time for you?"

If you are focused on yourself and don't take into account the dynamic of the relationship, then you shouldn't be surprised when your communication flatlines. It's in your best interest (and the other person's) to find a good time for both of you to listen.

Setting up a conversation for success allows you to get clear about what you'd like to express while getting buy-in from the other person. It's a small investment upfront that will provide the greatest chance of effective communication. This is a great example of *slowing down to speed up!*

◆ ◆ ◆ ◆ ◆

TalkRx Toolkit

How you know it's time to initiate a conversation

- **Three-Time Rule:**
  - *First time*: Notice and get clear about your reaction to something you've observed.
  - *Second time*: Store it in your mental filing cabinet (it's potentially becoming a pattern).
  - *Third time*: Ask for a conversation.

- **Sunrise Rule:** If you find yourself awake in the middle of the night thinking about an interaction, or if it's the first thing on your mind in the morning, it's time to set up a talk.

The i-Five Setup

1. **Topic:** What would you like to talk about?
2. **Time:** How much time do you expect it will take?
3. **Attention:** When would be a good time for the other person?
4. **How:** Choose a method that equals the level of importance for both of you.
5. **Where:** What setting would create the best environment for this interaction, public or private?

YOUR 1-FIVE MOMENT

- The questions and exercises in Chapter 22 of your *TalkRx Journal* (DoctorNehaTalkRx.com) will help you set up your conversations for success.

- Share with the TalkRx Community how you decide when it's time to say, "Can we talk?"

CHAPTER 23

LEARNING TO TRUST

Have you ever been torn between whether or not to have a conversation or take some sort of action? It's natural to feel internal conflict as you weigh the price versus the payoff of creating change. The decision may even be more complicated if it impacts not only you but also others in your life—your partner, your children, your friends, or your co-workers. It's true that there are always trade-offs—pros and cons for any particular action. One way people try to avoid making tough choices is by playing the waiting game, crossing their fingers, and hoping the need to make a decision will pass. If you do that, it's likely that your window of opportunity will close and you will have inadvertently made a choice—even if it wasn't the one you wanted.

It can be scary to step outside your comfort zone. As you contemplate the possibility of actually having a challenging conversation, you may recall prior times when things did not go so well. This is the point at which you may get uneasy physical sensations in your body. And this is often when people stop, because they're afraid. But it doesn't have to be your story.

Communication expert Kris King shared what one of her mentors once said to her when she was afraid: "There are two kinds of people in this world. The ones who are afraid and climb mountains and the ones who are afraid and don't. Which one are you? Because everyone's afraid."[26]

What strikes me most about that statement is that if we're waiting for self-doubt and fear to exit before we act, it's not going to happen. Moving forward starts with acknowledging our fears and then having the courage to take the next step anyway. This is one of the biggest challenges we face in step 5 of the i-Five Conversation. We have to learn to trust ourselves enough to take a step forward.

EXPANDING YOUR COMFORT ZONE

One way you might talk yourself out of taking action is by saying you want to keep your life a drama-free zone. I hate to break it to you, but trying to avoid drama in the present moment is the exact recipe for how to create even more drama in the future.

Of course, you can continue to numb, avoid, control, or bully your way through relationships. It may work in the short term, but in the long run, you'll encounter more stress in your relationships and feel frustrated and disconnected. Choosing an old course of action—the one you may be used to—is a decision to tune in to fear or self-doubt rather than tuning in to your own heart.

I can't guarantee that when you use the i-Five Conversation, there won't be any drama with others, or uncomfortable sensations inside you; in fact, there will be. Here's the deal: There's going to be discomfort either way. If you decide to listen to your own heart and take action in alignment with your values, initially you'll feel short-term discomfort. But the long-term payoff is that you'll expand your comfort zone, connect to your heart, and have a higher likelihood of getting what you want.

If there's an area of your life calling out for you to take action, you're at a choice point: Do you want the discomfort to last for only a few minutes or hours, or for a lifetime? This is where you don't *have to*, but you *get to* speak from the heart and genuinely communicate with others to create the life you want. This requires courage, which can cause you to feel vulnerable. Everything you've been doing up until this point has been preparing you to make these choices. If you've been practicing the tools in your everyday conversations, your communication skills have been honed and your confidence should be on the rise. Now it's time to trust yourself and to believe you have everything you need. Because you do.

MY STROKE OF CLARITY

It was May 2008, on what seemed like a regular Tuesday morning, when my pager went off. The call was regarding a 48-year-old woman named Sara who had just arrived in the hospital following a stroke.

You've probably seen this scene on TV: The patient's heart monitor was beeping loudly, her daughters were crying, and her husband was helplessly exclaiming, "She can't move! She can't talk, and she's drooling! When is a doctor going to get here?"

As I entered, I glanced at the monitor and saw Sara's blood pressure was abnormally high and her heart was racing. Once I had introduced myself, examined Sara, and was certain she was medically stable, I turned my attention to the anxiety in the room. "I need your help," I told her family. "You see these numbers on the screen? That monitor is letting us know that Sara's blood pressure and heart rate are too high. These elevated numbers might mean she needs additional blood pressure medication, but they might also be high as a result of the fear and anxiety in the room. Please have a seat. I'd like to ask her about it."

I took Sara's hand and said, "I know this must be scary, not to be able to talk, and to know that your family is so worried. I'd like to teach all of you a relaxation exercise that will help your anxiety now, as well as when you leave the hospital. This may bring your blood pressure and heart rate down naturally. It will definitely help me decipher whether or not I need to give you additional medications. Would you be willing to try it? Squeeze my hand once if the answer is no and twice if the answer is yes." She squeezed twice.

I turned to her family. "This technique is known as guided imagery. It's a scientifically proven technique where together we'll take some deep breaths and focus our attention on different parts of our body in order to relax them."

I took Sara and her family through guided imagery as a way to take action by using their thoughts to influence their physiology, their emotions, and their desires in the moment.

This is the exercise I took Sara and her family through. When you feel anxious, sad, or stressed, use guided imagery to shift how you feel.

1. Sit comfortably in a chair and focus only on yourself. You can keep your eyes open or close them, whichever is most comfortable. Begin by taking several slow, deep breaths, in and out, allowing your body to relax.

2. Let the weight of gravity bring your shoulders down toward the floor. With each breath, bring your attention to a different part of your body. Start with the top of your head, then your forehead, around your eyes, then move your focus down your neck and shoulders.

3. With your next breath, focus on your chest cavity. Pay attention to your rib cage expanding and contracting with each breath. Take a moment to settle in your heart space and focus on all the compassion you give to others—your family, your friends, your community, and the world.

4. Continue breathing, and move your focus into your abdomen, legs, calves, and feet.

5. Now gently move your attention back up into your chest and bring back to mind the love you give others. Then take a few minutes to experience what it's like to shower that compassion upon yourself.[27]

Watch my TEDx San Luis Obispo talk "The Community Cure" to hear me go through the full guided imagery and explain the science behind how we influence each other (DoctorNehaTalkRx.com).

As I walked Sara and her family through the guided imagery practice, I could feel a new sense of calmness enter the room. Then the monitor alarm went silent, and I asked everyone to shift their focus back to Sara.

"What just happened? Why isn't the monitor working anymore?" her husband asked with concern.

"It's actually working just fine," I answered with a smile. "It only beeps to let us know when Sara's numbers are too high or too low. Her heart rate and blood pressure have returned to just above normal now."

They looked at me in disbelief. "Is that because of what we just did together?" the husband asked.

I smiled. "Yes, guided imagery is a powerful tool to deal with anxiety and other uncomfortable emotions. And as you can see, this isn't just for patients. Anyone can use it."

After outlining what Sara was going to need to heal, I emphasized how important it would be for the other family members to manage themselves first. I glanced over at Sara and saw tears running down her cheeks. She motioned for my hand and squeezed it twice, indicating her agreement with what I had just told them.

As I left the room, Sara's husband went to stand beside her, and her older daughter followed me into the hall. "Thanks so much for spending time with us and teaching us how to do that," she said. "I promise we'll take good care of her."

When I finished entering Sara's medical orders and headed back to the elevator, I had a skip in my step. I felt alive. I loved empowering my patients and their families with tools that catalyzed their healing in their immediate physical crises and beyond.

I knew this opportunity would help Sara better manage herself and had helped her family experience the critical role they played in her healing. What I didn't expect was that later that morning, one of the emergency department staff would report me to the chief physician.

Choice Point

I was slightly bewildered as I walked down to Dr. Wilkers's office at the end of the day. With a serious look on his face, he began, "Neha, a nurse called to report that you were performing *voodoo* on a patient this morning. Is that true?"

Stunned, I replied, "I'm not sure what you mean. Did I miss something in Sara's medical care? Did her family complain?"

"No, I checked the chart. You gave her the right medical treatment. And no, her family didn't complain. The nurse who needed the bed for a new patient did. It would have taken under thirty seconds to order an antianxiety or antihypertensive medication so we could move the patient out of the emergency room. Instead, you did some sort of talk therapy that took extra time."

I felt my muscles clench, my heart race, and my throat tighten—signs I wouldn't have noticed a decade earlier. I took a few deep breaths to manage my shock and anger. "So you're saying that I gave her the appropriate medical diagnosis and treatment. But because it would have been quicker to sedate her than to teach her and her family how to manage their anxiety, I'm in trouble? Is that why you've called me here?"

"It's my job to make sure that you get patients from the emergency department up to the hospital floor as efficiently as possible so we can provide the quality care people expect. And this voodoo medicine of yours took fifteen minutes longer than the cutoff time. If everybody did this, we'd never meet our metrics for the month. It's got to stop."

As I looked across the desk at my chief, I felt nauseated. By this point, my throat was so constricted I could barely breathe. Clearly we had different priorities, and very different ideas of what quality care meant.

The crazy part was that we were in agreement about Sara's diagnosis and the traditional treatment of her stroke. Where we differed was in whether or not to also address her and her family's emotional response to this traumatic event.

My ride home from work was sheer torture. *Voodoo? Was he serious? Wow, if taking some deep breaths and focusing the power of my patients' thoughts to relax their body and empower them in their own self-care is modern medicine's definition of voodoo, I don't belong in this profession.*

But along with my feelings of anger, disappointment, and worry, I realized this wasn't the first evidence I'd been given that the hospital and I might be on different paths.

Each year, sicker and sicker patients were admitted. And each year, the doctors were expected to see a higher number of critically ill patients per day, while our patients were growing less satisfied with the time we had to spend with each of them. I'd had a growing sense of unease about my work environment over the past couple of years. For too long I had denied the truth that was now staring me in the face.

At this point in my career, I was a physician partner, which meant I was tenured in for life. As the daughter of immigrants, I valued stability—and partnership was the ultimate in job security. I had worked hard for this badge of honor, but now it felt more like a pair of golden handcuffs.

I spent the next four hours hunched over my dining table as Ritu consoled me. All my fears of failure and of giving up everything I had always thought I wanted came pouring out. "Just so you know," I cried, "I may not be able to pay the mortgage next month!" Ritu reassured me that it was all going to be okay and reminded me that right now, what I needed was a good night's rest. So I used a well-tested strategy that had served me for decades: I cried myself into a deep, deep sleep.

Somehow, when I was little, everything seemed to be better in the morning. The sun would be out, my tummyache would be gone, and it would be time to play again. But much to my dismay, the next morning I awoke with throat constriction, my stomach churning, and a heavy heart. How on earth was I going to find the courage to make a decision?

Then I remembered that in the deepest, darkest hours of my patients' lives, I had written them the Awareness Prescription as a way of asking their heart and soul for guidance. Their answers consistently revealed the action that would lead to their own healing. Perhaps the day had come for a dose of my own medicine. So I reached for my journal and my favorite pen. I lit a candle, took a deep breath in, and let it out with a heavy sigh.

Why this?

Why this . . . throat constriction? I must be afraid of speaking my truth.

Why this . . . nausea? I've done everything to please others—my parents, my colleagues—but in the process I haven't been taking care of my own needs. I think my body is telling me that I haven't been nourishing myself.

Why this . . . heavy heart? It can only be this heavy if I'm carrying an unfair share of the load. I'm making myself responsible for everybody else's happiness as well as my own.

Why this . . . dilemma at work? Because this is where I keep bumping into the greatest disparity between my values and my actions. I want to pave a new path in medicine, create change, and help heal people. I claim that I want to be a trailblazer, but I don't want to leave my comfort zone. I want my colleagues' approval, my job security, and a sense of belonging.

Why now?

Why have I come to this crossroads at this particular point in my life? I've struggled for a long time with the conflicts between my values and the traditional, medical establishment. But I haven't had the courage to be honest about what's in my own heart. But yesterday was the tipping point. I was reprimanded for doing what I value—inspiring my patient and her family in their own self-care. My body won't let me ignore the truth any longer: I've outgrown the environment I've chosen to surround myself with.

What might I have missed?

I've missed signals all along:

- The burnout I experienced should have alerted me that I need to think more broadly about my definition of health. Neglecting my physical, mental, and emotional health actually prevents me from practicing medicine and being able to serve others.

- I've been telling myself that the low energy I've been feeling for the last few months means I'm weak. But I'm not weak; this low energy is a signal telling me that I'm not practicing medicine in a way that inspires me.

- I've also neglected to recognize how energized I am when I have meaningful interactions and healing conversations with my patients.

- My patients have been encouraging me to be that doctor who speaks to companies, veterans groups, and the public to help them understand stress and communication long before they end up in the hospital. I have been too scared. I haven't understood what that would look like or believed that I could actually get paid to do what I love.

What else needs to be healed?

First of all, I need to look honestly at what my body, mind, and heart are telling me. It's time to heal my relationship with myself—to correct the imbalances in my life. I also need to heal my relationship to the practice of medicine; to move beyond the limits and restrictions of the hospital environment and have the courage to share what I've learned to heal a broader audience long before they get physically ill.

If I spoke from my heart, what would I say?

I have to balance the needs of others with my own. I have to replace my worries about what other people think by focusing more attention on what really matters to me.

I need to confront the discrepancy between what I have told myself I wanted—security, status, praise, and the approval of others—and what truly brings me happiness: living my truth, having the courage to trust my heart, and paving a new path in medicine that makes a lasting difference in the health and lives of others.

I now know security and happiness don't come from a physician partnership, my parents' approval, or my bank account. I have to believe in my experience with thousands of patients and the miracle that happens when I help them communicate what's in their hearts. And it's time for self-trust—to know that I'll find my way when the going gets tough. Even if I fail.

A part of me is scared. No, petrified. But even if I am, I need to venture into the world and show how clear communication changes everything.

FREE FALL

The next day I booked an appointment to speak to my chief's boss. When I showed up, his back was to me as he typed on his computer. "Go ahead," he said. "I'm just finishing up, but I'm listening."

Tears were flowing down my face. "I want to begin by saying thank you. You were the one who hired me, and I've learned a lot from being here.

"Although I originally signed on to be a traditional hospitalist, over the past several years my approach to practicing medicine has evolved. The methods that I know help my patients heal seem to run contrary to hospital procedure and metrics. I'm frustrated and sad that I haven't figured out a way to feel fulfilled practicing in this environment."

After 15 seconds of pin-drop silence, I blurted, "I made this appointment to let you know that I'm resigning my partnership."

Without turning around, he responded, "It sounds like you've made up your mind. Get it to me in writing."

That was it.

It definitely wasn't the conversation I had anticipated. I was devastated. Only then did I realize I'd been secretly hoping he would try to stop me. Regardless, I knew what needed to happen next. Four days later, I e-mailed him my official resignation.

In order to pave a new path, I needed to be gentle with myself and listen to my heart above all else. I needed to trust that I would be able to navigate the many decisions that were coming my way. Only then could I find the courage to change my role in the medical community.

PREVENTIVE MEDICINE

As you can see, the Awareness Prescription is an invaluable tool for much more than a health crisis. I had picked up my body's signals early and was able to use those five questions to guide myself as I reached a fork in the road. Using this tool, along with identifying the information coming from my body, thoughts, emotions, and desires, I was able to clarify what I needed to do next.

Realizing your values have shifted or have grown apart from those of your friends, your family, or your previous ways of thinking can be scary. But it's a fear you must face if you want to heal, change, and grow. When you pay attention early, these five questions will guide you to the truth of your heart and soul—a different kind of preventive medicine.

So go ahead. Invite fear to the table. Just make sure you invite self-trust, forgiveness, and gratitude, too. That's part of growing and taking risks. At least you're betting on yourself. And if you're not willing to do that, why should anyone else?

Like me, you'll need to trust that by showing up authentically in your life, the subsequent action will be revealed. You sometimes have to take the next step without being able to see beyond it, but I can assure you that the truth inside your heart is far more powerful than any voices of self-doubt you may hear. Yes, you may stumble. Your life may take an unexpected turn. You may even find that other people are uncomfortable when you start getting clear and taking action—because when you change, so do the dynamics of your relationships.

That scary, unknown future can present you with marvelous and unexpected gifts. It was the life-changing decision I made after treating Sara and talking to my chief that led me to you. And when I fearfully hit SEND on my resignation letter, little did I know that in two short years, that very hospital would become one of my biggest clients. Using all of the principles and techniques in this book, I'm now working with the hospital's medical teams to help them improve their communication skills—not just with their patients, but with each other.

Only this time, as I drive the same highway to the same hospital, my throat is relaxed and I feel only peace, anticipation, and excitement.

As the i-Five Conversation starts to become natural, you'll begin to trust yourself, and that will translate into a new level of confidence, clarity, and ease in your relationships. You'll be able to identify where a breakdown has happened, get curious as you address your part of the interaction, and express yourself clearly.

You've created a solid foundation as you've read this book. Now let's jump right in to what an actual i-Five Conversation entails.

◆ ◆ ◆ ◆ ◆

TALK RX TOOLKIT

The Awareness Prescription

- Why this?
- Why now?
- What might you have missed?
- What else needs to be healed?
- If you spoke from your heart, what would you say?

TalkRx Video: Watch my TEDx San Luis Obispo talk "The Community Cure" to hear me go through the full guided imagery and explain the science behind how we influence each other (DoctorNehaTalkRx.com).

YOUR I-FIVE MOMENT

- The questions in Chapter 23 of your *TalkRx Journal* (DoctorNehaTalkRx.com) will help you find the courage to listen to your heart.

- Join the TalkRx Community to connect with other brave souls who are engaging in clear, direct, compassionate communication.

CHAPTER 24

THE I-FIVE CONVERSATION

3, 2, 1—Action!

Buckle up. You're ready to change how you show up in everyday relationships—at work, at home, with friends. There is an art to taking action, and it works in challenging situations as well. You need to manage yourself, be specific about what you've observed, take personal accountability, get curious, and then listen deeply. This is how you do it.

HOW TO PREPARE

Step 1: Identify and interpret the signals coming into and from your body.

External data: What do you notice? What do you see, hear, taste, touch, or smell? In conversation, what body language, tone, or words have you picked up on, in someone else or yourself? What has changed?

Internal data: What are your internal physical signals—heart racing, stomach turning, sweating, etc.? (If you think you're reacting rather than responding, hit your pause button.)

Step 2: Identify and interpret the stories in your head.

Thoughts: What are the stories you've made up? Are they mostly about the other person or about yourself? What else could be going on (in the other person's life or environment) that you might not be aware of? What is your part in this situation? What might you not have taken responsibility for?

Step 3: Identify and interpret your emotions.

How do you feel (happy, sad, mad, glad, irritated, excited)?

Step 4: Identify and interpret your desires.

What do you want? What do you value in this relationship, situation, conversation, or request? What attitude (your internal state of being) do you want to bring to this conversation?

Step 5: Integrate the above four steps and take action by preparing what you will say, setting the conversation up for success, and then having it.

When I began using the i-Five Conversation, I wrote out what I intended to say. And sometimes I even brought my notes with me to make certain I remembered. You can do the same. Simply take notes such as:

- "I've noticed _____ ."
  [what you've observed in facts]

- "I think this means _____ ."
  [the story you've made up]

- "I feel _____ ."
  [insert a one-word emotion]

- "I want/want to know _____ ."
  [either make a request or ask a question to determine the accuracy of the story you've made up, or get curious about the other person's experience]

Once the conversation has begun and you've spoken, pause, breathe, and listen deeply at levels 3 (words), 4 (emotions), and 5 (values). After you hear what the other person says, together you can negotiate an agreement that works for both of you.

You can use this template to guide you in getting clear about your part in any situation. Realize that these are guidelines; natural conversation won't always follow this order. When you run into trouble, though, it probably means you've skipped one of these important elements of the i-Five Conversation.

> Watch the video "The i-Five Conversation" to better understand how you can incorporate these five easy steps into everyday conversations (DoctorNehaTalkRx.com). This framework also works to help you prepare for difficult conversations!

EVERYDAY I-FIVE CONVERSATIONS

Now that you understand just what goes into an i-Five Conversation, let's look at a few practical scenarios.

Scenario 1: Your Friend Is Late for a Dinner Date

Without the i-Five Conversation: You cross your arms and legs and look away as you begin, "What's got you so busy? I've been waiting for more than thirty minutes. Now that you're a big shot, you've forgotten us little people. I guess I should be honored that you would make time for me at all, huh?"

I hope you notice this "conversation" isn't really a conversation at all. It's a game of hot potato where you're tossing the blame at the other person. Not only are you not being accountable, but you also aren't curious. "What's got you so busy?" is a sarcastic dagger masquerading as a question. And the closed body language would likely discourage genuine interaction.

In the conversation, the only information you present is that you've been waiting more than 30 minutes. This is followed by a series of stories and limiting beliefs that you've made up. And you never ask for what you want. My prediction is that this conversation is heading for a communication disaster with defensiveness and hurt feelings on both sides.

With the i-Five Conversation: It's time to tune in to your body, thoughts, emotions, and desires.

Your body:
- External data: We agreed to meet at 7:00 P.M. and confirmed over e-mail. Today she showed up at 7:30 P.M. I've just finished my first drink and the seat across from me is empty. Last Thursday she showed up at 7:15 P.M. for the same reservation.

- Internal data: throat constriction, muscle tightening, jaw clenched

Your thoughts: She doesn't respect my time; she has more important things to do; maybe I did something that made her mad; I miss her. My stories are mostly projections about her; I wonder if traffic was bad. *My part in the situation is* that I've never told her that being on time is important to me.

Your emotions: hurt, disrespected, defensive

Your desires (for both yourself and your relationship with your friend):
- To ask if time with me is important to her
- To find out if her priorities have changed
- To get together on a weekly basis
- To strengthen our friendship
- To renegotiate our agreement about timeliness

How do you want to show up (your attitude or internal state of being)?

- Curious
- Honest
- Open
- Respectful
- As a good listener

Your action: To have the conversation with your friend. The new and improved version using the i-Five Conversation might sound like this:

> *You:* "The last two Thursdays we agreed to meet for dinner at 7:00 P.M. The first time, you came at 7:15, and last night you arrived at 7:30. By the time you got to the restaurant, I had already finished my first drink. My throat felt constricted and my body was tense, so I knew I was upset. But I realize that I've never told you how important being on time is to me.
>
> "The story I made up about you being late is that you didn't really want to come to dinner—that it was a burden, not something you were excited about. And I thought you might have just squeezed me in out of obligation. I feel hurt and disrespected. So what I'm wondering is this: Are our get-togethers valuable for you? Or do you feel obligated to come?"

> *Friend:* "Oh my gosh! I'm sorry you're upset. I never knew being on time was so important to you. I value our time together—so much so that I schedule these dinners early to maximize how long I can see you before I have to be home to relieve the babysitter. It sounds like when I'm late, you interpret it as my not caring or thinking you're not important. The truth is that with work and then traffic, seven o'clock is probably too early for me to get all the way

out here. I think meeting downtown is too far away and becomes unpredictable with traffic. Can we pick a location closer to my office? Or schedule dinner on the weekends?"

In this example, you begin by presenting external and internal data: the facts surrounding your agreements with your friend, the times she arrived, and the signals from your body. You then reveal the thoughts in your head, making clear that these are simply stories you have made up and not necessarily facts. Finally, you articulate your emotions and ask what you want to know in order to clarify the stories you made up and take ownership for your part in the situation. This is how curiosity helps shift you to personal accountability.

This clear, concise, and direct i-Five Conversation gives your friend a chance to respond openly and tell you what's happening for her. Once you realize you have never shared how important punctuality is to you, it's easier to be curious about what else you might be missing. And when you take accountability in a conversation rather than blaming, it opens the door for the other person to own her part of the interaction. Since you've already thought through your desires, as the conversation unfolds naturally, you will be clear about what else you want to ask about. You might decide to negotiate—suggesting, for instance, that if either of you is going to be more than five minutes late, you'll be sure to text. You will likely be able to reach a level 5 agreement to schedule future dinners at a restaurant closer to your friend's place of work or change the day of the week you meet.

Scenario 2: Your Partner Doesn't Do What He Said He Would

Without **the i-Five Conversation:** "It's like I'm the only one around here who lifts a finger. Everyone in this house thinks there's a magic fairy keeping the fridge stocked and doing laundry. Well, I'm not going to do it anymore. You can all take care of yourselves. This fairy is on strike because nobody ever takes me seriously! Especially you."

And your partner looks up, dumbfounded, wondering what on earth you're talking about.

With the i-Five Conversation: It's time to tune in to your body, thoughts, emotions, and desires.

Your body:

- External data: At breakfast this morning, I said, "Honey, would you please move the dog crate from the family room to the garage? We haven't had a dog in six months. I'd like to make room so we can start being more social." He answered, "Sure." However, when I came home from work today, I saw the dog crate was still in the family room.

- Internal data: fists clenched, heart racing, head pounding

Your thoughts: He doesn't take me seriously; he thinks I'm a push-over; he's got more important priorities than me; he doesn't care whether we have any friends; he's being passive-aggressive and disrespecting me. Wow, all my thoughts are projecting on him. I wonder if the kids needed him for something after work since no one's home. *My part in this is* that I think it's easier to do it myself. I guess I've pretty much trained my family that if they don't take care of something, I will. And when I finally do ask for what I want, I do it in a harsh tone because by that time I'm totally fed up.

Your emotions: frustrated, annoyed, disappointed

Your desires:

- To know why the dog crate is still in the family room
- To know why he said he would move it and then didn't do it
- To have a common space that's kept clean and spacious for socializing

- To renegotiate the house rules about what's stored in the common areas

How do you want to show up (your attitude or internal state of being)?

- Curious

- Open

- Honest

- Brave

- As a good listener

Your action: To initiate and have the conversation with your partner

You: "This morning at breakfast, I asked if you would please take the dog crate from the family room to the garage. When I came home from work this evening and saw the dog crate was in the family room, my heart started racing. I normally would just do it myself, but I realized that it's not healthy for me to do it just to avoid having a conversation with you. The story I'm making up is that you take me for granted. I heard you say, 'Sure,' and I think you conveniently forgot about what we agreed to. I'm frustrated and disappointed. So I'd like to know: What happened?"

Your partner: "Yes, I did hear you. Honey, I do take you seriously and I appreciate all that you do to make our house a home. Regarding the dog crate, I had no idea you wanted me to move it today. I agreed that the dog crate should be moved. Since it needs to be washed and I need to make room in the garage for it, I was going to take care of it this weekend when I had more time. I wasn't ignoring you."

In this example, by getting curious, not furious, you come to realize that you thought your request meant *now* and your partner thought he could do it over the weekend. In other words, you had only a level 4 agreement. As soon as you both agree on *when and where in the garage* the dog crate will be moved, you'll have a level 5 agreement.

Scenario 3: You Just Made a Pass at Your Best Friend's Fiancée

Without the i-Five Conversation: When your angry friend confronts you, you reply with a grin, "Dude, your fiancée is so hot that I can barely control myself around her when I'm sober. So I'm sure you understand how after a few drinks it was utterly impossible. We're good, right?" Backslap. Fist bump. Wink, wink. "Can I get you a beer?"

Your friend is speechless. He glares at you in silence, then stands up and walks out the door.

Okay, seriously, that's not how it should go down—but it often does.

With the i-Five Conversation: It's time to tune in to your body, thoughts, emotions, and desires.

Your body:

- External data: While my friend was in the restroom, I put my arm around his fiancée, Kathy, and whispered (something unrepeatable) in her ear. She pulled away, slapped me across the face, and got up to leave.

- Internal data: sinking stomach, insomnia, muscle tension

Your thoughts: I acted like an idiot flirting with my best friend's fiancée; I've ruined our friendship; I'm a creep; he's not going to trust me—hey, after two drinks, *I* don't trust me.

She was smiling at me. I think if I'd met her first, we'd be dating. This one is definitely about me. *My part in this is* that I use drinking as an excuse to behave obnoxiously. This isn't the first time it's happened.

Your emotions: guilty, anxious, regretful, defensive

Your desires:

- To acknowledge that I acted like a fool
- To apologize and ask for forgiveness from both of them
- To attempt to repair our friendships

How do I want to show up?

- Humble
- Apologetic
- Sensitive
- Accountable
- As a good listener

Your action: Have a conversation with your friend and his fiancée

You: "Hey, Conrad, I wanted to talk to you and Kathy about my behavior last weekend. It will take about a half an hour. This has been weighing on me. I'd like to talk as soon as you're both available, and I'm happy to come to your place."

Conrad: "Sure. Kathy told me what happened. Now is fine."

You: "Thanks. I wanted to apologize to you both for my behavior last weekend. I haven't been able to sleep. Kathy, I'm sorry for making a pass at you. It was completely inappropriate. I thought it would be funny, but as soon as you slapped me, I realized it was having the opposite effect. Conrad, we've been friends since grade school. I'm scared this has ruined our friendship. I'm embarrassed. I got carried away after a few drinks, and I want you both to know it won't happen again. I really care about you guys, and I'm wondering: How can I make it right?"

This conversation will undoubtedly be uncomfortable. When you're apologizing for making poor choices or hurting someone else, it's extra important to set up the conversation for success. Once you've said what you intended to, it's time to breathe, slowly and deeply, and shift into levels 4 and 5 listening. Your friends might be livid, and you'll need to listen to the impact of your behavior on them. Or your friend may have brushed it off as inconsequential or not even remember, as he was more drunk than you. You have no idea. They may or may not accept your apology. This is where self-trust and knowing you can handle what happens next comes into play. And this is where curiosity and levels 4 and 5 listening will (hopefully) get you out of the doghouse.

Scenario 4: You're Passed Over for a Promotion

Without the i-Five Conversation: Every chance you get, you tell your colleagues at the office how unfair management is. "Barry's just a brownnoser. He never comes in on time and has nothing intelligent to say in meetings. I'm the one who does all the work, but of course he gets the promotion. Well, they made a big, big mistake. This company just doesn't appreciate its employees."

With the i-Five Conversation: It's time to tune in to your body, thoughts, emotions, and desires.

Your body:

- External data: I read an e-mail announcing that Barry was promoted to manager. In my last review, I received a grade of "excellent" and my supervisor said my work "exceeded expectations." I have worked at this company for ten years, and Barry has worked here for five.

- Internal data: nausea, dry mouth, lightheadedness, racing heart

Your thoughts: I can't believe this. It's not fair. I'm not appreciated. I have been here so much longer than he has. Barry's such a kiss-ass. He knows how to play politics better than I do. I bet they're planning on letting me go. I'm being an equal-opportunity blamer. *The way I've contributed to this situation is* that I've made a lot of assumptions about what leads to getting a promotion. I haven't told anyone that I want to take on more responsibility. I just assumed it was obvious by how hard I work and how loyal I am to the company.

Your emotions: worried, angry, disappointed, surprised, betrayed

Your desires:

- To know why I was passed over
- To know what criteria are used to give a promotion
- To find out if my job is secure

How do I want to show up?

- Calm
- Curious
- As a good listener

Your action: Schedule an appointment with your boss and have the conversation in person

> *You:* "I read the announcement that Barry got promoted. My last review was excellent, and last week after the regional meeting, you said that my performance had exceeded your expectations. Even though you didn't say it directly, I thought you were implying that I was next in line for a promotion. I have been working here five years longer than Barry, and I was never even interviewed for the manager position.
>
> "When I learned about Barry's promotion, I was surprised and disappointed. Do you use other criteria besides tenure and performance in selecting who will be promoted?"
>
> *Your boss:* "I wasn't even aware that you were interested in moving into management. Barry formally applied for the

position and has been open about his desire to be a manager. To gain additional skills, he has been working on a special project for the senior leadership team, and we're impressed with his leadership and teamwork. You do an excellent job in your current position, but there are additional skills you would need to develop if you'd like a promotion."

You: "I'm ready to take on some additional responsibility, so could you tell me what I need to do in order to be a stronger candidate next time? Next week, during our one-on-one meeting, can we discuss my career path?"

Your boss: "Great idea. Consider it done."

By listening deeply, following up with a recap of what you heard your boss say, and asking for suggestions on how to build your skills, you can make a great impression on her—plus you'll get some helpful information on how to improve. No matter what she says, she'll likely be impressed with your communication skills, which I'm sure is a prerequisite to moving up in management. When you're clear about what you want and have the courage and self-trust to ask for it out loud, it's easy to make an agreement that will move you forward.

Scenario 5: A Written Level 5 Agreement Is Broken

Without the i-Five Conversation: You live in a condo building. You have just enough time to get to an appointment, but as you open your garage door, you see there is a car parked in the driveway. You knock on your neighbor's door. As soon as she answers, you start with, "What's your problem? You can't block me in my own driveway! Don't be surprised if *you're* blocked in the next time you want to leave."

Your neighbor replies, "It's not that big of a deal. You act like you're the only one who lives here. You need to learn how to compromise."

With the i-Five Conversation: It's time to tune in to your body, thoughts, emotions, and desires.

Your body:

- External data: My neighbor (and co-owner) signed a legal agreement guaranteeing me free access into and out of the garage. When I was leaving, I was unable to get out because her friend's car was in the driveway. Twice in the past month similar situations have happened: once with a contractor and once with her boyfriend. As a result of having to contact them and wait for the cars to be moved, I was ten minutes late for appointments on both days. Dealing with this has now made me late for the third time. She's breaking our legal agreement. When I spoke to my neighbor, her response was "It's not that big of a deal. You act like you're the only one who lives here. You need to learn how to compromise."

- Internal data: tight muscles, shallow breath, right shoulder and neck pain

Your thoughts: She doesn't even ask if it's okay. She acts entitled, like she's the only one who lives here, and then accuses me of that very thing. I think she should follow the rules. My stories are mostly about her. She values flexibility and spontaneity. She may not know that the contractor or her boyfriend blocked me in. *My part in this is* I assume she read the agreement she signed. I'm scared that this will happen when I have a more important engagement and I'll be stuck. I'm avoiding having the vehicle towed because I want to have a good relationship with my neighbor.

Your emotions: surprised, annoyed, mad

Your desires:

- To stand up for myself

- To be able to get in and out of my garage with ease

- · To figure out how to enforce our agreement

- To confirm the repercussions of violating the agreement again

How I want to show up:

- Respectful

- Clear

- Direct

- Curious

- Honest

Your action: Initiate a conversation with your neighbor

You: "When we bought our condos, we signed an agreement that neither of us would park in the driveway. This is the third time this month it's happened. There's a car blocking me right now. I'm frustrated and annoyed. Do you know whose car it is? Do you have a different understanding of our agreement?"

Neighbor: "I know what we signed. Why are you so agitated? He just got here, and I was about to move the car myself."

You: "I can tell you value flexibility and spontaneity. I appreciate your willingness to move the car right now. The problem is, I'm still going to be late. How can we make sure this doesn't happen again?"

This, my friend, is where you've entered into slippery territory. You still listen to what your neighbor has to say—because you're that kind of a guy (or gal). The most common hope of people who know they're doing something wrong is to pray they won't get caught—that you won't notice, or that if you do, you won't have the courage to say anything. Other common responses are to make some new, vague promise, justify their behavior, or try to blame you. Even if you made a level 5 agreement with them, and even if you set up the conversation for success, you may also need to clarify the consequences of breaking the original agreement again.

Neighbor: "I'm sorry. I promise it won't happen again."

You: "I appreciate your apology. And since we've had a similar conversation twice before, and you made the same promise, I want to give you a fair warning. If I encounter a car blocking the driveway again, I won't be getting curious about whose it is; instead, I'll have it towed."

Yes, there are times that, despite your best efforts to clarify an agreement, you may have to make an unpopular decision by drawing boundaries. In this case, a repeat offense would require mustering the nerve to call a tow truck.

In the previous scenarios, did you notice the difference between reacting with strong statements of threat and blame versus responding with accountability and curiosity? More often than not, the latter will get you much closer to what you want. When you show up with accountability and curiosity, you dissolve barriers and build an invisible bridge between your hearts—and the best part is, both of you will experience a different outcome.

◆ ◆ ◆ ◆ ◆

TALKR$_X$ TOOLKIT

i-Five Conversation

- Interpreting Your Body
- Interpreting Your Thoughts
- Interpreting Your Emotions
- Interpreting Your Desires
- Integrating into Action

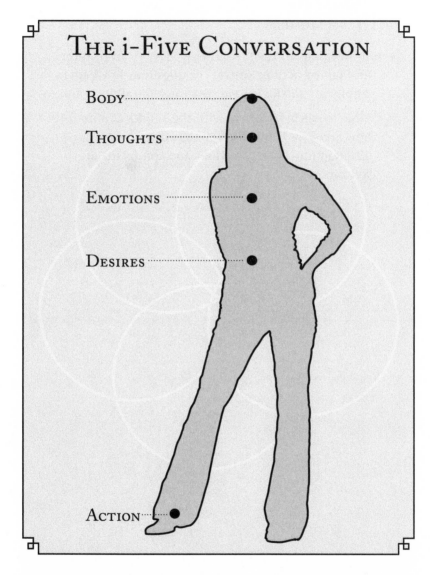

THE i-FIVE CONVERSATION

BODY

THOUGHTS

EMOTIONS

DESIRES

ACTION

TalkRx Video: Watch "The i-Five Conversation" to better understand how you can incorporate these five easy steps into your everyday conversations (DoctorNehaTalkRx.com).

TalkRx Video: Watch "The Communication Cure" from TEDx Berkeley to hear the actual speech that inspired this book (DoctorNehaTalkRx.com)!

Your i-Five Moment

- To integrate all the pieces of an i-Five Conversation into taking action, answer the questions in Chapter 24 of your *TalkRx Journal* (DoctorNehaTalkRx.com).

- Time to celebrate! Share with the TalkRx Community how an i-Five Conversation helped you create a different outcome. Questions and comments are welcome.

CHAPTER 25

SURRENDER

One final thought—even if you use everything you've learned, diligently complete the exercises, and apply all the tools of the i-Five Conversation, other factors are at play when you attempt to engage with those around you. You can't force someone else's readiness. You can't make another person listen or change. As hard as you try, you can't *want for another*. Despite your accountability and curiosity, you may discover that you and someone else have grown apart or that there is no overlap in your desires. As a result, the outcome of a well-constructed conversation may not be what you wish for, envision, or anticipate.

And that's okay.

It's not always about getting the outcome you want. It's about aligning your choices with your heart—and trusting that that's the outcome that's healthiest for you. Sometimes the key lies in your ability to *surrender*.

For those who love control, *surrender* can seem like a swear word. Sometimes you hold on to what's familiar, even if it's painful and no longer serving you. Letting go can be hard to do, but it doesn't mean giving up. When you face competing intentions, whether in yourself or in relationships with others, sometimes surrendering is the best action you can take. It means letting go of the old and trusting what the future holds.

Letting go is a human experience that transcends culture, race, and religion. It can feel like you're losing something, when in fact it may be your best chance of getting what you want most. What if you were intentional about letting go rather than fighting it?

When I resigned my medical partnership, I had to let go of all hope that I could change the hospital environment in order to match my style of patient care. It was hard to accept that I had grown and changed. Sadness and anxiety set in as I gave up my job security and faced an uncertain future. But as soon as I surrendered to the reality of the situation—that I was trying to control the hospital's practices—I was free to create a path that led me where I am today, connecting to my heart and my purpose by practicing the medicine I believe in and being healthier and happier than I've ever been.

The reward of letting go is inner peace and freedom. There are many ways to release what no longer serves you. If you're ready to let go (of a behavior, a relationship, etc.), ask yourself the following questions:

1. How has this behavior, relationship, job, or community served me (e.g., offered protection, brought happiness, met a need)?
2. What's the price of continuing to be attached to it?
3. What physical signals arise at the thought of letting go of this? Close your eyes and tune in to the physical sensations your body is sending (location, quality, and intensity).
4. What emotion(s) arise at the thought of letting it go?
5. If you let this go, what will you be creating space for?

Now take a deep breath in and fill your lungs with oxygen. Imagine your breath traveling to the physical space where you feel attachment. Use your next breath to lean into that discomfort. As you exhale, visualize releasing what no longer serves you. You might picture it dissolving, evaporating, melting, or washing away. With your next deep breath, allow any emotion you're experiencing to move through you.

You may need to take a few more deep breaths in order to let the physical and emotional presence of your attachment resolve. Imagine that with each subsequent breath, you are inviting gratitude, self-trust, and healing to fill you up. With each exhalation, become aware of the space you've created for new possibilities.

As you begin the process of letting go, be patient with your-self. You may think an issue has been resolved, only to find that there is a deeper layer that needs to be healed. Just repeat the same exercise. You may want to write in a journal or talk it out with a friend or a professional.

In the short term, your feelings of loss may be painful and your vision of the future may seem uncertain and frightening. But in the long term, if you surrender to the outcome and stay true to your highest values, you'll be heading in the right direction.

◆ ◆ ◆ ◆ ◆

TALKRX TOOLKIT

Five Steps to Surrender

1. Notice where in your body you feel attachment to the behavior, relationship, experience, or object you wish to let go of.

2. Take a deep breath in and imagine oxygen moving into that area of your body.

3. As you exhale, visualize releasing what no longer serves you. You might picture it dissolving, evaporating, melting, or washing away.

4. Repeat steps 2 and 3 as you continue to let go, and allow any emotions to move through you.

5. Invite gratitude, self-trust, and healing in. Become aware of the space you've created for something new.

YOUR I-FIVE MOMENT

*   Record any insights, discoveries, or realizations in Chapter 25 of your *TalkRx Journal* (DoctorNehaTalkRx.com).

- Share your struggles, successes, and questions with the TalkRx Community. This may seem like the end, but it is just the beginning . . . welcome to the TalkRx world of communication. You now have the awareness, the tools, and the community to support you.

REWRITING HISTORY . . .

Everything changes when you do. Armed with the Awareness Prescription and the i-Five Conversation, you hold the power to create your own health and happiness. My work with Brandon, Lilly, Juan, Mary, and Sara, along with thousands of other patients, revealed the profound connection between health and communication. With e-mails, cards, and flowers, they thanked me for the healing power of our time together—for listening, for asking them those five simple questions, and for inspiring them to get clear about the conversations they needed to have. Not one of them thanked me for the medications I prescribed.

Each of them came to the hospital seeking the science of medicine, but the art of medicine is what gave them hope and connected us to each other. Thanks to the courage they showed in speaking from the heart, I had the honor to serve as a catalyst for their physical, mental, and emotional healing.

But sometimes I wish I could rewrite history for them.

Could Brandon at some point have called his father and said, "Dad, I've been thinking about how hard I drive myself, and I'd like to talk to you about it"? And let's just suppose his dad said, "Son, what is it? Let's talk now." Brandon might have replied, "Thanks, Dad. I'd rather talk to you in person. I'd like to talk about something I remember from when I was a young boy. It should take half an hour. When is a good time?"

Do you think his dad was proud of him? We'll never know—but I sure have made up a lot of hopeful stories about it. If Brandon had gotten curious, might he have discovered that his father was in fact proud of him but didn't understand the importance of expressing it?

We already know that by slowing down and becoming aware of what was driving his stress, Brandon reduced his dependence on sleep medication and actually gave his body the rest it needed to heal. But I wonder . . . If Brandon had paid attention to the signals coming from his body earlier and had known how to communicate clearly, could he have created an authentic connection with his dad and avoided the stress that ultimately led to his stroke?

What about Lilly? How much richer might her life have been if she had been surrounded by the love of her son, daughter-in-law, and grandchildren for all those years? If she had been willing to challenge the stories she made up when her son married outside of their faith, could she have avoided the chronic emotional stress of being separated from what she valued most—her family?

I wonder . . . If she had built a bridge to them a quarter-century earlier, might Lilly have boosted her immune system and protected herself from that terrible pneumonia?

And Juan? Might the quality of his life have been different if he had understood Emotions 101? What if he had had the courage to ask a mentor or friend who already had strong relationships what the secret was? And suppose this friend had told him, "When I open up, it's sometimes uncomfortable, but that's when I feel the most connected to others."

Juan made great strides to heal his relationships. Not only had he reversed the typical depression that often plagues heart attack victims, but just six months later his physician told him that his heart had regained normal function.

I wonder . . . If Juan had allowed his emotions to flow freely after the war, healed his trauma earlier, and stayed connected to his family and friends over the years, would the arteries in his heart have remained open as well?

And then there was Mary. Would she have had a different experience with her family if she had known how to ask for what she wanted? By figuring out the conversations she needed to have with her mother, husband, and sons, the reward was freedom and inner peace for the last few months of her life. Getting clear about her desires allowed her to make videos for her sons that would keep her as an ongoing part of their lives. Rather than letting anxiety, guilt, and resentment eat away at her, she chose to embrace meaningful connections in the time she had left.

I wonder . . . How much more fulfilling might her life have been if she had courageously expressed her desires earlier? With hope, clarity, and connection, might her immune system have been stronger and given her a few more months or years?

And finally there was Sara. Her situation wasn't a "what if." The power of her and her family's transformation happened right before my eyes. As a result of the guided imagery exercise, together, we witnessed Sara's heart rate and blood pressure return to normal. She and her family experienced the critical link between health and communication and were on their way to healing.

I didn't wonder how Sara would do. I had confidence she would do well. She had everything she needed—the appropriate medical treatment; the awareness of how her thoughts, emotions, and environment impacted her health; and the support of her loving family. With courage and awareness, she would be able to successfully navigate the next steps in her healing.

As Brandon, Lilly, Juan, Mary, and Sara discovered, it's never too late to use the power of clear, direct communication to reduce stress, improve health, and create solid relationships. Every conflict, miscommunication, and drama can serve as an opportunity to learn, connect, and transform.

Together my patients and I traveled a sacred journey, never quite sure of what we were about to discover. For the lucky ones, our exchange was a wake-up call for them to re-engage in their lives. They had each been given a precious second chance. The only question that remained was: *How were they going to use it?*

I wonder . . . If these patients had had the Awareness Prescription and the i-Five Conversation before I met them, would they have ended up in the emergency room? Or might their lives have taken a different turn?

All you have to do is be willing to learn and grow with each conversation. Be accountable. Be curious. Be true to your values. Have the courage to ask for what you want. Stay connected to your heart while remaining open to new possibilities.

If Brandon, Lilly, Juan, Mary, and Sara could speak to you now, I bet they'd say, "You can't rewrite history. But you can rewrite your future. Now you know how."

Each day is another opportunity to do it the way you wish you could. And each time you choose to communicate with clarity, you'll improve your connections, your health, and your happiness. You'll find yourself navigating confidently into the unknown with your heart leading the way.

I wonder . . . if this is *your* wake-up call.

NOTES

1. "Monthly Population Estimates for the United States: April 1, 2010 to December 1, 2014, 2013 Population Estimates," U.S. Census Bureau, U.S. Department of Population, January 2014 to December 2014; "Drugs: Safe Use Initiative Fact Sheet," U.S. Food and Drug Administration, October 16, 2012, http://www.fda.gov/Drugs/DrugSafety/ucm188760.htm.

2. "Stress," University of Maryland Medical Center, January 30, 2013, http://umm.edu/health/medical/reports/articles/stress.

3. A concept called the Awareness Wheel, which you can read about in Sherod Miller et al., *Straight Talk: A New Way to Get Closer to Others by Saying What You Really Mean* (New York: Rawson, Wade Publishers, 1981), was adapted for the i-Five Conversation.

4. Albert Mehrabian, *"Silent Messages"—A Wealth of Information About Nonverbal Communication (Body Language)*, 1981, http://www.kaaj.com/psych/smorder.html, 1995–2011; Jeff Thompson, "Is Nonverbal Communication a Numbers Game?" *Psychology Today,* September 30, 2011, http://www.psychologytoday.com/blog/beyond-words/201109/is-nonverbal-communication-numbers-game.

5. James S. Gordon, M.D., is the author of *Unstuck: Your Guide to the Seven-Stage Journey Out of Depression* (New York: Penguin, 2008).

6. Other resources to help you ground your body can be found in *The Tapping Solution* by Nick Ortner (Carlsbad, CA: Hay House, 2014); *Unstuck* by James S. Gordon, M.D. (see note 5); and through the HeartMath Institute, heartmath.org.

7. I first learned about soft belly breathing at a conference put on by Dr. Jim Gordon and the Center for Mind-Body Medicine.

8. "Physiology," *Encyclopedia Britannica,* 2014, http://www.britannica.com/EBchecked/topic/287907/information-theory/214958/Physiology.

9. "Humans Are Hardwired for Connection? Neurobiology 101 for Parents, Educators, Practitioners and the General Public," interview with Amy Banks, M.D., Wellesley Centers for Women, September 15, 2010, http://www.wcwonline.org/2010/humans-are-hardwired-for-connection-neurobiology-101-for-parents-educators-practitioners-and-the-general-public.

10. If you want to delve more into this topic, read Byron Katie, *Loving What Is* (New York: Crown Archetype, 2002); Louise Hay, *All Is Well* (Carlsbad, CA: Hay House, 2013); or Geneen Roth, *Women, Food, and God* (New York: Scribner, 2010).

11. Denis Grimes, "An Analysis of Patient-Physician Discourse: Comparing Physician Diagnostic Scripts to Patient Social Script Expectations," University of Wisconsin–Milwaukee, December 2012, http://dc.uwm.edu/cgi/viewcontent .cgi?article=1202&context=etd.

12. David Stuart Sobel and Robert Evan Ornstein, *The Healthy Mind, Healthy Body Handbook* (New York: Time Life Medical, January 1996), p. 156.

13. Daniel Goleman, *Social Intelligence* (New York: Random House, 2006), p. 42; Sandra Blakeslee, "Cells That Read Minds," *The New York Times*, January 10, 2006, http://www.nytimes.com/2006/01/10/science/10mirr.html?pagewanted=all& _r=1&; Marco Iacoboni, "Imitation, Empathy, and Mirror Neurons," *Annual Review of Psychology*, 2009, http://www.adineu.com.ar/IMITATION%20EMPATHY%20 AND%20MIRROR%20NEURONS%20IACOBONI.pdf.

14. William H. Frey and Muriel Langseth, *Crying: The Mystery of Tears* (Minneapolis: Winston Press, 1985), pp. 9, 17, 20, 26, 45; Jane E. Brody, "Biological Role of Emotional Tears Emerges Through Recent Studies," *The New York Times*, August 31, 1982, http://www.nytimes.com/1982/08/31/science /biological-role-of-emotional-tears-emerges-through-recent-studies.html.

15. Frey and Langseth, *Crying*, pp. 73, 75; Audrey Nelson, Ph.D., "The Crying Game," in "He Speaks, She Speaks," *Psychology Today*, January 2, 2011, http:// www.psychologytoday.com/blog/he-speaks-she-speaks/201101/the-crying-game.

16. Sobel and Ornstein, *The Healthy Mind, Healthy Body Handbook*, p. 167.

17. University of Utah Health Care, "Heart Attack Risk Rises in Hours After Angry Outburst: Study," March 3, 2014, http://healthcare.utah.edu/ healthlibrary/related/doc.php?type=6&id=685429; Suzanne V. Arnold, et al., "The Hostile Heart: Anger as a Trigger for Acute Cardiovascular Events," *European Heart Journal*, March 4, 2014; Dana Crowley Jack, "Understanding Women's Anger: A Description of Relational Patterns," *Health Care Women International*, June 2001, http://www.ncbi.nlm.nih.gov/pubmed/11813786.

18. "The Numbers Count: Mental Disorders in America," National Institute of Mental Health, October 1, 2013, http://lb7.uscourts.gove/documents/12-cv -1072url2.pdf..

19. About 30 percent of adults have symptoms of insomnia. "Insomnia," American Academy of Sleep Medicine, http://www.aasmnet.org/resources/factsheets /insomnia.pdf.

20. Candie Hurley, "Top Ten Human Fears—Presenting Is Number One!" IBM: Mandel Communications, June 2, 2010, http://www.ibm.com/developerworks /community/blogs/f439d619-6757-42bf-9598-e5de87392dce/entry/top _ten_human_fears_presenting_is_number_one1?lang=en; Jerry Seinfeld comments, www.youtube.com/watch?v=kL7fTLjFzAg; Sora Song, "Health: The Price of Pressure," Time.com, July 19, 2004, http://content.time.com/time /magazine/article/0,9171,994670-1,00.html.

21. Robert L. Leahy, "Are We Born to Be Afraid?" *Psychology Today*, May 9, 2008, http://www.psychologytoday.com/blog/anxiety-files/200805/are-we-born-be -afraid.

22. I heard resentment explained this way at a communication workshop with Kris King in Eugene, Oregon.

23. Heather L. Stuckey and Jeremy Nobel, "The Connection Between Art, Healing, and Public Health: A Review of Current Literature," *American Journal of Public Health*, February 2010, pp. 254–263, http://www.ncbi.nlm.nih.gov/pmc /articles/PMC2804629/; B. A. Esterling, et al., "Empirical Foundations for Writing in Prevention and Psychotherapy: Mental and Physical Health Outcomes," *Clinical Psychological Review*, January 1999, http://www.ncbi .nlm.nih.gov/pubmed/9987585; K. J. Petrie, et al., "Effect of Written Emotional Expression on Immune Function in Patients with Human Immunodeficiency Virus Infection: A Randomized Trial," *Psychosomatic Medicine*, March–April 2004, pp. 272–275, http://www.ncbi.nlm.nih.gov/pubmed/15039514.

24. Gary Chapman, *The 5 Love Languages* (Chicago: Northfield Publishing, 2010).

25. I learned this exercise at the Center for Mind-Body Medicine during a professional training program.

26. Kris King said this in the communication workshop I attended in Eugene, Oregon.

27. To read more about the research and science supporting guided imagery, see Marty Rossman, M.D., The Healing Mind website, thehealingmind.org.

RESOURCES

Visit **DoctorNehaTalkRx.com** for free resources and additional materials that will help you master the i-Five Conversation.

- *TalkRx Journal* PDF—get the personalized questions that will make TalkRx relevant in your life
- Blogs—find inspiration for everyday conversations
- Podcasts—listen as you drive, walk, or work out
- Videos—get up close and personal with my clients as I work with them live
- Doctor Neha's Library—my favorite authors to complement your TalkRx journey
- Doctor Neha's Rolodex—the practitioners and organizations that I recommend

Connect with me online and on social media:

- Website: doctorneha.com
- Book: DoctorNehaTalkRx.com
- Facebook.com/DrNehaSangwan
- YouTube: bit.ly/nehatube
- Twitter: @drnehasangwan
- Instagram: doctorneha
- Google+: Dr. Neha Sangwan

Also join the online conversation at **DoctorNehaTalkRx.com** to connect with other readers, ask questions, post comments, and share thoughts. I'd love to hear from you!

To book Dr. Neha Sangwan to speak at your event or offer leadership and corporate trainings, please contact her team at hello@doctorneha.com.

Acknowledgments

As I complete this book, it feels like I'm the one who has been rewritten. This process has healed my relationships with myself and with those I love, and it has strengthened my belief that with clear, direct communication, compassion, and a rock-solid team, anything is possible. I send my deepest thanks to all of you who made this journey both transformational and fun.

Kathy Trost, thank you for walking beside me every step of the way. I treasure the memories of our healing Saturdays, of our weeklong writing retreats in Tahoe (when you could have been on an actual vacation), and our dance parties and champagne to celebrate each and every milestone. Thanks for your friendship and your certainty that this book would become a reality.

Thank you, Angie Chen, William Lewis, and Leigh Ann Loggins—my friends with superpowers. With healing hands and loving hearts, each of you has guided me, believed in me, and reminded me of my purpose here on earth. Leigh Ann, you were right—you told me many years ago that this day would come and I would be an author. Bev Martin, thank you for being the midwife to my creation. Yes, birthing a book is a thing.

Kris King, with elegance and wisdom, you taught me to honor my own voice. I heard your voice in my head and heart many times as I was writing. I hope that I can inspire others as much as you've inspired me. Bev Foster, you showed me the value of honest conversations and you have been a true friend. Sue Muck, your wisdom and wit have taught me not to take myself so seriously. Sheryl Brown and all my friends in Eugene—thanks for giving me a second home.

Thank you, Reid Tracy; you're a man of few words—but most important a man *of your word*. Somehow you convinced a woman who wanted to be a facilitator and speaker to spend more than two years writing a book. Your unwavering confidence, flexibility, and open communication allowed me to create the type of relationship with my publisher that I advocate for in this book.

To my agent, Stephanie Tade, thanks for your guidance and for choosing only to represent books that make a positive difference in the world. I hope this one lives up to your high standards.

Huge thanks to my editors: Peter Guzzardi, whose gut instinct about connection and belonging were spot on; Laura Gray, Patty Gift, and Anne Barthel at Hay House for your patience, flexibility, and support in working with an author who needed this to be an interactive, experiential process. Laura, your input was invaluable. Cathy Shap, thanks for flying to California for my in-person, two-week writing tutorial. Andrea Vinley Jewell, dare I say you made writing a book fun. Your wit, drive for excellence, insane organizational skills, and willingness to embark on Google+ changed everything. Michael Hauge, imagine my facing you and bowing in gratitude. You, my friend, are a true master of story. It was not by accident that our paths crossed at the 11th hour—and this book and I are all the better for it.

Thanks to Louise Hay for your vision many decades ago. Nancy Levin, Donna Abate, Craig Johnson, and the Hay House team, you're the behind-the-scenes heroes who make it all happen. I'm honored to be part of the Hay House family.

To the i-Five team: To the best speech coach ever . . . Patricia Fripp, thank you for your precision, for your gift of honest feedback, and for a fabulous British accent that had me at hello. My photographer-extraordinaire Octavia Hunter and videographers Luke Goodman and Max Basch, thanks for working your magic. Jen Roggia and Michael Minucci, thanks for helping me look and feel my best. Thank you, Monica Gurevich, Katy Putnam, Lexie Rhodes, and Michelle Nielsen for your graphic design, branding, and creative genius. To Sara Pollan DiMedio—I love your style! Holly Cara Price, your spirit, your laugh, and your social media magic rock my world! Jason and the Peaceful Media team—Love.

Jim Gordon, thank you for your friendship and for trusting me to represent your work in Saudi. I admire your bold vision and your willingness to question the way the world has always been. To Dr. Paul Rosch, Dr. Abdullah, and Prince Abdul Aziz for allowing me to share our adventures on the TEDx Berkeley stage and in this book. Thanks to my colleagues at The Center for Mind-Body Medicine. Your virtual encouragement has lifted my spirits.

Mark Hyman, you're a bright light in the world. Thanks for believing in me, for being willing to have honest conversations, and for your endless drive to change the paradigm of medicine. To Rachel Remen, a wise and beautiful role model who pioneered this movement long before it was hip and cool. David Sobel, thank you, my friend. I admire that you didn't need anyone to tell you that the mind and body were connected. You already knew.

Speaking of health care's early adopters of communication, thanks to Bill Greif, Linsey Dicks, Alan Chan, Sujata Easton, Julie Sher, Vickie Catanzaro, Abdul Wali, Mary Staunton, Terry Stein, Joan Beltran, Terri Pillow-Noriega, Diana Longacre, Becky Chism, Brenda Catt, Michael and Gabriela Orosco, Dave Deriemer, Tom Jackson, Deepak Sonthalia, Carmen Lindsey, Dean Gilbert, and all the thousands of medical staff in Northern and Southern California who invested in learning these skills both personally and professionally.

In pure entrepreneurial fashion, Michael and Xochi Birch, thanks for once again being ahead of the curve. Jordan Shlain, thanks for being a fellow trailblazing soul, paving a path to the future of medicine. David Eagleman, you're the best friend I've ever made in flight. Thanks to you and Sarah for putting your stamps of approval on my neuroscience fun facts! David Kerr—so grateful that you challenged my communication more than a decade ago that catapulted me on this journey. Rich Fernandez for being a wisdom pirate and inviting me to bring honest communication to the corporate world. Gopi Kallayil, thanks for your friendship and for continually challenging me to live an extraordinary life. Thanks to Gopi, Erinne Lambden Cohen, Renee Blodgett, and Jennifer Barr, for inviting me to speak on the TEDx Berkeley stage, which ultimately resulted in this book.

To Tom, Amy, Demi, and Tori Trezona, thank you for the crackling fire and your love as I wrote straight through the holidays. Amy, thanks for reminding me that I had to eat if I wanted to write. I'm bummed the fish-bullying story didn't make final edit!

Mad love to my family, Karma, Indu, Ritu, Sarika, and Simrin, who have consistently served as mirrors to reflect back what I value most. Thanks for having the courage to let me share our life experiences in the hopes that others might benefit. I couldn't have done this without Dad's morning chai, Mom and Savitri Nani's cooking, and everyone's collective love and support. And thanks to my extended family—Vidhu, Nidhi, Ajay, Pushpa, Usha Rajvir, and Zain Mausaji—for spending our airport layovers and India vacations learning communication and giving your theatrical input. Thank you, Raj, Kavita, Anshu, and Richa Singh, for acting as if learning the i-Five Levels of Listening was a normal after-dinner activity. And to all my cousins and especially Soni Singh, for her enthusiastic advocacy of this work.

To Rachel Hyman and the House of Truth, Kelly Graham Melcher for our final read-through, Alison Covarrubias, Linzi Oliver, Galit Szolomowicz, Marsha Nunley, Kamal Sran, the Larsons, Lori Johnson, Nona Lim, Jennifer Tuck, Roselyn Thomas, Sonia Madera, and the countless others who so lovingly cheered me on—my deepest gratitude.

Speaking of gratitude, how could I forget Café Gratitude— where I would travel every third day to stock up on the healthiest, most savory food I could have wished for. Your question of the day and your smiles gave me much more than physical nourishment. You warmed my heart and soul.

To my patients, who continue to be my greatest teachers; you are the ones who taught me that our inability to communicate literally makes us sick. Our heartfelt conversations empowered me to take the leap.

And finally, thanks to YOU—the reader of this book, the TalkRx Community—for doing your part to learn honest and compassionate communication. You make the world a better place—one conversation at a time.

About
the Author

CEO and founder of Intuitive Intelligence, Dr. Neha Sangwan is a first-generation American who grew up believing there were only two career choices: engineering *or* medicine. As soon as she realized they weren't mutually exclusive, she pursued them both. However, she's not your typical scientist. Her entrepreneurial spirit has led her to combine the science of medicine with the art of communication. With practical tools, she empowers individuals, leaders, and organizations to communicate clearly, strengthen relationships, reduce stress, and improve health.

Doctor Neha earned her Bachelor of Science in mechanical and biomedical engineering from Michigan State University. She worked as a manufacturing engineer for Motorola before attending medical school at the State University of New York at Buffalo (SUNY–Buffalo). She completed her Internal Medicine residency at Temple University Hospital and became board certified. She worked as a hospitalist until burnout forced her to pay attention to her own health and healing. Only then was she able to diagnose and treat her own limiting beliefs about medicine and her traditional role as a physician. With the help of thousands of patients, she discovered that physical ailments aren't always rooted in a physical cause. Upon leaving her physician partnership at one of the country's largest health maintenance organizations, she founded her own company, Intuitive Intelligence, to educate and inspire others. Now in her private practice, she's become a different kind of physician—one who addresses the root cause of stress, miscommunication, and interpersonal conflict, often healing chronic conditions such as headaches, insomnia, anxiety, and depression.

As a speaker, author, and coach, Doctor Neha has shared her unexpected discoveries on the stages of TEDx Berkeley ("The Communication Cure") and TEDx San Luis Obispo ("The Community

Cure"). Doctor Neha speaks for and partners with organizations such as the American Heart Association, American Express, Kaiser Permanente, and Google. She also enjoys teaching annual retreats for the public at Kripalu Center for Yoga & Health.

Join Doctor Neha on the path to bridge the gap between health and communication at www.doctorneha.com.

Follow her on:

Facebook.com/DrNehaSangwan

YouTube: bit.ly/nehatube

Twitter: @drnehasangwan

Instagram: doctorneha

NOTES

NOTES

NOTES

NOTES

NOTES

Hay House Titles of Related Interest

YOU CAN HEAL YOUR LIFE, the movie, starring Louise Hay & Friends
(available as a 1-DVD program and an expanded 2-DVD set)
Watch the trailer at: www.LouiseHayMovie.com

THE SHIFT, the movie, starring Dr. Wayne W. Dyer
(available as a 1-DVD program and an expanded 2-DVD set)
Watch the trailer at: www.DyerMovie.com

◆ ◆ ◆ ◆

The Art of Extreme Self-Care: Transform Your Life One Month at a Time,
by Cheryl Richardson

The Fear Cure: Cultivating Courage as Medicine for the Body, Mind, and Soul,
by Lissa Rankin, M.D.

*Jump . . . and Your Life Will Appear: An Inch-By-Inch Guide to Making a
Major Change,* by Nancy Levin

The Tapping Solution: A Revolutionary System for Stress-Free Living,
by Nick Ortner

All of the above are available at your local bookstore,
or may be ordered by contacting Hay House (see next page).

◆ ◆ ◆ ◆

We hope you enjoyed this Hay House book. If you'd like to receive our online catalog featuring additional information on Hay House books and products, or if you'd like to find out more about the Hay Foundation, please contact:

Hay House, Inc., P.O. Box 5100, Carlsbad, CA 92018-5100
(760) 431-7695 or (800) 654-5126
(760) 431-6948 (fax) or (800) 650-5115 (fax)
www.hayhouse.com® • www.hayfoundation.org

◆ ◆ ◆ ◆ ◆

Published and distributed in Australia by: Hay House Australia Pty. Ltd., 18/36 Ralph St., Alexandria NSW 2015 • *Phone:* 612-9669-4299 *Fax:* 612-9669-4144 • www.hayhouse.com.au

Published and distributed in the United Kingdom by: Hay House UK, Ltd., Astley House, 33 Notting Hill Gate, London W11 3JQ • *Phone:* 44-20-3675-2450 *Fax:* 44-20-3675-2451 • www.hayhouse.co.uk

Published and distributed in the Republic of South Africa by: Hay House SA (Pty.), Ltd., P.O. Box 990, Witkoppen 2068 • *Phone/Fax:* 27-11-467-8904 www.hayhouse.co.za

Published in India by: Hay House Publishers India, Muskaan Complex, Plot No. 3, B-2, Vasant Kunj, New Delhi 110 070 • *Phone:* 91-11-4176-1620 *Fax:* 91-11-4176-1630 • www.hayhouse.co.in

Distributed in Canada by: Raincoast Books, 2440 Viking Way, Richmond, B.C. V6V 1N2 • *Phone:* 1-800-663-5714 • *Fax:* 1-800-565-3770 • www.raincoast.com

◆ ◆ ◆ ◆ ◆

Take Your Soul on a Vacation

Visit www.HealYourLife.com® to regroup, recharge, and reconnect with your own magnificence. Featuring blogs, mind-body-spirit news, and life-changing wisdom from Louise Hay and friends.

Visit www.HealYourLife.com today!

Free e-newsletters from Hay House, the Ultimate Resource for Inspiration

Be the first to know about Hay House's dollar deals, free downloads, special offers, affirmation cards, giveaways, contests, and more!

 Get exclusive excerpts from our latest releases and videos from *Hay House Present Moments*.

 Enjoy uplifting personal stories, how-to articles, and healing advice, along with videos and empowering quotes, within *Heal Your Life*.

 Have an inspirational story to tell and a passion for writing? Sharpen your writing skills with insider tips from *Your Writing Life*.

Sign Up Now!

Get inspired, educate yourself, get a complimentary gift, and share the wisdom!

http://www.hayhouse.com/newsletters.php

Visit www.hayhouse.com to sign up today!

 HAY HOUSE

 HAYHOUSE RADIO *radio for your soul*

HealYourLife.com ♥